# Equestrian Education

## PROFESSIONAL DEVELOPMENT FOR INSTRUCTORS

## Jill K. Hassler-Scoop AND Kathy Kelly Ph.D.

*With contributions from Beth Clarke and Nicholas Fowler*

**GOALS UNLIMITED PRESS**
**Huson, Montana**
**2002**

*Edited by:*
Melinda Artz, Tanya Boyd,
Russell Scoop and Gayle and Mike Stike


*Front Cover art by Frank White*
*Book art by John Baker*


*Published by:*
Goals Unlimited Press
c/o Equestrian Education Systems
25155 Huson Road
Huson, Montana 59846




Library of Congress Cataloging-in-Publication Data

Hassler-Scoop, Jill K., 1944–
    Equestrian education : professional development for instructors /
Jill K. Hassler-Scoop and Kathy Kelly ; with contributions from
Beth Clarke and Nicholas Fowler.
        p. cm.
    Includes bibliographical references (p. ).
    ISBN 0-9632562-7-0 (alk. paper)
    1. Horsemanship—Study and teaching.  I. Kelly, Kathy, 1959–
II. Title.

SF310.5 .H368  2002
798.2′3′071—dc21
                                                            2002017528

*Equestrian Education uniquely puts together the many elements of teaching that most instructors struggle for years to identify, and then gather that information throughout their careers. Jill and Kathy are offering a clearly organized and comprehensive program that is a great review for experienced instructors and an enormous benefit for those entering the vocation.*

*As an instructor of more than 25 years I could easily identify my own progress from the "young and eager" to the "older and wiser" stages. Much of the information offered would have helped me progress in a more organized way, and accomplished my goals without so much trial and error.*

*It is my dire wish to see a core of well trained riding instructors in USA to teach the many who seek honest and correct trainers. This book will help to accomplish this goal.*

Cathy Frederickson

*Equestrian Education is a valuable source of information for every instructor who is trying to improve and refresh their skills.*

Jim Wofford

# ACKNOWLEDGEMENTS

### JILL WANTS TO THANK:

Kathy Kelly for her tireless, enthusiastic hours of discussion, debate, writing, and rewriting that helped us create the Stages of Rider Education – An American System of Learning. Kathy and I had lots of fun and both of us learned a lot from each other as together we organized our years of teaching experience into the information presented in this book.

Russell, my husband, for his patience, editing, guidance and encouragement through this very involved process of creating not only a new book but also a system of education.

### KATHY WANTS TO THANK:

My family – you have been "in this" from the beginning, watching me develop from a "horse-crazy kid" to a "horse-crazy adult" with amazement, some disbelief, but most importantly, tons of love and support. I thank you from the bottom of my heart.

My friends - for being patient with me as I "went underground" for long periods of time, surfacing only to discuss the finer points of equestrian education, then to disappear once again. That I still have you all to thank is a testimony to your loyalty and persistence!

My husband – your patience, encouragement, and never-ending belief in me has been my lifeline. Words cannot express. . . .

And, a final note of thanks goes to Jill Hassler-Scoop, for the honor and joy of working with her on this book. Our shared sense of energy, passion, and beliefs makes it seem as if we have found in each other a teaching "soul mate." Jill's incredible curiosity, vast fund of knowledge, practical horse sense, and keen mind never failed to make this project educational, inspiring, intellectually stimulating, challenging, and . . .fun! Thank you Jill, for being you.

### WE BOTH WISH TO THANK:

Elizabeth Clarke and Nicholas Fowler for the wonderful insights and valued expertise shared in their chapters.

John Baker, not only for his innovative art and attention to the little "horsey details," but also for his patience with our ever-changing ideas and deadlines!

Melinda Artz, Tanya Boyd, and Gayle and Mike Stike, who spent countless hours editing against deadlines imposed by Kathy and Jill because of our busy teaching schedules.

Our colleagues, Natalie DiBerardinis and Tanya Boyd, for their knowledge, advice, support, and hard work as we put this book together. We have truly enjoyed sharing this experience with you!

A special note of thanks is due to the many instructors and students with whom we have come in contact, past and present. You all have been, and continue to be, the backbone of our educations. Your efforts to learn, improve, and be challenged have provided us with the incredible learning opportunities from which we have drawn so heavily for this book.

And, last, but not least . . . *the horses,* who through their incredible patience, generosity of spirit, and capacity for forgiveness, continually amaze and inspire us. We hope, through the publication of this book, that we are giving back to these noble creatures just a fraction of what they give to us everyday.

We are excited to share our experiences and education with our readers. We hope the materials in Equestrian Education will offer new and useful tools to help you along your way in your work to develop satisfied, successful, and independent riders on happy, comfortable, and obedient horses.

# TABLE OF CONTENTS

**Equestrian Education: Professional Development for Instructors**
*Written by Jill K. Hassler-Scoop unless otherwise noted.*

**Stages of Rider Education – An American System of Learning**
*This section written jointly by Jill K. Hassler-Scoop and Kathy Kelly, Ph.D.*

# PHILOSOPHY

Equestrian Education System's approach to equestrian riding, learning, teaching, and education is based upon our values and beliefs about the nature of the horse/human connection. We hold as a guiding principle that the true beauty of the horse and human partnership reveals itself when there is mutual understanding, respect, and cooperation between species. Our goal is to help instructors teach their students to strive for this ideal, at whatever level of education they may seek. We believe all riders can develop to become independently thinking, feeling, and aware riders who, through classical training, learn to ride their horses by staying ever present to what is natural and comfortable to the horse. In doing so, these partnerships become characterized by relaxed, comfortable, and classically correct riders sitting on top of relaxed, comfortable, and classically correct horses.

Core to our philosophy is integration. The continual search for new knowledge and information, when built upon the foundation of one's core beliefs, can help instructors not only improve the quality and effectiveness of their teaching, but of their personal lives as well. Happy and content instructors not only search out new information about the theories of riding and teaching, but also about who they are, what they want out of life, and how they plan on going about getting it. They then integrate this knowledge into their own "life philosophies," which guides and propell their teaching philosophies. This kind of personal knowledge and growth is critical to being a good instructor, as teaching someone in the art of equestrian riding is about so much more than a set of specific instructions on "what to do." It is teaching students about how to handle relationships, limitations (real and perceived), frustration, anger, and loss. It involves sharing with your students the experiences of joy, exuberance, and the articulation of dreams, hopes, and wishes. Teaching riding also opens your students up to the complexities of intimacy. These include the sharing of weaknesses, fears, and vulnerabilities; not only with you, their instructors, but also with their horses. To this end we encourage instructors to learn as much about themselves as possible. Self-knowledge makes instructors much more effective as they help riders and horses navigate successfully through the myriad of experiences and skills needed to enter into an honest and authentic partnership with a horse. There are many wonderful learning opportunities available – this book is only one of them! Good instructors just need open mindsets, organized minds and the desire to be life-long learners to take advantage of them.

Our philosophy also includes the belief that positive results are attainable for ALL riders who want to learn. Although riding is an art and an athletic endeavor, it attracts riders with a wide-range of natural "artistic-ness" and athleticism. We encourage instructors to help their students, through the use of realistic and honest evaluations, learn to identify their own definitions of "success" within their particular horse activities. We believe that we can help our students achieve their successes by providing the groundwork for a systematic approach to setting attainable goals. To help students become more skilled on their horses we advocate unmounted cross training experiences, such as other forms of physical exercise (yoga, t'ai chi), meditation, relaxation, massage, and sport psychology. These different approaches, along with many others, have proven to be valuable and effective supplements to a students' riding educations.

As a result of our many years teaching, learning, and integrating, we have created an American system of learning called the Stages of Rider Education. It is our hope that instructors will find this approach to be useful as a guideline for their own instructional programs. Based upon our philosophy of balance across body, mind, and spirit, this system integrates classical riding principles and sound instructional tools and techniques with knowledge and information from many different areas, such as education, meditation, and psychology. We hope this system sets the stage for instructors to teach their students the joys of the human/horse partnership through the process of classical education, integration, goal setting, communication, and self-discovery. Our deepest wish is that through the application of our system of learning, more riders and horses will demonstrate the qualities that make it possible to attain that wonderfully special and unique relationship - true partnership with a horse.

For those of you who share our philosophy, *Equestrian Education* will serve as a validation of your approach and mindset to riding education. It may solidify your current ways of thinking and/or provide some new ideas to help make your teaching even more successful. For those of you who may have a different outlook or approach to teaching and learning, we simply ask you to read on and see if some of the ideas may be applicable to your situations or beliefs. Experiment with the ideas presented in this book, and maybe you will find something useful to integrate into your own style and philosophy. We thank you for giving us the opportunity to share some of our insights, beliefs, exercises, and techniques with you on your journey to professional and personal development. Happy reading!

# Introduction

*"The human individual is equipped to learn and go on learning prodigiously from birth to death, and this is precisely what sets him or her apart from all other known forms of life."*
— from George Leonard's, Mastery

Riding instructors first learn how to ride, and then they spend a lifetime trying to teach others to do the same. Yet mastery of equestrian sport, as riding students everywhere quickly find out, does not have an end-point. It is an on-going process. As such, instructors find themselves on a life-long path of learning and challenge. What is so fascinating about this learning process is that it *always stimulates self-growth and development.* It is nearly impossible to connect intimately with horses and not be touched in all areas of our being: mentally, physically, emotionally, and spiritually! Therefore, as life-long learners, instructors need to be prepared to work on personal and professional growth issues throughout their teaching careers.

*Equestrian Education* is designed to support and enhance instructors' personal and professional development processes. We hope this book proves to be a valuable resource for instructors from many disciplines as they seek to better themselves and master the elusive art of equestrian riding.

*The more we learn and live, the more we have to integrate into riding and teaching. And, the more we know about riding and teaching, the more we can learn and live!*

**Integration** and **Professional Development** go hand-in-hand in the pursuit of mastery. When instructors seek out new information and use it to improve or expand upon what they do, they are demonstrating the power of integration. Through the power of integration, these instructors are developing their professional skills. There are many sources of information that are important and relevant to riding instructors. All the chapters included in the Professional

Development Section are designed for instructors to learn more about themselves and human behavior so they can better assist their students as they pursue their love of riding. This includes topics related to instructors' career development, personal motivations for teaching, and knowledge and use of ethics and psychological principles when teaching. Inserted throughout the chapters are valuable charts, checklists, and helpful tips to provide further guidance.

Until now, very few books on teaching have included information specifically for those who are new to the instructing profession. To address this oversight, *Equestrian Education* provides a **New Instructors Section**, which was written with the beginning instructor in mind. Useful ideas are provided for getting started and also include information on the basics of teaching. It is our hope that this section will be a resource for those new instructors who want to start teaching with a solid foundation when they enter the riding ring and face a student for the first time.

STABLETALK WBIT 1680 AM

effective listening builds confidence

To be an effective instructor, a person needs to know more than just how to ride. The riding world is full of excellent, talented riders who kindly offer to teach others what they know. The problem is that the skills needed to teach well are quite different and distinct from those needed to ride well. For some riders, this shift is easy to make, as they are "natural" teachers. For others, making the transition from rider to teacher is fraught with frustration and difficulty. In this book, we have researched and adapted the important core teaching skills developed in the field of education and have put them to use for equestrian instructors. These **Fundamental Teaching Skills** include communication, developing your eye, goal setting and a solid but flexible lesson structure. Of particular importance is an instructor's ability to know when and how to shift from being a "teacher" to being a "coach," as each role has its own skills and emphases. A chapter is included on this important topic.

Throughout *Equestrian Education* you will see Instructor's Reminders and Important Points. The Instructor's Reminders are brief tips for instructors that highlight specific techniques, points, concepts, or exercises that can be useful as your students progress through the stages.

INSTRUCTOR'S REMINDER

This book is focused on mounted Equestrian Education, and as such, does not include the unmounted aspects of horsemanship such as knowledge about horse care, nutrition, conformation, lameness, etc. Instructors are strongly encouraged to supplement their students' riding educations with unmounted lessons in horse-manship. A true horseman is well-rounded and is equally at home in the barn or on the back of a horse! ⚞

Two **Important Points** to keep in mind as you are using Equestrian Education:

1. How long does learning take? Progress through the Stages is very individualized and is related to each horse and rider partnership. The length of time each stage takes is influenced by the student's age; fear or confidence level; athletic ability; personality; learning levels, both mental and physical; previous experiences; life circumstances (including time and money); and the horse's aptitude, training, personality and suitability.

2. Students do not start off being independent learners; they need to learn how to become independent thinkers and riders. This is important because most Americans learn by spending considerable time riding without instruction, thus instructors will find it essential to teach students how to learn as well as how to ride. Thus we are teaching them to become good students early in their riding careers!

Equally important to "how" to teach is "what" to teach. Technical expertise is considered a fundamental requirement for all teachers, in any field! There is a saying in education, "Junk in . . . junk out." No matter how good a teacher someone is, if he/she is not teaching the correct things, more harm than good will be done. Nowhere is this truer than in equestrian education. This is because equestrian instructors first and foremost have a primary, ethical responsibility to the horse. The information an instructor provides to students *must be in harmony with the natural and physiological prerequisites of the horse.* This belief is the basic underlying principle behind every classical system of equestrian riding and training.

> *No matter what discipline you teach, the fundamental skills remain the same.*

One of the biggest problems voiced by American instructors (and trainers, clinicians, judges, etc.) is the proliferation of educated and talented riders (and horses) who lack the fundamental basics associated with a classical education. The enormous success of the German system in Europe demonstrates the value and effectiveness of having an organized program of study that takes students through a gradual progression of skills. In the German system, riders are held to established standards as they progress through the program. In America, there is little to no regulation over the horse industry. While this freedom has its benefits, it also has its price. Anyone can call himself or herself an "instructor" or "trainer." This has led to vast differences in the kind and quality of instruction available to American riders. Many students, because of their geographic locations, ignorance, lack of financial resources, or just plain bad luck, end up learning to ride without the benefit of any kind of a system or program. This is one of the reasons so many American instructors express frustration with the variety of problem horse and rider combinations that enter their riding rings seeking instruction. How, they ask, did these riders progress so far with so little?

*The goal of this American system is to help students arrive at the same final endpoint as students do in the German system – classically educated riders and horses who can move together in balance, beauty, comfort, and cooperation.*

The last part of *Equestrian Education*, **Stages of Rider Education - An American System of Learning,** describes a system of rider education that was created to help instructors work with the specific challenges and realities seen in America today. Please note that this system is based on *classical principles and standards,* but has been modified to make it easier for instructors to shift between stages and steps instead of pro-

AMERICAN SYSTEM OF LEARNING
Stages of Rider Eduation and Wheel Shows Flexibility

xvi

gressing in a linear fashion straight through. The Stages of Rider Education parallel those of the German Scale of Education for the horse. Instructors are encouraged to read these chapters together in order to gain a fuller understanding of the classical principles behind the German system, along with how the Stages of Rider Education allow instructors the flexibility to mix and match stages and steps. These are the signs of a true partnership between rider and horse.

Mastery of equestrian sport is a life long pursuit, to be sought after while enjoying the process. Therefore, riding instructors have a responsibility and an obligation to ensure that their students have the tools, skills, support, and encouragement to work through the inevitable frustrations, anger, lows, and plateaus that make up everyone's riding experience. As well, instructors are in positions to champion their students as they experience progress and accomplishments along the way. Learning to ride, as well as learning to teach, is often as much about learning to be the best person you can be as it is about riding horses!  It is our sincere hope that *Equestrian Education* offers you, the instructor, your own set of tools, skills, support, and encouragement as you progress down your own learning path.

# INTEGRATION
# INTRODUCTION

The former director of the Spanish Riding School, Alois Podhajsky, *wrote, "In the outward appearance, riding should present itself as an art. Horse and rider, in all movements, should give the impression of two living creatures merged into one."*

How is this achieved? Each part of the well-trained horse is responsive to the highly refined communications of the rider. The rider has worked long and hard to train body, mind, and spirit and to understand the body, mind, and spirit of the equine partner. The art of integration has to have been in constant use for this to happen.

Integration is a process that allows one to sift through the vast amounts of available information, choose what is relevant to a particular problem or need, compare new information with previously established beliefs and tools, and finally blend both new and old information. Ideally, the process becomes a second-nature response to new information collected from factual, psychological, and social awareness.

Integration is a powerful educational tool. To get the most out of integration, the reader must understand his/her own riding and teaching philosophy and be an avid, educated consumer of as many resources as possible.

Integration is the thread of development that has most influenced my career and life. It was a natural learning process for my curious mind. It started with my love of horses and my respect for the riding instructors I had as a member of the United States Pony Club (USPC). Integration continued with horses teaching me about parenting and people and my working hard to provide students with the skills to become riders, independent in both seat and mind. While I did not recognize integration as a primary source of learning until I was in my early forties, since then, one of my life missions is to encourage as many people as possible to enrich their lives with the use of this effective tool.

In 2001 the latest step in this journey has moved from Integrated Approach to Teaching and Learning (IAT&L) to Equestrian Education Systems (EES). IAT&L was a valuable learning experience for everyone involved in its development and the creation of Equestrian Instruction: An Integrated Approach to Teaching & Learning. To take the idea to the next step and add more ideas for personal and professional development, as well as more individualized options for riders and instructors, plus the addition of a new focus on technical development, Equestrian Education Systems was founded. EES is a support system for learning, designed to provide a variety of resources to aid instructors and riders in their professional and personal development. Integration is at the heart of this system.

Mastering integration, like mastery of all skills, is an ongoing process that involves being an educated consumer with a curious mind and a well-defined understanding of your ultimate goal or destination for your own riding and teaching. The integration process can enrich your life by creating a dynamic interaction between relationships, career, avocation, and community life. In recent years, the horse world has expanded beyond the traditional approach to horsemanship with a renewed awareness that there are many contributions from other areas that can expand riding skills. Professionals have developed and promoted many new concepts: Mary Wanless, Sally Swift, Linda Tellington Jones, John Lyons, Pat Parelli, and Monty Roberts to name a few. Each of these have offered concepts or approaches with lots of valuable information; however, by using integration with each of these concepts, you have the opportunity to expand not only your current basic framework/philosophy, but also to improve upon these new concepts by adding information you already have in your knowledge base to these new ideas. The end result of this integration process is a dynamic blending of traditional and contemporary ideas and philosophies, which is uniquely tailored to your specific goals and beliefs.

To become and remain a top professional in any field requires a solid foundation in the basic principles of the discipline and a deep commitment to remaining current with the latest information. New information must not replace correct foundation knowledge. Using the skills expressed in the educated consumer chapter of this book will help you to be certain that your basic fundamental knowledge is correct. Integrating new ideas will enhance basic understanding and make it more useful. Integration is a never-ending process of adding and revising. The more experience we have, the more processing opportunities we have. Staying on top of our field of expertise is a direct result of our ability to integrate, constantly building on our own knowledge and thus having more to offer our students. Often, instructors automatically integrate, but sometimes they fail to take advantage of this refreshing process. It is fun to go into a lesson and share with your student something you recently learned!

Integration requires that we be well-educated, discriminating consumers. We must also teach our students the skills of the wise consumer as well. The art or practice of being an educated consumer provides not only a valuable thinking process for our students, but it also helps them to own the information and take an active role in their own learning programs.

The following two chapters will give you more information on integration. "**Power of Integration**" explains how to use integration, and "**Educated Consumer**" helps you identify information and sources that are credible and worth the time and effort to evaluate for future integration. I hope you refer back to these two chapters as you move through the rest of the book. EES is providing instructors with resources, some proven traditions, some on the cutting edge, and you will want to integrate the information new to you via the process of being a well-educated consumer.

# EDUCATED CONSUMER

*Listen, evaluate, and investigate to decide if new information is right for you.*

Well-balanced and educated riding instructors assess the usefulness of new information from three different perspectives based on the wisdom of their own experiences. First is from an awareness of up-to-the-minute trends in the market-place. Second is from the standpoint of their willingness to experiment for themselves with the vast number of learning opportunities our world provides. The third perspective is from their readiness to experiment with the application of new information as it might fit their students' learning styles.

AH... YOU LOOK MARVELOUS!

Because instructors play such a vital role in their students' lives, they need to be educated consumers themselves and teach their students to be the same. The value of integration is directly related to being able to sort through the vast amount of information that floods the market and determine what warrants the investment of an instructor's time and attention.

I start every lesson with a new student with this statement: "Please feel free to ask5e questions if anything I ask you to do is one, different from what you identify with, or two, is confusing to you." I continually explain that all information must be evaluated before it is integrated into one's individual learning or teaching philosophy. Every instructor realizes that there are many methods, philosophies, and theories on training horse and rider, and that students have most likely been exposed to a number of those opinions already. This makes it essential that riding instructors become educated consumers who can effectively evaluate and then integrate ideas and teach their students to do the same.

Whether information is new or old, traditional or non-traditional, integration of information requires initial evaluation to examine its credibility. While most information can be useful one way or another (even if we learn what we don't want to do), it is important to conduct critical research before accepting the information of any self-proclaimed authority.

Instructors constantly update their professional knowledge. Carefully choosing respected professionals as mentors and utilizing additional sources of information, such as videos, books, and magazines, are key to furthering one's confidence and making steady progress toward educational goals. To evaluate new information for integration, consider taking these three essential steps:

1. Inventory your current knowledge, practices, and understandings.

2. Be clear on what you want to learn and what you want your students to achieve.

3. Seek inspiration and education that will expand and reinforce these goals.

These three steps will help you sort through the information you need to make a useful investment in your education.

One of my favorite authors, Waldemar Suenig, charges every rider to "Know thyself." Reading his book in my early twenties made me wonder; how do we come to know ourselves? I now realize that Suenig's words sparked my life-long search for balance, a search that has influenced the way I approach teaching, parenting, and nurturing of relationships. Progressive instructors challenge each student with Suenig's charge, "know thyself," and become educated consumers in the process.

Lots of books and articles are written. How many are applicable to you and your work at the time you see them? How much is of actual value to you? Can you use part of it, or do you need all of it? What attracts you to the information? What reservations do you have about the information? How much influence on your acceptance of the information is based on whether or not the author is famous? What has made the author famous? Your answers to such questions can help you evaluate what you read.

---

### Important Questions to Ask When Seeking Professional Help

1. What are the standard qualifications for a member of the profession?
2. Does this person meet these standards?
3. How many years experience does this person have working in the profession?
4. What do other clients have to say about their experience with this professional?
5. How do I feel about working with this professional?

Chart 1

Riding instructors are professionals. Like psychologists, physical therapists, and others who provide services to the public, we may choose to follow one of the profession's certification programs, or we may abide by our own standards and ethics. Our reputations will be based on the evaluations of our clients and our ability to provide ethical, quality information. Our actions and results will speak louder than our words.

Equestrian Education Systems encourages referral whenever appropriate. When we recommend another professional to our students, we must be certain the professional has a high degree of ethics and training. This requires the investigation of the professional from the standpoint of an educated consumer. We owe this to our students.

I encourage you to be a discriminating consumer in the world market of information and ideas. Exercise your analytical and experimental skills and teach them to your students; it will help create involved, independent students who will enjoy lasting results from having worked with you.

Ideas and resources for information to assist you in being an educated consumer: See Resources in back of book.

# THE POWER OF INTEGRATION

Combining what you know with what you want to learn or are learning and turning that combination into a useful asset in your bank of knowledge is a constant life process. Whether we are instructors, trainers, riders, or bystanders, we are always students. As such, we are constantly making discoveries. These discoveries either confirm what we know or give us information to add to what we already know. Much of

INTEGRATION OF OLD WITH THE NEW...
TO CREATE A MORE BALANCED PERSPECTIVE

what we discover can be used to help us succeed in reaching our goals.

Integration is the act of examining what you are exposed to and then making the choice to put new information into your own information bank for further exploration or use. One such integration opportunity for me was one of my first clinics with John Lyons. John introduced his seven steps to a "small give". Even though I had taught bending, it never occurred to me to break it down into seven steps. As I watched Lyons work, I had mixed feelings about what I was seeing and hearing; however, the clarity of each step impressed me. I decided to experiment with these seven steps with my students. I did not like his idea of "no leg", so I integrated the seven steps in my teaching while I continued to include use of the leg. This integration process revolutionized my teaching, enabling me to help many students create the proper connection from inside leg to outside hand. Could something have gone wrong in adapting his techniques for my own use? Certainly. Lots of things could have gone awry, but since I did not throw away the classical foundation skills, I was able to keep the old and refine it with new information.

The process of integration leads to a more harmonious whole, whether it is in our riding or in our lives. Integration allows skills and information to be interactive, filling in gaps and bringing parts together. Consciously using integration will help make each learning experience more valuable because it creates a broader, more balanced perspective and basis for advancement. In all that we do, this balance gives us more tools to use to meet our needs.

Sources of information worthy of integration can come from daily rides, taking part in and watching lessons or clinics, reading, and from our day-to-day life outside the horse world. A curious mind will soon discover similarities between life skills and riding skills. From performances to relationships, aspects of all areas of life provide many learning opportunities that can enhance all our skills.

Essential to training progress are the fundamental elements of being a good student. One of the roles of a well-skilled instructor is to help students learn how to become good learners. The following list of fundamental learning ingredients has proven helpful to both instructors and riders.

1. Know what you want to do with your riding and/or teaching. What is your motivator? What are your long-term goals?

2. Make a realistic appraisal of where you are in your learning process so you know the next steps you need to master. Consider asking for help from an "outside" evaluator to confirm your current appraisal.

3. Seek the technical knowledge needed to attain your goal. Of singular importance to instructors and riders is the recognition of the value of a traditional, solid foundation of skills built carefully over time—a process for which there are no shortcuts.

4. Have a clear understanding of what success will feel like so you will know when you have achieved it and can move on to the

next goal. This is a conscious process of understanding what gives you pleasure, satisfaction, or fulfillment; instructors can help riders figure this out. Pleasure is one aspect of success. We can have a sense of pleasure without satisfaction or feeling successful. The difference is what gives us pleasure that is associated realistically with our motivation. Instructors have the tough job of doing this for themselves, so consider talking to trustworthy colleagues to help you get your bearings. Awareness and review are key tools in this process.

5. To make the most progress as a student, find an instructor who shares or understands your personality, learning, and communication styles as well as your same basic philosophy about riding and learning. Instructors also need to find instruction from an instructor of their own or other instructors and like-minded professionals.

6. Nurture the desire to own what you learn and use it instinctively/ naturally.

7. Always be ready and eager to learn more. Successful people constantly develop their personal and professional skills. An open mind, coupled with the desire to learn more, is one of the hallmarks of success and a key factor in integration.

8. Seek to integrate new information with trusted experience. Integration is the on-going process of adding to our base of knowledge. It can happen in a few minutes, or it can take years. When we are introduced to new information or take a lesson, we must understand its relationship to our goal and how it will help us move from where we are at the moment. As educated consumers, we need to examine what is offered and evaluate it with an open but critical mind in order to give the new information a fair chance for our own benefit.

9. Keeping an open mind, keeping the goal in mind, and keeping one's mind in the moment is a universal mindset for success, no matter what learning style we may have.

10. As is true for many art forms, most new information in the art of horsemanship takes plenty of practice time to prove its value. After giving the new information a fair chance, we evaluate its usefulness and make the decision whether or not to integrate. Is it moving us toward our goal or not?

Life and our pursuits give us the opportunity to be students of many subjects. Thus learning to be a better student helps us in many ways, including becoming better riders and/or instructors. It is important to keep an open mind and body to as many learning opportunities as possible. Add integration to allow information to interact with any stage of knowledge. It is exciting to expand and develop a solid foundation that promotes independent thinkers and decision makers, thus creating successful horsemen and women.

Maintaining a keen awareness to integration in your reading and experiences combined with being an educated consumer will expand your learning and teaching skills. ⚬

---

**Integration Questions to use for Clinics, Workshops, Symposiums & Seminars**
The questions below are designed to spark new ideas and understandings to be integrated into your personal learning philosophy, riding and life. Please use these questions to reflect upon your experience in a way that clarifies and gives direction to your riding program. Attend a clinic or a workshop, audit lessons or watch a professional video and answer the questions below. Describe the situation. Until you get in the habit of automatically evaluating and integrating, this questionnaire helps organize awareness.

Name and date of event: _____
1.  What made you decide to attend the event?
2.  What did you expect to get from attending?
3.  Did you get what you expected? If not, how did you benefit?
4.  What exciting points do you want to be certain to remember?
5.  Did you disagree with any of the information given? If so, what and why?
6.  What points do you want to learn more about?
7.  What points do you feel you want to experiment with before you decide if they are good for you?
8.  What sparked your creative thinking?
9.  Did anything in the event inspire you? If so what?
10. Was the information presented in an open and encouraging way, or was it presented to convince you that it was the only way?
11. Was the information presented in an objective fashion?
12. What was the highlight of the event for you?
13. What gave the information credibility for you?
14. What are the three most important points of information you gained from attending or taking part in this event?

Chart 1B

---

# PROFESSIONAL DEVELOPMENT INTRODUCTION

*The instructor's task is to impart to the pupil his knowledge of handling and riding horses in a way that will guarantee good sport, enjoyment, and safety. It is therefore obvious that a good instructor must have suitable qualifications as well as many years of experience.*

—From the Complete Riding & Driving System: Book 1, Official Instruction Handbook of the German National Equestrian Federation

Learning does not end when one becomes an instructor, but rather continues with an even greater responsibility. One is not learning just for one's self, but also for the benefit of students. Instructors must continue to be students, gathering useful information from multi-faceted resources: their own riding, clinics, media, other instructors, their own students, and of course, horses! One of the goals of this book is to provide instructors with tools for integrating this wealth of information. Professional curiosity obliges responsible instructors to seek out information from many time-tested traditions, as well as from new ideas, in the ongoing effort to remain a constant source of value to both students and the horses they ride. Integrating information expands our toolbox, making the job of communicating the learning process to students fun and effective for everyone involved.

Staying abreast with current information, as well as keeping our professional skills up to date in our fields of expertise, is very important. See the **Essentials to Development** chapter for ways to help stay up to date with current information.

Professional success is one key to our professional development. We need to define our successes, and we need to help our students understand and apply realistic parameters for their own satisfaction and success in riding.

The chapter **Defining Success** outlines the principles that define successful teaching.

Our obligation as professionals is to follow a strict code of ethics that ensures that each of our students can come to enjoy full trust in us. Trust is the basis of confidence. Students need to have confidence in both their horses and their instructors. As explained in the **Ethics** chapter, a solid code of ethics lays the groundwork for this trust and builds confidence.

Instructors deal with both horse and human behavior in each lesson. Feelings, thoughts and actions play a large role in the riding arena. The chapter, **Why Psychology for the Equestrian Instructor?**, provides an explanation for many of the challenges we deal with in the arena. Combining a basic understanding of psychology with **Tapping Into Students' Motivation for Learning**, gives us valuable information that will help instructors to better understand each student. No matter how experienced we are, we all encounter challenges with our students upon occasion. **Counseling Skills for Instructors,** provides us with the simple counseling strategies that will enable us to move through some of the common problems we encounter with more success. Finally all instructors find themselves faced with **Burn Out** from time to time. Recognizing it and preventing it is much easier than dealing with it when it hits us. This entire section is filled with vital information for ALL instructors.

With our motivation, definition of success, and personal code of ethics in place, each instructor needs to develop and enrich personal career goals. This can include, but is not limited to, being clear on what and who we enjoy teaching, what we feel most competent doing, and what defines satisfaction within career and life activities. The chapter on career development provides ideas and helpful information to measure our progress.

A commitment to consistent professional development allows us to create happy horses that will perform willingly, going the extra mile for their riders. Happy horses plus evolving, advancing riders create fulfilled instructors.

# THE ESSENTIALS OF
# PROFESSIONAL DEVELOPMENT

Commenting on his own education, Alois Podhajsky, former director of the Spanish Riding School, wrote that for more than half a century, the horse was his teacher. In his sensitively written book, *My Horses, My Teachers*, Podhajsky says, *"I have come to value his [the horse's] qualities and to tolerate or to pass with indulgence over his weaknesses, which are so insignificant compared with his honesty and affection, his good will, loyalty, and undeniable share of intelli-gence. My horses not only taught me riding, but they also made me under-stand many a wisdom of life besides."*

Podhajsky knew his motivator and his greatest teacher. He showed a passion for it throughout his professional development that was influ-enced by this clear understanding. Do you know your passion? If you do not, *In Search of Your Image* has chapters dedicated to helping you find it.

Investing in your own professional development is fueled by your motivator and satisfied by your success. Ten guidelines can enrich the investment:

1. It is essential to keep up to date on professional reading.

2. Seek insight and information from all areas of horsemanship and life. Work with it, then share what you have learned with your students.

3. Remain open to new ideas, but delve only into what serves your current interest or need. Trust your curiosity to lead you to what you need to learn next.

4. Watch your students' lessons at clinics with respected clinicians. This is an ideal way to expand and evaluate your own technical know-how as well as to gain a fresh perspective on your students and your own teaching techniques.

| Curious? | | | |
|---|---|---|---|
| **SUPPLEMENT** | **Personally using this skill** | **A desire to learn more** | **NOTES FOR CHANGE:** |
| Visualization | | | |
| Relaxation / Meditation | | | |
| Positive Self-Talk | | | |
| Goal Setting | | | |
| Massage | | | |
| Lunging | | | |
| Yoga, T'ai Chi. Pilates | | | |
| OTHER? | | | |
| | | | Chart 2 |

5. Take lessons and clinics yourself, not only to expand your technical knowledge and teaching style, but to remind you of what it feels like to be the student.

6. Observe top professionals as they train and give lessons. Many new ideas can be picked up this way.

7. Get together with other teaching professionals in your area. You can all benefit from each other's experiences and ideas.

8. Maintain your own standards of physical and professional fitness, especially when the highs or lows of success tempt you to take a break from your disciplines for health and well-being.

| On-Going Professional Development Checklist | | |
|---|---|---|
| **Checkpoint** | **How Often?** | **Dates & Comments** |
| Read professional literature: magazines, books, watch videos and review internet sites. | | |
| Investigate other horsemanship disciplines. | | |
| Seek insight and ideas from non-horse related areas for teaching hints and cross-training. | | |
| Watch your students in clinics, take time to discuss & evaluate the experience with them. | | |
| Take lessons and attend clinics as a student. | | |
| Observe respected professionals teach. | | |
| Discuss teaching issues and ideals with others, especially other professionals. | | |
| | | Chart 3 |

9. Honor your professional lineage and model that respect for your students. Name the sources of your information in print and in person.

10. Follow the Golden Rule of riding: ask of yourself what you ask of your horse and your students; that they be strong, supple, sensitive, and sincere.

It is essential that instructors teach only in areas in which they are well-versed and confident in their ability to impart information to others. If instructors are teaching above their level or outside of their discipline, they will most likely suffer steady deterioration of self and student confidence as expectations of progress are not realized. That said, some of the best instructors are not the best riders. Many are not even currently competing or riding; however, their instruction is solidly founded on experience and education in the material they are teaching. Top instructors have the ability to pass on their wealth of knowledge using an easy-to-understand, systematic approach their students are able to follow.

To become the best riding instructor you can be, you must take time to develop a thorough understanding not only of horses, but of humans as well, and most particularly of yourself.

# DEFINING SUCCESS

*"Success in life could be defined as the continued expansion of happiness and the progressive realization of worthy goals." "Success is a journey, not a destination."* From Deepak Chopra's *The Seven Spiritual Laws of Success.*

Riding and learning are activities riders choose for pleasure and enjoyment. It is the instructor's job to make learning both pleasurable and gratifying for student and horse. A happy horse will perform willingly, going the extra mile for the rider. Happy horses plus evolving, advancing riders create a successful and fulfilled instructor.

A HAPPY HORSE WILL PERFORM WILLINGLY...
GOING THAT EXTRA MILE FOR THE RIDER!

Success means different things to different people. Success is the achievement of something desired, planned, or attempted. Our deep desires fuel our aspirations to succeed. Our motivation produces satisfaction, delight, and gratification; in other words, happiness. Each area in our lives has its own powerful motivator. The lucky individual is one who can enjoy the small successes in life's journey. The first step is to recognize and acknowledge our motivators and thus our definition of success. What is your definition of success?

*My definition of success is to help students learn to get the most out of their horses toward a harmonious performance that meets their goals as they progress in their training, while maintaining and creating a comfortable, performing horse on each and every ride, while becoming independent from me.*

How would your definition differ? There is no right or wrong definition. We must each find our personal idea of success in order to achieve enjoyment and satisfaction from our lessons.

Once we understand our underlying motivators for success, we are able to use them while giving lessons. We can also use this information to create a plan that expands our teaching tools and skills. This plan will help us enjoy each lesson even more, thus becoming more successful at our profession.

First, we must honestly identify our motivators. How do your motivators help you measure your success? Be certain you have identified your motivation and then match it with your 'feeling' after a lesson. How we 'feel' is one of the measuring tools for motivation. Do you know your motivator?

> *You are what your deep, driving desire is.*
>
> *As your desire is, so is your will.*
>
> *As your will is, so is your deed.*
>
> *As your deed is, so is your destiny.*
>
> — Brihadaranyaka Unpanishad IV.4.5

---

### Review Your Motivators

Realizing that none of these common motivators is by nature worse or better than the other.

Rate the following: (1{lowest}—10{highest}…...or N/A {not applicable})

_____Desire to share you knowledge
_____Interest in student's progress
_____Interest in horse's progress
_____Improve quality of horse's performance
_____Make money
_____Feel sense of achievement
_____Improve horse/rider partnership
_____Create harmony between horse and rider
_____Meet student goals
_____Meet your own goals
_____Student/instructor relationship
_____Exercise authority
_____Feel personal power
_____Create independent rider
_____Be popular or well-liked

Review your Motivator ratings, what does this tell you about yourself?

Chart 4

---

Success is related to progress that satisfies our motivators. It is a great idea to fill out the following chart for 10 or more lessons and compare results.

Review your motivators and your satisfaction results. What do these results tell you?

Combining our motivators and our definition of success with sincere professional ethics will set the stage for student success. For example, if earning money is your primary motivator, and you devote yourself to giving the student a lesson dedicated to improvement, your efforts will be both ethical and successful. If, however, you sit in the arena and look forward to the end of the lesson and collecting your check, you are fulfilling your primary motivator but will not feel or be successful with yourself or your student.

Another important aspect of success is to know your assets and limitations. Being realistic, your skills and teaching those students you are qualified to teach allows you to provide ethical services. Instructors need to be at least two stages above their students in order to have the needed technical knowledge. This skill level will allow you and your student to experience lasting success.

Motivators can change, as can your definition of success. At least once a year, it is a good idea to reflect on the past year and review both your motivators and your success rating. Knowing and reviewing these two points will help you remain fresh, satisfied, and happy with the process. Your students will share this with you. As Deepak Chopra said, "Success is the journey, not the destination."

What if instead of feeling success, you feel exhausted or drained? It is important to do something about this as soon as possible. Tired, exhausted instructors will soon find their students becoming unhappy, so it is our ethical responsibility to remain emotionally fresh as well as professionally up-to-date. When you notice you are in a slump, take time to examine your day, your motives, and your students. See what might be wrong. This is a time for reflection and review. (see Burn-out later in this section)

Some important questions to ask yourself when you feel drained:

- When was the last time I felt successful at the end of the lesson or day's teaching?
- Are there certain students I feel successful teaching? If so, why?
- Are there students who drain me? If so, why?
- What about the rest of my day? Do I feel better, worse, or the same as when I teach?
- When was the last time I took a break from teaching?
- What is the best part of my week?
- What do I look forward to the most each day?

Follow the answers to your questions to uncover a solution and then take time to make the necessary changes. There is no time like the present.

The greatest inspiration for instructors is successful, progressing students. A key requirement of professional development is refreshing your awareness of your motivators and your definition of success. Knowing and recalling this about yourself allows you to understand and relate to your students' needs and goals. Helping each student toward success and each horse toward a better performance will feed success no matter what your motivator.

# ETHICAL ISSUES FOR THE RIDING INSTRUCTOR

## By Elizabeth Clarke

*I have to take this call. I have been playing phone tag with this person all week, and this student is not getting what I'm trying to say anyway. It'll only take a minute. . . .*

*How will Sue know if I tack a couple thousand onto the price of this horse? She can afford it, and I need the money right now. . . .*

*I am so tired of nagging those kids not to jump if there's not an instructor around. It's their parents' problem if they do not listen and someone gets hurt. . . .*

*I have to finish this Christmas shopping even if it does make me late for my first lesson. She never lasts the hour anyway. . . .*

*This horse has no business doing the regular hunter circuit. He always comes home sore. But that rider is paying the bills, so I'll just give him some more Bute. . . .*

*I do not have any problem with that girl, but she makes the other clients uncomfortable, so I guess she has to go. Seems a shame. . . .*

*If I pay my assistant "on the table", I'll have to pay all those other taxes and worker's comp insurance, and I really cannot afford that. I can pay her more if I do not report it, so we are both better off. . . .*

Ethical issues arise for the riding instructor when the interests of the instructor differ from those of another party. What is good for the instructor is not always what is best for the student, what is best for the horse, what meets the greater interests or values of society, or even what is required by law. When a choice is to be made between what benefits the instructor at the expense of another party and what is "right" but against the best interests of the instructor, a value based choice has been made. Whether or not it is an ethical choice depends upon the amount of harm done to another to benefit oneself or how much one sacrifices one's own interests to comply with the law, social norms, or the best interests of another. In the world of riding, choices are often made more difficult by the fact that it is often the risk of harm rather than actual quantifiable harm that must be weighed. When a student or instructor perceives a potential harm, but does not think it very likely to occur, otherwise easy choices can become difficult ones. **It is very easy to assume the worst cannot happen and ignore the risk because it rarely does happen. The problem is that when the unexpected does happen, it is often devastating.**

Such choices come up in lessons and lesson barns all the time. Many are economically driven. To do or require the "right thing" might cost more money or time or might cause a student to go elsewhere, leading to the loss of revenue that student represents. In general, while riding instructors can generally see the economic implications of a given choice, they often need a good deal more education on the legal side of "ethical" choices. When the law does not impact the choice, then it is often a matter of living better (making more money) vs. living with oneself. **The law impacts ethical choices more than most equine professionals understand.**

As an example, the law of agency (acting as a fiduciary to represent the interests of another party) frequently comes into play in the buying and selling of horses. Often, the agent/instructor/trainer sees an opportunity to make a little extra money at the expense of a client who has engaged the agent's services to help find a horse. But the law of agency dictates that once one has agreed to act as an agent on behalf of another, the agent cannot act to benefit himself at the expense of the client (the "principal"). Secret profits are prohibited. So are other actions that would benefit the agent but act to the client's detriment. The law prohibits acts such as buying a horse the client cannot ride well simply to make an-

YOUR HONOR, ALL EYES SHOULD BE ON THIS HORSE...
WHO TOOK ADVANTAGE OF MY CLIENT WHILE ACTING AS HIS LEGAL AGENT.

other commission on the resale or seeing a horse that is better than expected and buying it for oneself or another client who will pay more without first giving the opportunity to the client who has arranged the shopping trip. Many equine professionals seem surprised that these actions are actually prohibited, though somewhere deep down they know there is something "wrong" about them. Should the client choose to pursue legal remedies in one of these instances, they are there to be had. **It is simply wrong to take advantage of someone who has engaged you to protect their best interests, tough as it may be to pass up some additional personal benefit, and regardless of how much the student can afford it more than the instructor can.**

Let's take this idea into the arena. The student has hired the instructor for a set period of time for the instructor's help and guidance. The student is expected to pay the full lesson fee. Should not the instructor be expected to pay full attention? If I buy a tool kit at the hardware store and some of the parts are missing, I go back and get a refund or a replacement. If someone paints half of my house, I will not pay him for painting the whole thing. If I take a lesson with an instructor, should I not get a full lesson, an honest evaluation, and help with what to do next? All too often, the instructor will answer a phone call, chat with someone watching, greet an unexpected visitor, or stop to help someone else who is riding at the same time but not part of the lesson. Maybe the instructor is watching the student while she is distracted and feels this is good enough. That is providing part of the product. The instructor owes the student her full attention. Even if the instructor is paying attention, she may fail to raise a fundamental problem because it is difficult to work through. Many an instructor has been heard to assure a student that the horse is going well, when it could be much better, simply to keep the student "happy". It is a rather condescending attitude to assume that the student who is paying for education would rather have meaningless stroking. Boosting confidence is one thing. Boosting ego and revenues with false praise is another. Professionalism and the instructor's duty to the student dictate that the student who has set aside time, shown up, and is eager to improve gets what he is paying for. There are many ways to "cheat" clients, some more subtle and more seemingly innocent than others. The law will not intervene here as it will when there is a formal agency relationship, but the concept is the same. **The instructor owes the student the duty of looking after the student's best interests and delivering a good product.**

I once hosted a clinic given by a true master. All of the horses and riders in the clinic were competing at Prix St. Georges level dressage or above with good scores. The clinician was a brilliant rider and a brilliant teacher, but only when he was interested. If the horse was seven or eight years old and well on its way to the Grand Prix movements, the lesson the rider received was quite impressive, and the horse much improved

> *It is simply wrong to take advantage of someone who has engaged you to protect their best interests.*

at the end of the session. If the rider was having trouble, but the horse interested the clinician, he would often get on and apparently effortlessly achieve a near miraculous transformation of the horse. He did it in such a way that the rider could get back on and experience the feeling of the improvement with no apparent anxiety for the horse. The man was the closest thing I have ever seen to true magic with horses. If the rider was less talented or the horse was older, however, the clinician sat in a chair in the corner of the arena, chatted with whomever was around, ate a little, maybe said a few words to the rider occasionally, but clearly expressed total indifference to any progress for either horse or rider. I asked him at the end of the first day why he would not pay more attention to the riders on older horses, and he explained that they simply did not interest him. If a horse was no't going to be internationally competitive at Grand Prix, he did not want to bother with it. Then I asked him how he could accept money from these riders and not at least try to teach them something, even if it would only improve the rider a bit for future horses. He answered that those riders should not be in the clinic but that was not his fault. He deserved his fee whether or not he was provided with students he considered worth his efforts. On the second day of the clinic, a very accomplished rider entered the ring at the appointed time. I was where I could see but not hear what was going on. Fifteen minutes into a session scheduled for 45 minutes, I saw the rider exit the ring. I went to talk with her, expecting her to be angry. Her response surprised me. "I have had one problem that has been plaguing me with this horse for months, and I just could not break through it. I asked him to help me with that problem, and he did. He could see what I could not feel and gave me just the help I needed. After I understood what was needed, the horse performed the problem movement quite well twice in a row. We both agreed we should reward the horse by stopping at that point. It may have been short, but it was probably the best lesson I have ever had." This clinician exhibited one of the key requirements of an ethical instructor. He had educated himself to a level where he could really help his students without frustrating or wearing out the horses in the process. He was lacking another requirement: that he have the best interest of every student at heart and feel truly obligated to give every student value for the money, time, and effort put into the lesson. **An instructor does not need to teach every person who asks for a lesson, but he does need to put thought and energy into teaching every student to whom he agrees to give a lesson.**

Perhaps less objectionable from a purely ethical standpoint, but probably more dangerous, is the instructor who absolutely pays attention every moment and puts her whole heart into every lesson, but who is not sufficiently advanced in her own horsemanship skills to be able to really help her students. We all know those patient souls who will teach students to groom, tack up, ride the three basic gaits, post on the correct

I DON'T EVEN WATCH THOSE DARN KIDS ANYMORE... THEY DON'T LISTEN WHEN I TELL THEM NOT TO JUMP UNLESS THERE'S AN INSTRUCTOR AROUND.

diagonal, and canter on the correct lead. The horse industry would not be here without them, and most of us would not be riding today if it were not for one of them. They may be the same individuals who can take those riders to the highest levels of their chosen disciplines, but more often not. The teacher who is great with beginners, but who has not made it to the top levels herself, needs to know when it is time for a student to move on to a more advanced instructor. To take someone's money for lessons when one has hit the limit of what one can teach them is just as bad as taking money but choosing not to put any effort into the teaching. The difference here is that trying to teach beyond one's own ability level can be dangerous as well. If an instructor wants to keep students as they move up in skill level, that instructor must pursue the advancement of her own education in order to stay ahead of them. **The instructor should not agree to teach students to whom she cannot offer a substantive increase in knowledge and experience.**

Once an instructor meets the basic requirements of skill level and dedication to deliver a good product, ethical choices move into the day-to-day interaction with students. Common ethical problems arise when the instructor chooses to do what the student wants rather than to insist on what the instructor knows is right. The most frequent bad choice I see in connection with riding instruction is also one of the most obvious and the most stupid. In barns where the horses are impeccably groomed, the tack carefully fitted, and the arenas dragged to perfection daily, one enormous life changing detail is left unattended. It is a conscious choice to allow students to unnecessarily risk their lives by riding without protective headgear. There is an applicable body of law called the doctrine of negligent supervision. The short version of the doctrine of negligent supervision says that if you are holding yourself out as an expert, someone is paying you to teach them, and you know there is something that could significantly enhance their safety in a potentially dangerous situation, you are automatically negligent simply by not requiring the additional safety equipment. Instructors have a legal duty to make sure that those paying for their expertise are protected from harm to the extent it is practical. It does not matter that they are on the steadiest horse in the world. It does not matter that the student argues for ten minutes about the effect of a helmet on her latest hairstyle. What matters is that the expert, given the information available in the industry, knows or should know that a helmet can make the difference between death or serious head injury and a normal active life after a fall and chooses to let the student take the additional preventable risk. The instructor is the expert. It is her job to know and uphold the industry standards that a prudent person in the same industry would uphold. There is little question about the additional protection helmets provide. Yet instructors leave themselves open to the kinds of monetary damages awarded in head injury cases simply because they will not require students to wear helmets. Or let them jump before they have a secure enough seat. Or let them ride a horse that is too hot or too green for the rider's skill level, simply because the student is enamored of the horse and will not stop begging. **Every instructor must put the safety of the riders and horses foremost.**

Forget the law for a moment. Let's just say that you know that by putting on an ASTM/SEI helmet, a person reduces the risk of a devastating head injury by a significant measure. Let's say that a student refuses to wear a helmet and threatens to go down the road to the next instructor who she is sure will not make her wear the helmet. Let's say that you let her ride without a helmet because the training money she pays you pays for your daughter's skating lessons. Let's say that the horse does uncharacteristically spook at something, and the rider does go headfirst into the fence. Let's say you could have saved her life by requiring the helmet and you did not. How do you feel then? How does the equation of living better vs. being able to live with yourself balance at that point? **Basing a decision on the fact that something which is entirely possible "is not very likely to happen" at your barn is a warning sign that you are making the wrong choice.**

"It will not happen to me." "It will not happen with this horse." Those are two of the most dangerous expressions of denial ever heard. If it can happen to anyone, it can happen to you, and it can happen with that horse. Standing firm around issues of safety with a student may cost you that student. Taking the path of least resistance with a headstrong student who is an "accident waiting to happen" is a great way to lose your horses, your business, your home, and many other objects you hold dear. It is also the best way to ruin the student's life. You are the expert. You have the duty to control the situation. This is not a tough choice, because it is the best one for both you and the student. Yet time and again instructors bow to the wishes of a student simply to avoid an unpleasant confrontation. When it comes to safety, ethical choices are usually pretty obvious. The excuses for avoiding them are many. **If you are worried about losing students simply because you enforce safety rules, it is time to rethink what it is you have to offer as an instructor.**

The willful student problem takes many forms beyond the wearing of helmets. The student who insists on buying a fancy horse that is too much horse for her at the moment endangers the student, often tortures the horse, and can risk the safety of everyone else around. An instructor cannot stop her from buying the horse, but she can advise against it, and she can refuse to help her make the mistake if it is a dangerous one. Being willing to take a stand that shows the instructor is willing to lose the client in order to stand by what is right often earns the instructor that client's respect, as well as enhancing the instructor's position with the others who know of the situation. The student who insists on trying advanced feats (a larger cross country course, a hundred mile trail ride) without having first mastered the basics of riding skill and horsemanship presents the same kind of dangers to self, horse, and others. If she is not willing to trust her instructor's judgment regarding her skill level and what she is ready for, she is not likely to be receptive to other kinds of advice from that instructor either. These are not tough calls. At risk for the student is her safety. At risk for the instructor is the loss of a client who probably is not very satisfying anyway. If that client leaves the instructor's program, it may be the best thing that ever happened to the instructor's business. If an instructor takes a stand for what is right for the student and the horse, either the instructor regains the respect of the student or the student leaves. In the latter case, gone from the barn, where anything can happen with horses in an instant, is a person who puts appearance over safety, thrill over the welfare of the horse, and who does not respect the instructor's judgment regarding her ability. The instructor, the other students, and the horses will all be safer as a result. The act of standing up to that student will attract those who do value safety and appreciate the instructor's desire to keep them safe. Such positions are often rewarded in ways we cannot always perceive. **In the case of enforcing safety standards, making the tough choices and enforcing them is rewarded by what does not happen, what does not go wrong, and who is not injured.**

> *In the case of enforcing safety standards, making the tough choices and enforcing them is rewarded by what doesn't happen, what doesn't go wrong, and who isn't injured.*

When there are competitive aspirations involved, the willful student presents another potential problem. In many cases, the student is not acting beyond his capacity, but is asking beyond what the horse is able to or should be expected to do. Short of obvious and flagrant abuse or violations of anti-drugging rules, the law and even the horse show associations will not help the poor horse. The drive to get more points, qualify for the year-end shows, or earn one more title can be irresistible. It can also be contagious. It is the instructor's job first to recognize the problem and not be drawn in by the lofty goals just beyond reach of the horse, and then to speak up when the horses are suffering or at increased risk. It has often been said, "First see to the horse's needs, then to your own." That applies in planning a competition or lesson schedule just as much as it applies after a day of hunting or a schooling session. Sometimes, it is hard to remember that this sport is about the horses. There is often a pressure to forget that they are sensitive beings and to treat them as mere assets or tools. **The expertise for which clients are paying cannot stop at how to jump a bigger fence. It must encompass good horsemanship in all its aspects.**

Everything with horses is a balancing act. Many of us remember with great fondness the days when we could run out to the barn, jump onto our ponies bareback, and go for a good gallop, hair streaming behind us. Some of us also remember with a shudder the friend whose hunt cap did not protect her head from a horse's hoof or the kid riding double who went off backwards and hit her unprotected head on the ground. Finding the balance with students entails making the right choices without becoming oppressive and without eliminating all the fun. Safe practices are critical, but operating always to avoid the risk of litigation can become destructive. Ignoring the rules and laws meant to protect horses and clients can have even more destructive results. **Finding the balance with students means being educated enough to make good judgments about horses and riders at the levels you are teaching. It means knowing the difference between a challenge for which the student is ready and an unacceptable risk.**

How is an instructor to know which way to go, especially when the line is not clear? Instinct is often the first sign of an ethical issue. If you find yourself uncomfortable with a situation, it is worth further thought. Writing out the pros and cons can help, as can running the situation by another person whose opinion you respect. Often, just hearing yourself explain the dilemma can clarify issues you had not even recognized as present. Sometimes, just counting to three before letting yourself answer gives your brain time to hear the various sides and prevent impulsive decisions. Just like any other businessperson, a riding instructor should familiarize herself with the laws and regulations affecting her business. Obeying the laws around ethical choices is basic. Beyond that, an instructor should draw some clear lines around how far she is willing

> **Questions to Ask Yourself When Feeling Uncomfortable**
>
> A few questions that can help to clarify choices and clarify your position around choices that will help explain them to others in a non-offensive, non-defensive way.
>
> - What is at stake, and who stands to lose or gain what from this decision?
> - What is right for the horses who can't speak for or protect themselves?
> - If I do what is easiest today, will it move me in the direction I want to be heading in the long term?
> - Will I feel good about this tomorrow if everything doesn't go smoothly?
> - Will making a little more money today be worth it if I get caught?
> - Am I building a better long-term relationship with this client?
> - Does this client add something to my life that is worth risking this?
> - If something goes wrong, how will it impact my student? Myself? My family?
>
> Chart 6

to go when the pressures are pushing toward choices that may sacrifice the interests of self, family, clients, and the horses.

If you can answer these questions to your comfort and satisfaction, you are on the right track. Will they prevent you from ever regretting a decision? Of course not. Hindsight always lends its own flavor to life. But they may ensure that you are at least confident that you made the best decision you could at the time with the information you had. That is all anyone can ask.

# CAREER DEVELOPMENT

*Defining, Refining, and Enhancing a Career*

## RIDER TO INSTRUCTOR

Riders usually become instructors in one of two ways. One common way is based on a rider's success. Students recruit great riders and competitors to become their teachers. Another common starting point for becoming a teacher is having a passion for horses and for helping people become better riders. Riding instruction is an excellent and obvious way to combine these passions. No matter the starting point, riders who want to become instructors must begin to learn how to teach and, most importantly, become a well-skilled, experienced rider.

People often assume that anyone who can win in the arena or train a horse can teach. Would a college allow even a highly renowned CPA to walk in and begin teaching math and accounting principles and practices? No, the accountant needs to successfully complete a series of education courses to learn how to teach the subject. Similarly, a good instructor must learn the principles and practices of equestrian education.

### Success as Rider and Competitor

How often do people who once enjoyed or are currently having successful careers showing their own horses become riding instructors? Frequently. I got into teaching this way. As an active Pony Clubber and a successful hunter/equitation rider at sixteen, riders in my area began to ask if I would teach them. Flattered and needing money to support my passion for horses, I eagerly obliged. I shudder to think of the mistakes I made from a lack of teaching skills, yet my students were successful in the show ring. Their success fueled my confidence. All I knew at the time was what I had learned from my father's instruction, Pony Club lessons, reading, and competitive experience. I did not know what I needed to know about "how" to teach. What I did have was a curious, open mind that absorbed information like a sponge. In the beginning, I had limited integration skills, did not recognize the need for them, and did not take full advantage of what can result from combining diverse information and skills.

I went to college intending to teach math or science. Since I loved to teach riding, it seemed logical that I would love to teach the subjects I excelled at in high school. Once in college, it did not take me long to realize that I had no desire to teach the same academic subjects day after day, year after year. I re-examined my intention to teach math and science, and decided I needed the variety that I so enjoyed in teaching horse and rider together. Each combination and each lesson provided a new set of challenges. Here was the variety and challenge I sought.

Life circumstances presented an opportunity to develop my equestrian teaching and business management skills. I have barely used my math and science training, but my love of teaching and horses has remained a stable foundation in my career. Did I plan this career? No. I followed my love of horses and my deeply rooted desire to help horses and humans, and this led to becoming a riding instructor. Knowing that I needed horses in my life surpassed everything else and gave me a strong basis for both personal and professional development. It was this need to be with horses combined with my commitment to and love of learning that provided me with many innovative ways to improve my teaching skills. My underlying motivator has always been to help students meet their goals, with improved skills, to create a comfortable and happy horse.

As I started working with the first Pony Club I founded, I was challenged to provide weekly instruction to the twenty members with varying levels of riding skills. Family and other work demands kept me from teaching each lesson, so I organized a program to help experienced local adult riders learn how to teach. This was my first effort to provide a learning framework for potential instructors. I used the same program for the Pony Club 'B' candidates who had to teach to receive their Pony Club ratings. These students received high scores on the teaching aspect of their exam. As I look back on this period, even though my efforts met with success, I recognized my limitations due to lack of education in the area of how to go about the business of teaching riders and the teaching of riding teachers.

## Riders who Love Horses and Become Instructors

Riders who want to become instructors have several options they can pursue to become riding instructors. The process is often much easier for young people involved in organizations designed to give them guidance to become instructors. Few similar opportunities exist for adults. Meeting the needs of adults wanting to become instructors is one of the goals of EES.

Young riders have several opportunities to follow their desire to become instructors. One is to follow the ratings and levels in Pony Club and 4-H. Others wait until they go to college. In the horse world, being a successful rider is the main criteria for receiving your teaching credentials. How will these teachers learn to teach? Several opportunities are available:

- Young people who have access to riding and to youth organizations, such as Pony Club and 4-H, are in an excellent position to begin getting teaching experience as they progress through the ranks of the organization.

- Those who are successfully competing as riders, but are not members of Pony Club or 4-H, can add teaching to their skills either in a carefully selected college program or by following an EES study program.

- Students enrolled in college may choose to expand their riding and teaching skills while they get their degrees by working part time with a trainer as a working student or a full time paying student.

Ann was a student who had a more difficult path to follow than most, but it worked out well for her. She had loved horses as long as she could remember, but her family could not afford for her to ride. To fulfill her need to be around horses, she volunteered at a local barn to do barn work and groom horses. Eventually, she was able to earn one lesson a week. Since she did not have a horse, she was unable to benefit from Pony Club or 4-H opportunities. Ann made an agreement with her parents. If she got good grades and earned a scholarship, they would pay for her to ride at college. She met her goals and rode in college while she studied equine science and education. When she graduated, she had limited experience as a rider, but had gained the skills in education she would need for her career as a public school teacher and as a riding instructor. After college, Ann got a job teaching fourth grade and also took a job at a local riding establishment. For the next four years, Ann exchanged teaching beginners for riding once a week. She took a summer job at a New England camp and gained even more experience. Up until the time Ann got married, she spent summers teaching camp, winters teaching school, riding once a week, and teaching a few beginners. Ann became a successful and popular instructor for beginners because she had honored her personal limitations of technical knowledge and experience and stuck with a group she was comfortable teaching. When she began to raise her family, she was able to continue her instruction three days a week. The work gave her some income and, more importantly, allowed her to continue to enjoy what she loved, teaching and horses.

Adults who decide they want to teach riding will:
- Find an instructor who will mentor them.
- Observe riding lessons, read books and articles, and put into practice what they have learned with students.
- Investigate certification programs that will help prepare them to become educated and certified to teach.
- Consider contacting EES for advice and an individualized program; we have something for anyone interested in riding instruction, no matter where they live or what discipline or level they want to teach.

Emily had been a happy horse owner for years, riding primarily for pleasure with her friends. Her love of horses and people was so obvious that her friends began asking her for help with their own riding. She enjoyed these opportunities and, after a while, decided to become a riding instructor. Her research into practical ways to achieve this goal revealed that both USDF and ARICP offered certification; however, she had no idea how she was going to learn how to teach to take the certification tests. Emily began asking local instructors if she could watch them give lessons. About six months into this, an instructor suggested that she attend an instructors' workshop being offered. The workshop was too far away for her to attend; however, after talking to workshop organizers, Emily decided to try combining an independent study program with a couple of workshops being offered closer to home. After one year of combined study and practice, Emily was ready to take her ARICP exam. She passed with flying colors and now confidently teaches her friends as well as other students in her area.

As you can see, career exploration can occur when you are a young Pony Clubber, about to graduate from college, in the midst of a flourishing career within the horse industry, or in another field. There are three typical career challenges that instructors may run into regardless of how they first came into teaching.

## THREE CAREER CHALLENGES
### Defining Your Career Path

What if you are fresh out of high school and cannot decide on a career path? Do you want to work full time with horses? What careers in and out of the horse world appeal to you? How important is money to you? How do you see your life in five years?, in ten years? What can help you decide on a career with horses or a career that does not involve horses? Can you combine two careers and do both?

Sally, in her junior year in high school, was torn between a riding career and higher education. After meeting with both her counselor and her riding instructor, she chose to do both. Instead of going to college full time, she took two courses a semester while working in a well-respected equestrian center. It took her six years to graduate from college, but she ended up with two professions, one in business management and the other as a trainer. Sally combined the two, starting her own business and continuing to train several horses a day.

## Refining Your Career Path

What if you love horses and riding but are tired of your current non-horse career? All horse lovers must be careful when they consider a change of career that will turn their avocation into a vocation. Should you become a riding instructor, trainer, barn manager, or groom? This needs to be carefully examined given the long hours, low pay, and limited social time that characterize jobs in the equine industry.

It is natural for people to consider career changes throughout their lives. How do you decide if this is the right move for you? There are many questions to ask yourself. Make a list of what you like and do not like about your current life, both with horses and your current employment. What do you most enjoy in each week with horses, employment, family life, and social life? Other important considerations are your financial needs and how much time you want to dedicate to each area of your life. Evaluating these needs and projecting your life with a clear view of it in five years and then in 10 years will help you evaluate and thoughtfully decide on a career change.

Tom's decision offers an ideal example. At fifty-five, he had grown tired of his law practice. His leadership skills set the stage for his interest in teaching; he had taught in the local pony club while his kids were members. His children were now grown, educated, and had their own families, and he wanted to spend more time with horses himself. He did not know what to do next, because his profession had provided for a luxurious lifestyle. After careful self-examination and consultations with friends, Tom decided to give up his law practice, develop a law consulting service and teach a limited number of riding students. The complex schedule was no problem, given Tom's successful competitive schedule of the past fifteen years. The adjustment presented some challenges, but two years later he found himself happier with less money, less pressure, and more satisfaction in each day.

## Enhancing Your Career Path

On occasion, well-seasoned instructors experience a bout of boredom or a spark of enlightenment that leads to a desire to change their instructional focus or expand their services. They may decide to combine riding instruction with other skills such as management, exercise programs, psychology, and/or coaching. If you discover an area you would like to combine with your existing instruction program, how do you institute a change in your career? The first step is to examine what has prompted your desire for the change. It is usually ignited by curiosity or an experience that has had a dramatic effect on something in your life. Once you know why you want to make a change, determine how it can compliment your existing career or what changes will be required in your career as you currently know it. Take Cynthia, for example. Cynthia loved riding and was an accomplished instructor for low-level riders. Following her desire to expand her education, she explored yoga, t'ai chi and Pilates. Cynthia found that Pilates was a very useful tool for her and felt it would be great for her students. As an educated consumer, she decided to pursue certification as a Pilates instructor. She now teaches Pilates to riders and non-riders and has helped many riders improve their riding performances in a unique way she would not have been able to do otherwise. Not every instructor will want to add additional skill sets to their teaching operation like Cynthia did, but for those of you who already have unique areas of additional skills, integrating them into your riding can be a very rewarding experience for both you and your students.

If you recognize in yourself the need or desire for a more satisfying career, the first step is self-examination of all aspects of your life. This gives you a clear vision of what you want to consider changing. As is often the case, you may find it difficult to recognize by yourself what you need or your unique gifts. Career counseling is readily available—do not hesitate to take advantage of these services to guide you while you make decisions that will lead to a satisfying career plan or change.

*When help would help. . .*
*Need a career change?*
*Feeling burned out?*
*Depressed?*
*Do you lack satisfaction?*
*Find yourself avoiding the*
*   barn or arena?*
*Has a new idea inspired you?*
*Are you....?*

To remain professionally fresh, recognize when you need a change or new inspiration along the path of your career. It is essential to evaluate what you are doing related to how you feel at the beginning and end of each day. See if you can design your career around the elements that give you the greatest joy and satisfaction. The balance between motivation and success creates enthusiasm and satisfaction. This fuels our daily lives and helps us make intelligent decisions as our careers develop.

# WHY PSYCHOLOGY FOR EQUESTRIAN INSTRUCTORS?

## BY KATHY KELLY, Ph.D.

Psychology is the study of human behavior. Every day, deep within the hallowed halls of academia, psychologists study the myriad of feelings, thoughts, and actions displayed by the human species. Some of these findings stay buried within the walls of science, as psychologists talk endlessly to other psychologists about what they found. However, other findings do make their way out to the world at large. Indeed, many of the public's beliefs and ideas about people and "how they tick," come from the world of psychology. Charts 7 and 7A contain a few of psychology's words and phrases that have become part of our common vocabulary.

In addition, the psychological insights and principles found in the science lab have found their way into such fields as education, communications, business, engineering, management, neuroscience, and health care (to name just a few). Given this wide and diverse range of influence, one could make an argument that the field of psychology is suffering from multiple personality disorder!  However, the truth of the matter is that psychology is interesting to so many people because it has important, practical significance for our everyday lives. Just look at the sheer volume of books dedicated to psychology and its related topics in bookstores!  In other words, psychology is popular because it is fundamentally useful.

# SO WHAT CAN PSYCHOLOGY
# DO FOR INSTRUCTORS?

Riding instructors deal with people everyday. Perhaps more significantly, instructors deal with people who are dealing with horses every day. This fact alone should qualify instructors for an advanced degree in psychology! As most instructors will tell you, human nature can get triggered in full force when people and horses combine. The sheer presence of the horse, along with riders' efforts to understand and communicate with them, brings up an intensity of emotion that is rarely seen in other teaching professions. Riding instructors not only have to work with a large animal, who has a natural flight instinct, but also with the wide variety of human beings sitting on top of that large animal, trying to learn to ride it. Thus, instructors are often on the front line of many difficult and intense interactions, not only between rider and horse, but also between instructor and rider (and sometimes between instructor and horse!). This can be an untenable position – and one that requires considerable tact, talent, and skill.

The world of psychology can help! By providing riding instructors with practical and useful knowledge, skills, exercises and techniques, psychology can help them develop both personally and professionally.

## Personal Growth and Development

Many instructors seek out opportunities for their own personal growth and development. They want to feel happy, content, and fulfilled in life, within and beyond the world of horses. Whether they try counseling, read self-help books, or attend seminars or conferences, these instructors are searching for a way to work through personal issues or problems so that they can be more successful and effective in their lives. In this book, the **chapter on burnout** provides an example of how psychology can address the personal growth of instructors. It discusses some of the specific stressors experienced by riding instructors, and describes in detail the various signs and symptoms associated with the different stages of burnout. This chapter ends with a list of suggestions for the prevention and treatment of this serious problem.

## Professional Growth and Development

Instructors are also seeking ways to improve professionally. In their profession, instructors find themselves having to take on a multitude of different roles over the course of a day, and thus need to be well skilled across many situations. For example, one moment instructors may be trying to teach a technical skill, a moment later they need to handle a physical or emotional crisis! As well, instructors frequently teach across the whole age and developmental spectrum, from young children to older adults. And, instructors are often called upon to be mentors, role models and coaches, who are able to inspire, energize and sustain their students' interest in and motivation for their sport. The range of skills and abilities needed to be successful in all of these areas is considerable! Psychology can be of particular service for instructors in the professional development arena. In this book, the chapters on motivation for learning and counseling skills provide instructors with information and tools from the

| Common Words and Phrases from Psychology | |
|---|---|
| Unconscious motivation | Based on Freudian theory, this refers to motivations occurring outside of a person's conscious awareness |
| Introvert and extrovert | This is based upon Carl Jung's description of two different world orientations. Introversion refers to people who are focused on the inner world of ideas and introspection. Extroversion refers to people who are focused on the outer world of people and relationships. |
| Type A and B personality | These definitions stem from the psychology of stress. Type A individuals are described as time-driven, pressured in action and speech, interpersonally intense, and domineering. Type B individuals are more relaxed, less sensitive to time pressure, easy going, laid back, and tend to talk slowly and deliberately. |
| Oral fixation | One of Freud's early stages of development, when the infant uses their mouth as the primary means of pleasure. Used today to describe habits such as smoking, overeating, and drinking. |
| Anal retentive | Another of Freud's developmental stages, this term is used today to characterize someone who is seen to be excessively orderly, neat, and attentive to details |
| Transference | Another term from Freudian theory, this refers to situations in therapy when the client reacts to the therapist as if the therapist was someone else, usually a parent or significant other from their childhood. |
| Projection | One of Freud's defense mechanisms, this is when a person attributes their own unwanted or unacceptable impulses to others, and attacks them for it. |
| Regression | Another defense mechanism, this is when a person, under stress or trauma, returns to the behaviors and feelings of an earlier stage of development. |
| Self-actualization | A term used by both Abraham Maslow and Carl Rogers, which refers to the human desire to reach one's ultimate potential. |
| | Chart 7 |

fields of sport and clinical psychology, respectively. In learning how to identify the different motivations of your students, instructors can adapt and individualize their teaching style to their students, making them just that much more effective. In addition, the communication skills required by a clinical psychologist can be of enormous benefit to instructors, as they maneuver through the emotional minefield of getting their students to "change."

Each of the chapters in the psychology section of the book was written specifically with the riding instructor in mind. It is hoped that this information will provide instructors with some new "tools" that they will find helpful and therefore will put into their teaching toolbox. Ultimately, it is our hope that riding instructors everywhere will continue to experience personal and professional satisfaction from their career choice. And, may you all continue to provide students everywhere with the joy and wonder of becoming connected to that most noble and loving animal, our friend, the horse.

| Common Words and Phrases from Psychology | |
|---|---|
| Ego | Freud and Jung both used this term to describe an individual's felt sense of "I". This word has also come to mean an attitude of narcissism, as in "you have a big ego". |
| Schedules of reinforcement | Based upon B.F. Skinner's work on behavioral learning, this refers to the rate and frequency of rewards or punishments. A good example is intermittent reinforcement, which rewards people after random time periods. Slot machines operate on this principle! |
| Classical conditioning | This term stems from Pavlov's experiments of training dogs to salivate upon hearing a bell. This term describes any conditioning that is done by pairing up two different stimuli, then taking away one of them and using only the other. One example in the horse world is when vets train horses to urinate upon hearing a particular sound, such as rattling a can. |
| Neurotic | Stemming from Freudian theory, neurosis is when a person became rigid and inflexible in their personality style, such that they are hindered in their ability to be function optimally. Today, the term has come to refer to the "everyday weirdness" that characterizes everyone at one time or another. |
| | Chart 7A |

# TAPPING INTO YOUR STUDENT'S MOTIVATION FOR LEARNING

By KATHY KELLY Ph.D.

For many instructors, trying to figure out a student's motivation seems a lot like the search for the Holy Grail. Many frustrated instructors find themselves asking questions such as the following:

shhhh... listen!

J.D.BAKER 2001

LISTEN TO ENERGY

- What makes this rider tick?

- Why is one rider so happy despite not winning a ribbon, while another one, with a ribbon, is in tears?

- How come competing pumps up some riders, but not others?

- When do I push hard, and when do I back off?

Over the past few decades, sport psychologists have been trying to find the answers to these and other related questions. Their findings provide us with important insights into the mysteries of motivation, offer us some practical tools that can help us answer these questions and, most importantly, help us become more effective in our teaching.

## WHAT IS MOTIVATION ANYWAY?

Webster's New World Dictionary describes a "motive" as **"some inner drive, impulse, or intention that causes a person to do something or act in a certain way."**

And "motivate"? This means **"to provide with an incentive; impel."**

So, instructors, if you are looking to motivate your students, you are searching for their "inner drive, impulse, or intention." WHY? So that you can tap into these motives to provide "an incentive or impellent" to push your students forward in their learning processes.

**So what "MOTIVATES" riders and other athletes?** Research has found that one of the most powerful motivators for athletes is the feeling that they are good at what they do. In other words, athletes are motivated by competence! If athletes believe they are competent, they feel successful; and if they feel successful, they stay motivated to achieve. As the famous saying goes . . . "Nothing begets success like success"! Simple? Yes . . .and no.

Research has also found that not all athletes define success the same way! As instructors well know, what is success for one rider may be a disappointment for another. How does this work? Well, it seems that there are two major ways of defining success, which are called TASK and EGO GOAL ORIENTATIONS. Both task and ego definitions of success are valid and legitimate ways to approach any achievement situation. Actually, most of us identify a bit with both! However, people differ in the importance they give to these two goal orientations. And, whether one is dominant in one or the other has enormous implications for how instructors can tap into and sustain a rider's motivation for their sport. Let's learn more:

## How Do TASK and EGO Goals
## Relate to MOTIVATION for Learning?

**Task-Oriented Athletes** enter learning situations willingly. Since their goal is personal progress, they see any chance to learn something new, master a new challenge, or improve upon a past performance as a way to feel competent, thus successful. Bolstered by feelings of success, these athletes tend to try hard, persist through difficulty, and exert considerable effort in the learning process. These individuals are often called "natural students."

**Ego-Oriented Athletes** enter learning situations reluctantly. Since their goal is to demonstrate superior ability, the "learning curve" diminishes their sense of competence. They want to perform correctly right away and have little tolerance or value for gradual improvement. In fact, any activity or task that exposes their "holes" or weaknesses generates

| TASK GOALS | EGO GOALS |
|---|---|
| Goal = personal progress | Goal = superior ability |
| Task-oriented athletes feel successful when learning, improving, and mastering challenges. They participate in sports because they enjoy the activity (or task) in and of itself. These athletes concentrate on their own performance, paying little attention to the performance of others. In a word, task-oriented athletes are "self - focused" in their motivation. | Ego-oriented athletes feel successful when demonstrating their ability to others. They participate in sports because they want to show off their talent and skills. These athletes concentrate on comparing their ability with others and focus on "crushing" their opponents, being the best, and finishing first. In other words, ego-oriented athletes are "other-focused" in their motivation. |
| | Chart 8 |

frustration and fear of failure. Under conditions of repeated difficulties, ego-oriented athletes may begin to demean the activity, withdraw effort, and may even quit. However, if an ego-oriented athlete thinks they are doing "better than" others during the learning process, they will feel competent and successful and will maintain motivation. It is only under conditions that threaten their sense of competence, such as showing less ability than others, that these athletes withdraw motivation and effort.

**How Task and Ego Oriented are you? Take the following quiz and find out. . .**

---

## TASK & EGO QUESTIONNAIRE
### *What makes you feel "MOST" successful?*

*Please read each scenario and rate how much you agree or disagree on the scale from 1 to 5.*

**As a rider, I would feel most successful if . . .**

|  |  | Totally Disagree | | | | Totally Agree |
|---|---|---|---|---|---|---|
| 1. | I started placing first on a regular basis | 1 | 2 | 3 | 4 | 5 |
| 2. | I finished a competition with the best score among my peers | 1 | 2 | 3 | 4 | 5 |
| 3. | My performance at a show was a 'personal best' | 1 | 2 | 3 | 4 | 5 |
| 4. | I realized that I had finished ahead of a lot of other riders in the competition | 1 | 2 | 3 | 4 | 5 |
| 5. | My instructor told me that I was ready to move up to another level | 1 | 2 | 3 | 4 | 5 |
| 6. | I won a big competition that got written up in the 'Chronicle' | 1 | 2 | 3 | 4 | 5 |
| 7. | I worked as hard as I could during a lesson | 1 | 2 | 3 | 4 | 5 |
| 8. | During a clinic, it became obvious that I was riding better than any of the riders in my group | 1 | 2 | 3 | 4 | 5 |
| 9. | I finished a cross-country ride with no refusals after previous attempts to do so | 1 | 2 | 3 | 4 | 5 |
| 10. | I could do something others couldn't, like riding a strange horse better than anyone else | 1 | 2 | 3 | 4 | 5 |
| 11. | I did something new, like rode my first dressage test from memory | 1 | 2 | 3 | 4 | 5 |
| 12. | I overcame difficulties, like finishing a jumping class despite having fallen off early in the course | 1 | 2 | 3 | 4 | 5 |

Scoring for the Task & Ego Questionnaire:

> TASK ITEMS:  #'s 3, 5, 7, 9, 11, 12
> EGO ITEMS:  #'s 1, 2, 4, 6, 8, 10

Add up the numbers for all the task and ego items separately. Your task and ego scores should fall somewhere between the range of 6 and 30.

Scores:

> 6-14  Low Levels
> 15-23  Average Levels
> 24-30  High Levels

Chart 8A

# LEVELS OF MOTIVATION

## Highest Levels of Motivation

*High Task combined with High/Average Ego:* These are our "elite athletes." These individuals have a strong desire to succeed and a love of competing combined with a strong drive to practice and improve. As a result, these athletes can feel satisfaction no matter what the outcome. If they succeed, they feel GREAT! If they fail, they can fall back on their task orientation. They learn from the experience and work hard to improve next time. They like the challenge. Learning for these athletes is believed to be a lifelong requirement for enjoyment.

> *All people have a little of both types of goal orientation - Task and Ego. It is the specific combination of task and ego that is important when trying to understand one's motivation.*

## Lowest Levels of Motivation

*High Ego combined with Average/ Low Task:* These are the athletes most at risk for frustration, tears, anger, and "dropping out." These athletes get "high" on success and crash in defeat. When all is going well, they appear committed and work hard. However, under conditions of repeated difficulties or failures, their self-esteem takes a big hit, and they tend to withdraw or demean the effort to try. They do not feel a sense of accomplishment with "a job well done"; rather, they need external validation of success. Learning holds no personal interest to them. Indeed, early unskilled efforts often leave them feeling demoralized, inadequate, and inferior.

---

### TASK/EGO PROFILES

**High Task/High Ego** — very motivated, competitive, solid confidence
**High Task/Average Ego** — very motivated, semi-competitive, solid confidence
**High Task/Low Ego** — very motivated, not competitive, solid confidence

**Average Task/High Ego** — well-motivated, very competitive, okay confidence
**Average Task/Average Ego** — well-motivated, semi-competitive, okay confidence
**Average Task/Low Ego** — well-motivated, not competitive, okay confidence

**Low Task/High Ego** — MOTIVATION AT RISK, very competitive, fragile confidence
**Low Task/Average Ego** — MOTIVATION AT RISK, semi-competitive, fragile confidence
**Low Task/Low Ego** — NOT MOTIVATED, often not in sport, lacks purpose or desire

Chart 9

---

*THE MOST EFFECTIVE AND HAPPY LEARNERS ARE HIGH TASK. The level of ego appears to be less relevant. Raise the task levels and let the individuals' ego go as high as they want. High egos folks with LOW TASK are most at risk!*

## MOTIVATIONAL CLIMATES

What can an instructor do to help create HIGH TASK students? Instructors can help students to become more task-oriented in their learning through a combination of a) how you structure your lessons and b) your interpersonal skills. In other words, what kind of "motivational" climate do you create?

Research has found three kinds of "motivational climates" to be present in sport activities. These are:

### Mastery Climate

This type of atmosphere focuses on learning. Instructors who foster a mastery climate value acquisition of skills, setting goals, personal improvements, and individual challenges. Social comparison is minimized and mistakes are viewed as part of the learning process. Instructors who create mastery climates encourage students to identify what they want out of riding, how they think they can get there, and try hard to instill in their students a love for the "road taken to get there," not just the outcomes. Some mastery instructors minimize the importance of outcomes; others use outcomes as information about how a student is doing. While some mastery-focused instructors eschew competition, many others encourage it; they just get excited about what winning may mean for learning's sake and not for winning in and of itself.

### Performance Climate

This type of atmosphere focuses on achievements and accomplishments. Instructors who foster a performance climate value superiority, excellence, and talent. Special skills are rewarded. Social comparison is used as a form of motivation. Mistakes can be treated negatively as a sign of lack of progress, laziness, or weakness. However, instructors who create a performance climate are often enthusiastic, have strong motivational skills, and can generate a strong competitive desire. Only problem is, the exclusive emphasis on winning and performance forces students into a "must win or be a failure" mentality – which is often NOT what the instructor intends! Too much emphasis on accomplishments in relation to others short-circuits the natural love of learning that many students start with – and instead generates a need to outperform others. This necessitates a focus on how others are doing, which has been shown to be detrimental to what sport psychologists, coaches, and trainers know is critical to maximal learning – a task focus.

## Autonomy Supportive Climate

This type of atmosphere focuses on the "soft, warm, and fuzzy" aspects of the student – instructor relationship. Instructors who provide autonomy support encourage the development of their student's independence as a learner. As a result, the emphasis is on personal goals, responsibility, and accountability in the learning process. The goal is to gradually decrease the student's passive dependence on the instructor for what is taught and how. This is all done in the atmosphere of a truly caring relationship. In other words, autonomy-supportive instructors seek to help their students become autonomy-supportive "self-determined" in their learning. Riders often describe these instructors as having the following strengths:

- Good with people
- Excellent social skills
- Handle their own and others' emotions well
- Provide their students with a sense of acceptance and confidence

Research indicates that sport environments that combine strong mastery climates with autonomy-supportive environments produce athletes with the **highest levels of task orientation**. High task orientation is associated with adaptive achievement strategies, such as effort, persistence, feelings of satisfaction, enjoyment, and high levels of involvement and commitment.

On the other hand, those sport environments that create strong performance climates without the inclusion of mastery and autonomy-supportive elements produce athletes with the **highest levels of ego orientation**. High ego orientation combined with moderate or low levels of task orientation are linked with maladaptive achievement strategies such as lack of effort, persistence, withdrawal, demeaning of activity, worry, tension, stress, and lack of fun.

# COUNSELING SKILLS FOR INSTRUCTORS
## *Help for Dealing with Difficult Situations*

By KATHY KELLY Ph.D.

### WHY DO INSTRUCTORS TEACH?

When asked why they teach, instructors often respond with some version of "because I want to help others learn what I know." When asked what makes them most satisfied when teaching, instructors tend to say, "when my students 'get it'." In other words, most instructors state that their primary goal when teaching is to be EFFECTIVE.

RESISTENCE/DEFENSE MECH

### WHAT OBSTACLES GET IN THE WAY?

For most instructors, teaching what they know is easy. What is harder, at times, is getting students to receive, absorb, and utilize this information. Not surprisingly, it is when the student is not "getting it" that instructors report feeling the least effective in their teaching. The following list includes some of the most common situations that instructors consider to be "difficult":

- Student's unrealistic expectations
- Disagreements with or conflicts around the instructor's method, viewpoint, or assessment
- Students who do not seem to be ready or willing to learn
- Lack of progress in student's riding despite regular lessons

It seems then that some of the most difficult teaching situations involve instructor/student discrepancies, such as what is being taught, needs to be taught, should be taught, and how it is being taught. A common thread running through all of these examples is the potential presence of CONFLICT. Most people do not like conflict. Instructors are no exception. One of the reasons instructors consider the above scenarios difficult is because the conflict can rise up and take over the lesson. So, the instructor (and sometimes the student) will often let the conflict go unresolved. The problem with this tactic? The conflict just sits there, festering, and becomes like that infamous white elephant sitting in the room, with no one acknowledging its presence. So how can instructors teach their students to change or modify their skills, attitudes, perceptions, and perhaps beliefs, with the least amount of conflict? It is to the world of counseling that we can turn for help and guidance.

## DEALING WITH CONFLICT — HELP
## FROM THE WORLD OF COUNSELING

At first glance, riding instructors and counselors seem like very different professions. Yet they actually share much in common. Both are helping professions. Both involve the development of a working one-on-one relationship. And perhaps most significantly, both professions **are in the business of change.** For instructors, students come seeking help with their riding, which means, by definition, changing something about how they currently ride. For counselors, clients come seeking relief from psychological stress and anguish, which often necessitates personal change of some kind. As we all know from personal experience, change is HARD. People do not typically seek out change. It is important to recognize that when change comes knocking on someone's door, it brings with it a host of uncomfortable feelings that can trigger defensive responses. As a result, the instructor's presence, through their very role as "change agents", can generate conflict. Why? Because lessons bring up students' ambivalence about change. While one part of the student recognizes and wants to change, another part of the student does not want to go out of their comfort zone. So, in order to help people work through conflict associated with change, both counselors and instructors need to understand the theory and background of ambivalence. Let's learn more about this common, yet fascinating human emotion.

### What Exactly Is Ambivalence?

Ambivalence is a state of conflicting feelings. During any change process, people will experience a multitude of feelings. When some of these feelings are in direct opposition to each other, we say a person is ambivalent. There are many reasons why riders might feel ambivalent during lessons. They may really want to ride at a higher level, but at the same time are put off by the time and effort that is needed to do so. Some riders may find themselves pushed out of their physical comfort zone when instructors try to change well learned, established riding patterns. Other riders may be conflicted because they are confused or afraid, and they are afraid to reveal their internal dilemma to their instructor. Understandably, any situation that creates such internal conflict can cause stress and discomfort! Therefore, people typically do not choose to stay in an ambivalent state and are often seeking a way out. There are three main ways that people can feel conflicted, thus becoming ambivalent:

- **Approach – Approach Conflict**:  Here, the choice is between two positive options. An example would be a student who cannot choose between two wonderful horse shows.

- **Avoidance – Avoidance Conflict**:  This involves a choice between two equally unappealing options. An example would be the student who cannot decide whether to work without stirrups or take a lunge line lesson. Both options are seen as boring!

- **Approach – Avoidance Conflict**:  The grand champion of ambivalence! This conflict serves to keep people stuck for the longest periods of time because the individual is both attracted and repelled by the same option. That is, the individual perceives costs and benefits to both sides of the issue. An example would be a student who wants desperately to compete in the jumpers but is concerned about jumping such high fences.

### Common Communication Traps

Instructors, upon stumbling into ambivalence, tend to respond in some characteristic ways that actually make the problem worse – by creating resistance in their students! What are some of these communication traps?

- **The two-sided trap**:  This is when the instructor, during a conversation, identifies a "problem." As the instructor begins to take action to address the problem, he/she unwittingly has begun to speak for one side of the student's ambivalence, leaving the student free to speak for the other side. In other words, instructor and student are each voicing only one side of a two-sided problem! This tendency of the student to get you to argue for one side of their ambivalence so that they can argue for the other is human nature. We all do this, and it is not due to any personality flaw or personal weakness on anyone's part. This two-sided trap is, however, very hard to get out of once you are in it, and it can be very frustrating for both parties, since nothing really gets accomplished.

- **The "Expert" Trap**:  This is when instructors, in their sincere desire to help their students, allow themselves to be perceived as having all the answers. The main problem with this trap is that the student can "react" against your expert opinion. This is similar to the problems associated with an authoritarian parenting style. Kids tend to rebel against it. So do students, no matter what age! If the student does unquestioningly accept the instructor's advice, the opportunity for self-discovery is lost. Any learning that takes place is likely to be only on a surface level, because the student has taken on a passive learning role. The biggest problem with this trap is that the student does not address his/her ambivalence about change.

- **The "My Way" Trap**: This is the classic "differing expectations" scenario. The instructor has one point of view, but the student has a different one. In other words, they are not "on the same page." This tends to produce lessons where the instructor puts a lot of effort into teaching, but the student often cannot reproduce their performance or explain what it is that they are doing. This trap, similar to the expert trap described above, encourages students to become a passive recipient of instructions as opposed to being an active part of the learning process.

- **Yes-No Trap**: This occurs when the instructor asks a series of close-ended questions that can be answered with a "yes" or a "no". The problem is that the instructor is putting in more effort than the student, the student is allowed to stay in a passive role, and the pattern allows little opportunity for the student to experience learning through self-discovery.

Each of these traps describes common ways instructors (and beginning counselors) tend to respond to students who are experiencing ambivalence. The biggest problem with falling into these communication traps is that they tend to create resistance on the part of the student. What do we mean by resistance, and what is the big problem with it?

## Resistance

In the world of counseling, resistance is viewed as any sign on the client's part that says, "I'm not with you." In the world of equestrian instruction, it can be seen as any behavior that suggests that the student is not keeping up with the lesson. That is, resistance is a student's way of indirectly saying, "Wait a minute, I do not get this," "I do not agree," "I'm unsure or scared," or even, "I'm not sure I trust you." The key word here is "indirect." If students could directly say to their instructors the above statements, much of the resistance in lessons would be immediately eliminated. However, students tend not to be that direct, for many reasons. They might be shy, afraid, embarrassed, or do not know themselves how they feel! For whatever reason, resistance pops out often in teaching situations and in various but identifiable ways. As you read through the following list of common resistances, (see chart 10) you may be surprised to find that you can provide personal examples of each one!

### THE PROBLEM WITH RESISTANCE

So what happens when instructors come face to face with resistance? Well, this depends much on the instructor; but many find themselves engaged in a classic **power struggle,** with often-disastrous results. What is a power struggle? A useful explanation is that power struggles exist

## FORMS OF RESISTANCE

| Resistance | Description | Common Phrases |
|---|---|---|
| **Challenging the Instructor** | The student directly or indirectly questions the instructor's point of view, knowledge, or directions. | "I've never heard THIS before." "This is stupid!" "Now how is THAT supposed to work?" |
| **Stopping Communication** | The student prevents the instructor from maintaining a dialogue by either talking over or cutting off the instructor before she is finished speaking. | "No, that's not it!" "Wait, wait. . ." "I don't want to talk about this anymore." |
| **Rejecting Responsibility** | The student does not acknowledge her role in the problem. This is done by either blaming someone or something else (the horse is a common target), making excuses minimizing the problem, disagreeing with reality, becoming pessimistic and defeatist, minimizing the risks, and rejecting the instructor's attempts to problem-solve. | "Yes, but . . ." the MOST COMMON "It's not that bad." "I'm not really out of control!" "What's the use?" "I'll never get it." "You're exaggerating; it's not that dangerous!" |
| **Passive Resistance** | This is seen in students who are purposely inattentive, disruptive, stay silent in response to direct questions, or answer questions by going off topic. When confronted, they often respond with "I don't know." They can also become submissive and quiet. Frequently, they appear sullen. These students are often angry or fearful, but don't feel comfortable expressing themselves. | "I don't know." "Hey, look at that!" "Did I tell you...." Sullen stares. Shrugged shoulders Silence |

Chart 10

when the instructor and student are both (overtly or covertly) vying for "control" over the learning process. In fact, many instructors believe that since they are the "experts," they are in control of the learning process. However, research from the field of education and learning has demonstrated that students learn BEST by being in charge of their own learning. As well, studies show that when students lack choices and self-determination, "resistant" behaviors increase.

## Dealing with Resistance

So, how can instructors prevent themselves from becoming another statistic in the "power struggle wars"? Research has found that one of the most successful strategies is **to meet resistance with nonresistance**. Sounds simple, does not it? It is, but as with many simple things, doing it is another matter entirely. Resistance tends to create resistance. The more one person opposes another, the more the second person digs in and holds their ground. This interchange can have wide-ranging results, from one side "giving in" (a shallow victory in the education field), to the two opponents agreeing to disagree (in teaching, a stalemate), all the way to verbal and/or physical abuse. Luckily, the ability to meet resistance with nonresistance is a learned skill, but one that takes considerable practice.

The main goal of these strategies is to help the instructor move the student past the initial resistance to an understanding of their ambivalence behind the resistance. So each of these strategies is designed to encourage the student to expand on their initial comment, to keep talking, and to stay engaged in a dialogue so that they can better understand themselves what is stopping them from progressing. In other words, these strategies are designed to help the student through the process of self-discovery! 

## Communication Strategies
### Reflective Listening

Reflective listening means that the listener actively tries to understand the meaning behind the speaker's words. So often, we assume we know what the speaker is talking about, but we never check it out! In reflective listening, which could also be called "curious listening," the aim is to make an educated guess as to what you think the speaker means by what they are saying and check it out by repeating your guess back as a statement. Why not as a question, you may ask? After all, your feedback is a guess. However, statements have been found to work better because they generate less resistance than questions. See if you can tell the difference in how you might respond to the following two reflections:

**You're feeling anxious about the horse show this weekend?**
**You're feeling anxious about the horse show this weekend.**

The question can be answered "yes" or "no", but the statement begs for clarification or elaboration. Reflective listening requires the listener to take on a "beginner's mind," which means not making any assumptions about what the speaker means. THIS IS HARD NOT TO DO. We all make assumptions, and often we are right. However, when we are wrong, we do not realize it right away and chaos can rein supreme during the dialogue until someone figures it out! Here are some examples of reflective listening techniques:

## SIMPLE REFLECTION

This is one of the core tools of the counselor and a major skill in Active Listening (see Equestrian Instruction). It means that you simply reflect back what you heard your student say, but in your own terms. The point? To encourage students to clarify what they mean by their comments.

EXAMPLES:

1. *S: This exercise is so stupid!*
   *I: You do not think that there is anything good or helpful in this exercise.*

2. *S: I do not see how my horse can be unbalanced; we win ribbons all the time at horse shows!*
   *I: This is confusing for you, and you do not see how what I'm saying can possibly be true.*

## EXAGGERATED REFLECTION

This is basically the same as a simple reflection, but stated in a more extreme fashion. The goal is to encourage students to give voice to the other side of their ambivalences.

EXAMPLES:

1. *S: Those jumps look awfully big!*
   *I: You're thinking that you could NEVER jump fences of this size.*

2. *S: I really do not mind Bucky going that fast, it's no big deal.*
   *I: So you think that it's perfectly safe for you and Bucky to be going this speed.*

## TWO-SIDED REFLECTION

If you know the student is ambivalent, you can reflect back both sides of the conflict.

EXAMPLES:

1. *S: This is too much work!*
   *I: This must be hard for you! On one hand, you understand the need to have your horse truly forward and round, but on the other hand, it seems like all the fun has gone out of riding.*

2. *S: I do not see how this is going to help.*
   *I: I hear you saying that you are quite frustrated with how things are going in your riding, but also that you are not sure if what I want you to do is going to work.*

## STEP-ASIDE REFLECTION

Sometimes, the best way to deal with resistance is to step aside it, especially if it is a tough issue or one that requires more thinking time before responding. This is not an avoidance of the issue, just a detour.

EXAMPLES:

1. S: *I know you are going to tell me that I need a different horse, but I'm not going to sell Magic, no way!*

   I: *Slow down a bit! I'm just getting to know you. There is no way I'm ready to make any kind of recommendation at this point. So let's not worry about that right now, okay? What we really need to do right now is . . .*

2. S: *I have been trying to get Smokey's head down, but he keeps jerking it up whenever I ask him to canter.*

   I: *That sounds frustrating for you, and certainly something we need to look at, but I'm more concerned about some of the problems you mentioned at the walk and trot. Tell me a little more about. . .*

## ZIG-ZAG REFLECTION

This can be a very effective method for joining with your student, while at the same time nudging them in the direction of change. You first validate the student's perspective, but subtly (or not so subtly) provide a little twist in the direction of change.

EXAMPLES:

1. S: *Why does everyone keep after me about my contact? I HAVE to pull on Spunky, otherwise he will not stop! There are other things I need to work on too, you know.*

   I: *You make a good point. When you do not pull, Spunky will not stop - you know that better than anyone! Maybe we should work on some of the other things you've mentioned. Having a horse that does not stop is a problem that affects everything else – you are so on target! Why do not we begin with . . .*

2. S: *Flat work is not our "thing." We are much better over the jumps, because Snickers is more balanced and pays more attention to me.*

   I: *This certainly sounds understandable. You prefer to ride Snickers when he is listening to you and stays balanced on his feet. Who would not? It's great that you notice such a big difference between your flatwork and jumping. What seems important now is to find out what works so well over the jumps so you can get that same feeling on the flat.*

## REFRAMING

This is the grand master of reflective listening skills. All counselors learn to reframe because it is a valuable and very powerful tool. Basically, to reframe means to restate the speaker's main points, but ALTER the MEANING. This provides the speaker with a different way of looking at things, especially if they have been viewing something negatively, and you reframe it in positive terms.

EXAMPLES:

1. *Student: I hate riding this horse! She is so slow, I have to kick her all the time just to get her to move!*

   *Instructor: You are right about that! But you know, I cannot help but notice how good you are with your hands. You have such a soft contact and a really good leg. One thing you have avoided by riding such a slow poke is NOT to pull with your reins or take your legs off her side. Riding Miss Pokey has really helped you learn how to use your seat and legs and not pull with your hands. This will really help you when you ride other, more forward horses.*

2. *Student: I feel so bad – I know Bojangles is really talented, and here I am, learning on him. He is not being used to his potential.*

   *Instructor: So you recognize Bojangles' natural talent, but are wondering if you are doing the right thing by keeping him to learn on. You know, many horses that go on to the "big time" end up leading pretty stressful lives. Constant traveling, shifting owners, and very demanding work, with little to no guarantee they will stay sound. On the other hand, Bojangles has a great home, pasture time, friends to play with, and someone who loves him and takes great care of him, no matter how well he does in competition. And his workload is not likely to make him lame at an early age either! I wonder which option Bojangles would choose if he had the option?*

All of these communication strategies are designed to minimize or defuse situations where resistance rears its intimidating head. With practice, instructors can become skilled in their use, leading them to feel more confident when dealing with those "difficult situations." More importantly, through the skillful use of these reflective listening techniques, instructors will find that they are significantly more effective in guiding their students through the change process. And this is, after all, what teaching is all about. Good luck!

# Instructors and BURNOUT

By Kathy Kelly Ph.D.

## WHAT IS BURNOUT?

Over the past decade, sport psychologists have been exploring the effects of burnout on coaches, teachers, and trainers. Viewed as a serious and complex phenomenon, burnout is generally defined as:

**An individual's physiological <u>and</u> psychological response to chronic levels of high stress, resulting in a state of extreme exhaustion that is felt physically, mentally, and emotionally.**

Two different types of burnout have been identified:

**1. Stagnation Burnout**: Instructors with this kind of burnout describe their jobs as routine, repetitious, predictable, boring, unexciting, and uninteresting. They feel as if they have reached a "plateau" in their career and learning, with little to no opportunities to progress or grow personally or professionally. Early responses to stagnation burnout include a sense of boredom followed by loss of energy, creativity, withdrawing of effort, and a sense of teaching by "rote.".

**2. "Fast-Track" Burnout:** Instructors who experience this kind of burnout describe their jobs as intense, highly demanding, and stressful. They often balance numerous roles, multitask, and respond to a variety of changing and challenging situations. Early responses to fast-track burnout include heightened feelings of anxiety followed by a need to "do more" by working harder, longer, and faster.

## WHAT IS THE DIFFERENCE BETWEEN STRESS AND BURNOUT?

Stress is a "hurry sicknesss." Burnout is a "depletion sickness." These are two very distinct concepts. Burnout is not, as some people believe, simply excessive stress. Rather, it is a complex, human REACTION to stress.

What exactly then is stress? Stress is your body's response to any kind of event or demand, mental or physical. There is "good stress" (eustress), which stems from happy circumstances such as achievements, joyful moments, fulfillment, and happy surprises. There is also "bad stress" (distress), which is associated with frustration, disappointments, loss, problems, obstacles, and negative surprises. Whenever you are stressed, your body reacts by going into a "state of alert." Physiologically, this means that adrenalin gets pumped into your system, speeding blood to your brain and muscles and increasing your pulse and respiration. Unfortunately, the body is not designed to maintain this state of alert indefinitely. If instructors are under a chronic state of stress, their bodies will begin to give signs of stress overload, which include sleep problems, psychosomatic illnesses (psychological/emotional problems showing up physically), digestive problems, headaches, high blood pressure, teeth grinding, and fatigue. It is under conditions of chronic stress that the body can begin the slide into burnout. However, in order for burnout to occur, there needs to be specific psychological responses that interact with their body's natural physiological responses to stress. **In other words, burnout is the end result of a tired body <u>and</u> mind.**

## WHAT ARE THE SIGNS OF BURNOUT?

Burnout does not happen overnight – it is a slow, insidious process that creeps up on people. Research has found that people go through a series of stages before they are in a full-blown state of "burnout." The order through which one goes through these stages may differ for each individual, but to reach burnout, all stages are involved. Different signs and symptoms accompany each stage.

### Stages of Burnout

#### DEPERSONALIZATION

In this stage, instructors begin to try to protect themselves from the onslaught of stress by "zoning out" emotionally. They find themselves closing off their feelings from their students, their horses, friends, and family. They become uncharacteristically distant and reserved. They find it hard to empathize with others and, as a result, begin treating their students and horses impersonally.

| Signs and Symptoms - DEPERSONALIZATION | |
|---|---|
| • Sense of detachment | • Being callous |
| • Excessively distant and reserved | • Loss of empathy |
| • Resorting too easily to anger and punishment | • Teaching on "automatic pilot" |
| | • Feeling unconcerned for others |
| | Chart 11 |

## Declining Sense of Personal Accomplishment

This stage is marked by feelings of doubt about one's competency and career choice. Instructors lose confidence in what they are doing and where they are going in their professional lives. They question their goals and feel that they are not making any kind of significant contribution. Most telling, they no longer feel any satisfaction from their job. Instructors in this stage often complain that their students are not making any progress, and that they feel "stuck" in their teaching.

| Signs and Symptoms – DECLINING SENSE OF PERSONAL ACCOMPLISHMENT | |
|---|---|
| ▪ Loss of satisfaction from teaching<br>▪ Feelings of failure<br>▪ A sense of being "stuck"<br>▪ Questioning career choice | ▪ Resentment for giving so much for so little in return<br>▪ Lack of confidence in teaching<br>▪ A lack of goals or dreams |

Chart 11A

## Isolation

This stage signals real trouble. Instead of trying to cope and find solutions, instructors in this stage no longer have the energy or resources to fight back against the stress – they begin to withdraw from, and avoid, their friends, customers, and social situations. They start spending more and more time alone, trying to rejuvenate their sagging energy levels. In some cases, they may begin abusing drugs or alcohol. This stage often begins slowly and can come along so gradually that the instructor (and others around them) at first does not notice.

| Signs and Symptoms - ISOLATION | |
|---|---|
| ▪ Avoiding barn and social activities<br>▪ Stops communicating<br>▪ Spending a lot of time alone<br>▪ Substance abuse | ▪ Making excuses not to ride<br>▪ Arriving just before and leaving right after lessons<br>▪ Increased desire to sleep |

Chart 11B

## Emotional and Physical Exhaustion

This is usually the final stage – at this point the slow slide into burnout is complete. Here, instructors begin to break down emotionally, physically, or both. They no longer have any energy and, perhaps most telling, do not care. It is in this stage that instructors show the most obvious changes in their psychological state. They adopt a sense of 'defeatism,' where they feel beaten down, helpless, hopeless, and perhaps doomed. They develop negative self-views and cynical attitudes toward work, life, and relationships. They may describe themselves as feeling "numb" or "detached." Outside intervention is typically needed at this point.

| Signs and Symptoms —EMOTIONAL and PHYSICAL EXHASTION | |
| --- | --- |
| ▪ Depletion - physically and mentally | ▪ Cynical outlook on life |
| ▪ No energy | ▪ Feelings of hopelessness |
| ▪ Complete exhaustion | ▪ Lack of desire or caring |
| ▪ Negative self-concept | ▪ Increased emotionality |
| ▪ Sense of helplessness | ▪ Sleeping a lot, but still tired |

Chart 11C

## WHAT MAKES INSTRUCTORS BURN OUT?

Coaches, trainers, and instructors have been found to be particularly at risk for burnout. Why? Because these professions often require long hours of giving to others, physically, mentally, and emotionally. When the "giving outweighs the getting," burnout is the result. Some of the unique demands placed on riding instructors include:

- Dealing with student's intense emotions around riding and their relationship with the horse
- Having to constantly attend to safety issues inherent in horseback riding
- Boredom resulting from too much repetition in lessons
- Working the long hours associated with a horse career
- Taking on shifting and ambiguous roles, such as instructor, friend, coach, mentor, psychologist, babysitter, professional rider, trainer, etc.
- Parental, spousal, or family interference or indifference
- Intense personal involvement with and caring for students and horses

## HOW CAN I TELL IF I AM BURNED OUT?

Because the slide into burnout occurs slowly over time, instructors may not know that they are suffering from a complex, psycho-physiological response to chronic stress. Instead, they often feel something is wrong with them. Many blame themselves for feeling bad or not having more energy. Sometimes friends and family notice that something is not "right" and mention their concerns, only to be brushed off with, "I'm fine, just a little tired" or some similar comment. One way to find out if you may be suffering from burnout is to take the following questionnaire. It contains twelve questions designed to tap into the four stages of burnout. Please note: This test is only an assessment and is not meant as a formal diagnosis.

# INSTRUCTOR'S BURNOUT QUIZ

*Instructions:* Please read each statement carefully. First, indicate *how often* you feel this way by writing in a number from 1 to 7. Second, indicate *how strongly* you feel this way by again writing in a number from 1 to 7.

| How Often | 1 | 2 | 3 | 4 | 5 | 6 | 7 |
|---|---|---|---|---|---|---|---|
| Not at all often | | | | | | | Extremely often |

| How Strong | 1 | 2 | 3 | 4 | 5 | 6 | 7 |
|---|---|---|---|---|---|---|---|
| Not at all strong | | | | | | | Extremely strong |

| How Often 1 – 7 | How Strong 1 – 7 | |
|---|---|---|
| 1. ____ | ____ | I feel used up at the end of a day |
| 2. ____ | ____ | I am avoiding social activities that deal with horses |
| 3. ____ | ____ | I am treating my students and horses as impersonal objects |
| 4. ____ | ____ | I am making up excuses for why I am not riding |
| 5. ____ | ____ | I feel fatigued when I get up in the morning and have to face another day teaching |
| 6. ____ | ____ | I do not feel that I am positively influencing my students' lives |
| 7. ____ | ____ | I worry that I am beginning to harden emotionally |
| 8. ____ | ____ | I feel exhausted |
| 9. ____ | ____ | I do not have any goals; I am just going day-to-day |
| 10. ____ | ____ | I no longer gain satisfaction from teaching |
| 11. ____ | ____ | I am feeling distant and removed from people and horses |
| 12. ____ | ____ | I do not want to spend any more time in the barn or ring than I absolutely have to |

add each column

Modified from Weinberg & Richardson (1990)

## Scoring

| **How Often** | | **How Strong** | |
|---|---|---|---|
| **12 – 36** | Low Levels of Frequency | **12 – 36** | Low Intensity |
| **48 – 60** | Moderate Levels of Frequency | **48 - 60** | Moderate Intensity |
| **72 – 144** | High Levels of Frequency | **72 - 144** | High Intensity |

## Interpretation of Results

Low Frequency & Low Intensity - No cause for concern - normal stress
Low Frequency & Moderate Intensity -Early signs of stress
Low Frequency & High Intensity - Signs of stress overload

Moderate Frequency & Low Intensity - Early stage of burnout
Moderate Frequency & Moderate Intensity - Middle stage of burnout
Moderate Frequency & High Intensity - Full blown burnout

High Frequency & Low Intensity - State of chronic stress
High Frequency & Moderate Intensity - Full blown burnout
High Frequency & High Intensity - Extreme state of burnout

Chart 12

## WHAT CAN INSTRUCTORS DO IF THEY ARE EXPERIENCING BURNOUT?

Sometimes, when burned out, instructors try to "fix" the problem by making life-changing decisions. The only problem with this tactic is that they are in an unusual state of mind and may be responding from feelings of desperation and panic. Being burned out, these instructors do not logically and rationally think things through. Many an instructor has given up a job or position because they thought it "was not right." Instead, what was wrong was that they were burned out! The job was right, but the circumstances were not. Instead, some environmental and psychological changes needed to be made – not switching to another job.

 Being in **a state of burnout negatively impacts an instructor's ability to be safe or effective in their job.** Given the high-risk nature of equestrian activities and sport, an instructor who is not "up to par" places themselves, their students, and their horses at increased risk for accident, injury, or both. Therefore, once an instructor identifies that they are in a state of burnout, it becomes critical that some changes are made. t

## PREVENTION AND TREATMENT OF BURNOUT

The following list offers suggestions, strategies, and practices for both the prevention and treatment of burnout. However, when an instructor is actually in a state of burnout, **attention should first be focused on improving their physical and mental well-being.** Only then will the instructor have the tools and resources to make use of the other options on this list.

1. **Develop and Maintain Physical Health** — The body's ongoing physiological response to stress plays havoc with one's physical health. Key points:
   - Get a complete physical check-up from a doctor
   - Get enough sleep
   - Develop healthy eating habits
   - Exercise - ideally something outside of riding, like yoga, t'ai chi, biking, running, or weight training

2. **Develop and Maintain Mental Health** — The effects of burnout take a toll on one's mental outlook and emotional health. Often the result is depression. If severe enough, professional intervention may be called for. Some of the strategies people learn in therapy (or on their own) that can reverse or prevent burnout include:
   - Healthy communication - feelings need to be expressed to others who will listen, understand, and not judge. Bottled

up emotions eventually come out, either in an explosion or "sideways" (indirectly).

- Self-regulation skills - some people intuitively know how to deal with intense emotions. Others become overwhelmed and off-balance when feelings get stirred up, especially negative ones. Psychological techniques such as relaxation, imagery, and cognitive restructuring (appropriate self-talk) can protect instructors from the damaging effects of stress that lead to burnout.

- Self-knowledge - some personality types are more prone to burnout. For example, instructors with high relational styles of teaching (people-oriented, high caring) have been found to have higher levels of burnout than more goal-oriented (authoritarian, task-focused) instructors. Also, burnout is more likely among instructors who have low levels of assertiveness, high needs for approval, and who tend to be perfectionists. An understanding of your personality type and its strengths and weaknesses can go a long way toward helping instructors learn better ways of coping and dealing with their day-to-day stress.

3. **Time Management** — This topic always comes up when dealing with burnout. Some instructors are constantly adjusting their schedules to the needs of their horses and students. End result - a feeling of loss of control, an important component related to burnout. As well, some instructors become "addicted" to the adrenalin rush associated with chaos and crisis. Time is always stressful for this group, never enough of it to get things done! Unfortunately, the body never lets down its "alert status" and trouble begins. Some of the positive ways time management can defuse or prevent burnout include:
- Learn to say "no" (without guilt!)

- Proper use of delegating - no one is expendable, really!

- Personal time - this is not just a luxury, but also a mental health requirement! Amounts differ for each instructor, but regularly scheduled time off is a must.

- Organize your schedule to allow for short breaks after four hours or more of straight lessons. It is difficult to maintain enthusiasm and energy when giving hour after hour.

4. **Goal Setting** — Often, instructors struggle with balancing their own goals with those of their students. Whose comes first? Too often it is the students' goals that take precedent. Other times, instructors fail to set goals and get caught up in the day-to-day demands of teaching, only to find themselves lacking direction, clarity, or focus. Some common strategies used by instructors to prevent or overcome burnout include:

- Establishing personally realistic and meaningful goals.
- Dividing goals into short and long-term segments that are identifiable and achievable.
- Setting up goals for teaching. Many instructors focus only on riding goals and view instructing as something that is a necessary evil.
- Establishing a plan for attaining goals, and setting up new ones. It is very healthy to be constantly striving, learning, and reaching for new heights and accomplishments that hold value to you, the instructor.

5. **Establishing Balance in Life** — This is a constant and ever evolving, ever-changing quest. At different times and during different stages in an instructor's life, what constitutes a **balanced life** will change. For example, early on in one's career, it might mean focusing on time to ride and compete. At other times, it might mean more time at home with a young family. Still later, balance might include attention to one's students and their accomplishments. And so on. Importantly, a way of life that provides balance for one person most likely will not be "right" for another. Each of us is different and, as such, need to find our own sense of balance, much like our students and our horses! However, when one seeks "balance," there are some common factors that people everywhere search for:
- Opportunity for time spent alone or with family and friends.
- Opportunity to develop diverse aspects of oneself - especially 'non-horsey' aspects.
- Ways to live life that reflect your own set of values and priorities.
- Chance to engage in activities (not always work-related) that are personally meaningful.
- Recognition of when you are becoming depleted and need recharging. Some people "work hard, play hard," while others go along at a steady pace, with regular intervals of rest in between. Knowing what is right for you helps you to achieve balance.

SUMMARY

Burnout is a serious condition that affects instructors on both a physical and psychological level. In addition, riding instructors are vulnerable to the burnout process because of the myriad of stressors associated with the demands of horses, riders, and teaching.

- Some instructors burn out because their job has become stagnant, thereby losing its ability to inspire and challenge them.

For others, burnout occurs because they are on an "activity high" which comes from a career that is demanding and stressful.

- Burnout sneaks up on instructors quietly and slowly, so that for many, they do not recognize the signs and symptoms. Only when they have "hit the wall" by becoming both physically and emotionally exhausted do instructors realize they need help. If instructors find themselves in a deep state of depression, they should seek professional help.

- The prevention and treatment of burnout is the same - it involves exploration and consideration of the instructor's physical and mental health, time management skills, interests and values, goal setting, and establishment of a life balance.

- Burnout is a sign that something is amiss or unbalanced in one's life. Many instructors report that through their slide down into burnouts' murky depths, they have gained valuable skills and self-knowledge, which has allowed them to rebuild their life in a more meaningful and satisfying fashion. It can be a stepping stone toward self-realization and growth that ultimately helps guide you forward on your life's path. So hang in there, and **GOOD LUCK**.

# NEW
# INSTRUCTORS'
# INTRODUCTION

So, you have decided to become a riding instructor! Congratulations. You are embarking on an exciting career filled with many joys and challenges. We hope that this section will help you begin this new adventure with the knowledge, confidence, and professionalism that leads to success.

Ideally, riders new to teaching will have learned the basics of instructing before entering the arena to give a lesson. Teaching, like riding, has a system which when used helps create a solid foundation of basic skills. These basic skills can be enriched and deepened with practice teaching and observations of other teachers in action.

Every new instructor will discover a personal path to learning the skills needed for teaching. Basic skills can be learned from classes and books and, as with learning to ride, will come to life while being put into practice in the arena. You can learn a lot from reading, but you must get out there and do it! Basic teaching skills are the same for all who wish to teach. Everyone has particular strengths coming into the field that can be tapped right away. Perhaps you have been trained as a singer and understand how to project your voice. You may have managed a business and know how to organize tasks in an orderly fashion. Making use of these established skills helps build your confidence as an instructor, a vital ingredient in your success. When instructors are confident, students gain trust in them. Trust promotes faster progress for students.

Teaching riding is always a challenge and seldom a bore because we are working with two creatures, horse and human. This gives us many possibilities for enjoyment and success as well as challenges that go well beyond traditional classroom instruction. Nevertheless, many of the same teaching skills are needed in both the classroom and the arena. As in academic subjects, it is necessary for instructors to have a thorough understanding of their disciplines that extends beyond the levels they plan on teaching. Both classroom and riding instructors need a clear understanding of the need to teach the whole student—physically, mentally, and spiritually. With this understanding and plenty of technical information, instructors must also learn the basics of teaching and the fundamental principles of how riders learn best. The **Basic Skills for Teaching Riders** chapter is designed to provide new instructors with the overview of these key teaching skills.

**Guide to Getting Started** provides a basic plan for new instructors to follow as they begin to apply their knowledge and experience in the arena with their students. This guide for learning to instruct has proven very successful for many instructors, both well seasoned and beginners. This chapter is meant to serve as an initial guide to the system as a whole. The order of learning, as laid out in this book, is suggested, not mandatory. The system is designed to make learning safe, lasting, and balanced.

New instructors should review the next section, **Fundamental Teaching Skills**. Combining Fundamental Skills with the technical information studied in the Stages of Learning will put you on the path to a successful career.

# BASICS OF TEACHING

*General Teaching Principles to Produce a Deep, Secure, Balanced, and Relaxed Rider*

GOOD INSTRUCTORS

Beginning with the first lessons, the instructor's primary goal is to teach students to have **a deep, secure, balanced, and relaxed position** that will lead to more effective control of the horse as they advance through the Stages of Rider Education (Mastery of Technical Skills section of Equestrian Education). Teaching, refreshing, and confirming a solid foundation of skills produces students who have the tools to advance and to learn new movements that require more sophisticated coordination, faster reflexes, and a more finely tuned feel.

## FOUR COMMON DENOMINATORS OF ALL LESSONS: SAFETY, FUN, TECHNIQUE, AND FEEL.

Our first priority as instructors is to ensure safety and comfort for horse and rider (see Equestrian Instruction – Safety Consciousness). Our second priority is to provide enjoyable learning experiences for both horse and rider. Our third priority is to utilize useful and consistent techniques that follow the Stages of Rider Education. And fourth, we intend to encourage and develop the student's sense of feel.

Safety is directly related to security and confidence. It is essential to have a suitable horse to make learning safe. A safe, reliable school horse can be one of the most valuable assets an instructor can have to help a student develop a sound, confident foundation of skills. Unfortunately, these schoolmasters are not always available. When this is the case, instructors need to assess the full situation and determine how to ensure safety for both rider and horse.

After safety is established, the focus can be on fun. Students learn quicker when they enjoy the activity. It is important to be aware that each student has a different definition of fun, including but not limited to enjoyment, pleasure, meeting a challenge, creating harmony with the horse, enjoying the feeling of freedom while riding, and meeting performance standards and expectations.

Facts can be introduced with an orderly and simple presentation. When students feel safe and are having fun, they are more easily able to learn even complicated new behaviors and embrace unfamiliar ideas. This leads to the development of "feel" in a student. Riders must move from the cognitive process of how to ride to being in the moment, aware

---

### Key Teaching Points for Starting New Skills & All Lessons 1 -5

1. Give Consistent, Clear, Concise Commands.
2. Create positive habits from the start. A beginning student learns quickly when both words and the associated responses are repeated often. To instill good habits connected to repetitions, take the following steps for beginning students:
   - Request the action to be taken - "Prepare to trot."
   - Explain all the steps in order in as few words as possible - "Shorten your reins, lift your chest (one specific position reminder only), squeeze with your legs, and ask horse to trot."
   - Give the cue or command - "Now, trot!"
   - Acknowledge specifically what was correct and suggest what could be different or better - "Great! Your chest was open; your horse gave a good answer to your leg. Next time, take a deep breath to relax as soon as your horse trots."

 When teaching students who have reached Stage 3 of Rider Education (have good position, seats and use of aids), it is seldom necessary to use the above procedure. In Stage 3 it is often enough to ask the student to "prepare to trot and trot when ready." It is essential to notice the student's preparation and not let them skip the preparation step. If they do, they need to be stopped, reminded of its role and importance and then allowed to practice this a few times.

3. Use words denoting feel all along the way. In the above example the "feel" words used along the way were: *lift* your chest, *squeeze* your legs, take a *deep* breath. These words are indirectly drawing the student's attention to feel from the start.
4. Keep expectations simple, but expect prompt and correct response to what you ask.
5. If student fails to use a skill learned in an earlier lesson, be prepared to return to the familiar skill. Help him to understand that skipping important steps in the learning process will be detrimental later. However, we must also be aware that while learning a new skill the rider may 'forget' something that has been previously learned. We must use common sense in this case asking, "Is it a temporary but OK missing piece, or is it essential to the current subject being learned and practiced?"

Chart 13

---

of the horse's response and what actions must be taken to improve performance. One of the instructor's goals is to help riders respond to the horse's reactions as soon as possible. In the moment-to-moment movement of the horse, the rider acts from either natural instinct or from educated response. It is through training with feel that the rider is able to do the right thing at the right time. The development of feel is an ongoing process for riders at all levels.

Safety, fun, facts, and feel. Then what? **Practice, practice, practice.** Students, who look forward to their lessons and the chance to learn more, are very willing to practice.

Practice is often identified as the key to success in learning to ride, as it is with every new skill. How can students who do not have their own horse practice? This is where visualization skills and video reviews can play a major role in a student's life. Studies have proven that regular and correct visualization can improve riding faster than riding itself! One student discovered that watching a video of an expert and then taking time to regularly visualize herself doing the same, improved her riding a great deal even though she could ride only two days a week.

When we are riding, we can perform only to the level of our current skills. With the image in mind of how we want to look and feel, we can practice free of mistakes! Of course, mental practice must be coupled with the physical training and experience itself. In addition, certain physical exercises, designed specifically for riders to tone their muscles and develop the coordination for riding, offer excellent unmounted training.

If we present new material to students clearly, allow them time to practice until the acquired skill becomes habit, and then build skill upon skill, we will provide our students with a solid foundation in basic riding. The student can use this foundation for pleasure riding or continue to the top level of the riding discipline of their choice.

---

**Key Teaching Points for Starting New Skills & ALL Lessons 6 -10**

1. Reward success with appropriate and positive enthusiasm.
2. Correct with clear explanations and offer enough theory to deepen understanding.
3. An astute instructor will be able to give just enough theory to enhance understanding, but not so much that the rider spends too much time referring to the theory. The purpose of theory is to give the action a foundation in the overall understanding. Remember that one important key is to keep the rider moving as much as possible during the lesson. This can help prevent the rider from becoming stuck "in their head".
4. Evaluate student's needs and be prepared to jump between the Stages of Rider Education as you instruct.
5. Keep lessons interesting and fun; practice the same skills with different exercises.

Chart 13A

---

# TEACHING A NEW SKILL

There are three phases to the process of teaching a new skill. The first phase includes the transmission of the technical information and the first attempts to accomplish the skill. In the second phase, the student begins to put this information into practice, while the instructor prompts the student with questions before and/or after the execution of the skill. The third phase turns the learning task over to the student with the instructor's withdrawing to observe.

- Phase 1: When teaching a new skill or starting to teach a beginner, follow three clear steps. First prepare the student with a clear explanation of how the skill will be taught, how to get ready, and how to execute the skill. When this has been accomplished, prepare her for the first attempt with simple, clear directions (including the short, simple name for the action). When she is ready, ask for the action and then reward her with an affirmation of what was done well (even just having tried!) and one or two notes for change. Include explanations with all steps.

- Phase 2: Ask the student to begin. Before and after the action, ask her to say what needs to be done or what was done.

- Phase 3: Turn the whole skill and its actions over to the student and step back to watch from the sidelines.

The lesson is not over even after instructors have passed the responsibility for initiating and accomplishing something to students. Students often forget to take time to prepare themselves properly and frequently leave out one or more important factors. Instructors must remain observant. Throughout each lesson, instructors must make certain students are practicing new skills using all the steps, including everything they have already learned. When a step is skipped, it is often because the instructor has not provided the student enough opportunity to practice the new skill in order to confirm the habit or has not kept an observant eye on the student once the skill is taught. Perhaps the rider has become careless. When this happens, simply return to the beginning of the action. "You have decided to trot. Now, please tell me how you are going to prepare to trot?" Then have the student follow through with the action. This procedure will bridge the gap from students following your directions to taking responsibility for themselves.

# CONFIRM RIDER UNDERSTANDING

Once you feel a student has learned a new skill, it is time to ask non-threatening questions to draw her attention to technique and feel. Encourage her to answer concisely and simply. Angel had been working hard on developing a deep leg position and was beginning to feel it. She was asked what she wanted to work on in the quiet time at the close of her lesson. "I want to keep my leg relaxed under me and my heel down."

Angel's answer was simple and to the point. If her answer had gotten too long-winded or rambling, she could use some help learning to think about the new skill in more simple terms. When the student is describing her next step in too much length, during a pause, you will want to ask the student to stop. With an understanding tone of voice, interject something like, "You have the right idea. Said more simply, you will spend less time thinking and more time riding." Simplicity comes from experience, something the student is just beginning to acquire. Combining what the rider has said with what you hope will be taken to heart, simply state the next step. Ask them to keep it in mind as they take a few moments to confirm in practice the connection between thought and action. It helps to remind them to listen to their bodies as they do so, to sense the feel of the movements. This is usually the most direct route to understanding.

> *Remind them that mental analysis is a tool for problem-solving and preparation, not for establishing reliable performance.*

## TEACHING CHILDREN

As you begin integrating these principles into your teaching, remember that children and adults are two different kinds of students.

Children must be kept moving. They need less explanation; adults need more. How much movement depends on individual characteristics and the child's state of mind. Is the student timid? Ask for small moves that do not cause insecurity. Aggressive? Bigger, energetic exercises might be best. How capable does the student feel? How confident? Adjust your suggestions accordingly.

Because children have less negative life experiences, most have less fear to deal with than adults. They think and talk less about what has been asked of them and eagerly pick up new things through feel more quickly than adults.

Teenagers like challenge, and they alternate between a childlike need for action and an adult's need for discussion.

Adults are eager to learn, engage new learning with more complex life experiences, and usually need more time and theory.

## TEACHING BEGINNING VS. EDUCATED RIDERS

When you introduce a beginning rider to the basic skills of balance, position, and feel, you have the wonderful opportunity to create a problem-free student. More often, students have been riding for a while and are missing an important piece of their foundation. The process of reeducation begins with identification of the ineffective habit and suggestions for replacement. Each unique complex of needs must be met with innovative techniques or tools. This is where the creativity and the fun begin.

## TEACHING & LEARNING ORDER

The sequence suggested here for introducing basic skills allows new students to learn safely and realize steady progress toward their riding dreams. Students who plan to ride for pleasure will build a solid, safe foundation for any discipline that captures their hearts. Those who want to develop more sophistication in their riding will establish a secure basis for their advancement. Teach all students one step at a time, proceeding from one goal to the next, as each step has been learned and becomes a habit. Throughout this process, be careful to explain the purpose of each skill and have students practice each skill with exercises that are fun.

As each student advances, adhere strictly to the Stages of Rider Education. Training progress for either a novice rider or an advanced rider cannot be assured without the security each step offers. If a step is missing, instructors must convince the rider of the importance of taking the time to add the missing step to their technique. Making practice fun makes all the difference, replacing embarrassment with enjoyment, tedium with tenacity, and insecurity with safety and surety. The basics of learning are useful across any career and eventually lead to the sophistication of the rider's skill and performance.

## REEDUCATING RIDERS

Riders with holes in their understandings need to be persuaded to take the time to fill in the missing skills. Most riders who understand the reason why a skill is important, empowered with the instructor's suggestions on **HOW** to fill the hole, will usually agree to the task. Now is a good time to integrate goal setting.

Instructors must feel at ease jumping between both steps and stages when a rider has missing skills as described in the Stages of Rider Education. 🐎

Keeping the big picture in mind, instructors can begin to work systematically to reinforce the skill foundations of even the most haphazardly educated rider.

Responsible instructors want to develop independent, astute riders. As one instructor has pointed out, "By teaching students how to work

## Fun Riding Lessons Produce Positive Results

- Keep lessons FUN! Laugh, enjoy, and see the beauty; be positive.

- Enthusiasm for what you teach is essential.

- Teach your student to become a good learner.

- Follow a consistent order in all lessons.

- Involve the student.

- Use a feeling vocabulary, addressing elasticity, relaxation, and stretching as you teach each phase of riding.

- Discover what each student enjoys and thread opportunities for enjoyment into the lesson whenever possible.

- Add trail rides, games, patterns; anything that is fun whenever safe and possible.

Chart 14

through their challenges and think through them on their own, instructors are creating real riders, not just students who look good and can perform only when the instructor is present." The process starts right from the beginning of a rider's training. By presenting an orderly training program and allowing time for skills to become habits, instructors encourage development of a firm foundation in the basics and can feel confident in their role as guides for their students' ultimate independence and personal success.

# GUIDE TO GETTING STARTED

*A Step-by-Step Plan to Build Confidence While Teaching*

 NEW INSTRUCTORS. . . Before you begin this section, it is recommended that you read and understand all the chapters preceding this section. 🐎

As was discussed previously, many instructors "fall" into teaching. Coming from a successful riding career, they take their technical knowledge and the wisdom of experience and try to find different ways to share them with others. As the inevitable mistakes are made and

NEXT...IT SAYS MOUNT THE HORSE IN CROSS-LATERAL, OMNI-PRESENT MANNER!

J.D.BAKER 2001

learned from, new teachers know they could be doing better; but without a system of teaching to fall back on, they do not know where to begin the search.

Drawing upon years of teaching experience, the founders of EES suggest this developmental process that is particularly effective for those just beginning to teach. This suggested seven-step procedure has proven successful to many riders who want to begin a teaching career.

 It is very important to start the practice of keeping notes as you begin teaching. Since there is so much to the process of learning how to teach, taking notes helps you monitor your progress and choose future directions to explore. I will always be glad I kept fairly detailed notes when I began teaching. This process allowed me to put my thinking in order, but more importantly, it trained me to remember the key points in each student's progress. This gave me confidence, kept me on track, made each lesson progressive, and impressed the student. Many students indirectly learned to chart their goals when they began following my example. 🐎

| 7-Step Plan to Begin Teaching Lessons | |
|---|---|
| Step 1 | Evaluate your skills and interests |
| Step 2 | Adopt a consistent lesson format |
| Step 3 | Review and refresh your fundamental teaching skills |
| Step 4 | Arrange for your first lesson |
| Step 5 | Assess your progress |
| Step 6 | Advance your communication skills |
| Step 7 | Add goal setting |

Chart 15A

## Step 1 – **Evaluate your skills and interests**

Review your background and goals related to becoming a riding instructor. This helps you find your own ideal starting place.

| EQUESTRIAN BACKGROUND | | | | | | |
|---|---|---|---|---|---|---|
| **RIDING DISCIPLINE** | Currently riding | Rode in past | Total years riding | Total years competing | Total years Training | Describe primary method of attaining technical knowledge Self-taught, reading, professionals |
| Hunt Seat | | | | | | |
| Dressage | | | | | | |
| Hunter | | | | | | |
| Pleasure | | | | | | |
| Jumper | | | | | | |
| Therapeutic | | | | | | |
| Other | | | | | | |

Chart 15

Assess your skills and determine the age and ability level of the students you wish to teach.

| Who do you want to teach? | | | | | |
|---|---|---|---|---|---|
| | **Beginners** | **Intermediate** | **Advanced** | **Individuals** | **Groups** |
| Children | | | | | |
| Teenagers | | | | | |
| Adults | | | | | |

Chart 16

## Step 2 - **Adopt a consistent lesson format**

Once you know the level and ages you want to teach, it is time to understand the value and use of a lesson plan. While instructors need to remain flexible in *what* is taught during a lesson, a consistent format or plan for presenting each lesson is vital. A lesson structure provides students a healthy habit for learning and instructors with a reliable routine for teaching. See a summary of lesson structure in the Skills section of this book. For more information, you may wish to read Lesson Framework in *Equestrian Instruction*.

### Step 3 – **Review and refresh your fundamental teaching skills**
If you would like to learn more about each of the fundamental teaching skills – lesson structure, awareness, communications, and goal setting, Equestrian Education reviews these skills, and more detailed information can be found in *Equestrian Instruction*.

### Step 4 – **Arrange for your first lesson**
As you get started, it is ideal to have volunteers, such as 4-H members, pony clubbers, or friends as your first "students." Have an agreement that after a specific number of lessons, if they wish to continue their lessons, they will begin paying you. With volunteers, you feel less pressure to "give them their money's worth" while you are learning how to do that. You can also ask your own riding instructor to observe your lessons and offer suggestions. This feedback from a qualified professional will go a long way in refining your teaching techniques and style.

When you arrange for these first lessons, talk to your students ahead of time to find out the key information you need to create a lesson plan. Use the same format you would use if a prospective student called you up for lessons. Your questions might include:

- What would you like to achieve by taking lessons from me?

- What discipline are you working in?

- What level are you now?

- What level is your horse?

- Do you or your horse have any health or conformation issues that we will need to consider?

With this information, you can come up with a general plan. As the lesson begins, watch the student's warm-up and revise your plan to match the needs presented.

After the lesson, allow time to make an entry in your lesson journal. Note how closely you were able to follow your original plan, what diversions you need to take, what you want to do in the next lesson, three main good points in the lesson, and three key points to work on in the next lesson.

### Step 5 – **Assess your progress**
After you have had approximately three lessons with the same student or students, it is time to assess your awareness and observation skills. Review the Awareness/Observation section in this book. Continue to keep your journal and begin evaluating your success in observing rider and horse and using appropriate corrections and solutions.

Self-assessment and correction is a life-long process, so become even more aware, remain aware, and you will continue to learn. ⚞

### Step 6 – **Advance your communication skills**

As soon as you feel comfortable with your observation and educational decision-making skills, it is time to move deeper into communication skills. One of the key ways to "get on the same page" with your student and ensure effective interaction is to take time to improve your ability to both talk plainly and listen carefully. In your lesson review and journal writing, pay particular attention to your developing communications skills.

### Step 7 – **Add goal setting**

Of the basic skills, goal setting is the last to focus on because most instructors know the importance of having a plan for their students. It is also very important to involve each student in the plan. A consistent lesson structure and a process that invites student feedback leads directly to effective goal setting. Routinely review both long and short-term goals and continue to involve your student in the process.

Each of these steps should be considered and reviewed on its own and then in conjunction with the other steps. Take your time in this learning process and slowly add new information to your existing skill set. It is essential to remember that throughout our teaching careers, we need to expand and review these basic skills. The framework we use in our lessons is the foundation; but awareness, communications, and goal setting play a vital role in each individual lesson.

You need to feel professionally solid and confident, not only in your lesson structure, but also in your key teaching skills (awareness, communications, and goal setting) before expanding your teaching to include supplementary information from sources such as sports psychology or unmounted exercises. Once you gain some teaching experience, you will find many resources for enriching your teaching for both yourself and your students.

Ideally, instructors who feel confident having taken these seven steps will then begin to explore the supplement sections both in this book and in *Equestrian Instruction* to see how integrating skills and information from the supplements can give you and your students even more learning tools.

# INSTRUCTOR'S LESSON JOURNAL

Student:_____ Starting Date:_____

Address:_____

Birth date:_____Phone:_____

Training history:


Motivators:

Long Term Goal:

## Lesson Records

| Date | Key Starting points of Lesson | Key Points Reviewed | Notes for next time |
|------|-------------------------------|---------------------|---------------------|
|      |                               |                     |                     |

| Date | Key Starting points of Lesson | Key Points Reviewed | Notes for next time |
|------|-------------------------------|---------------------|---------------------|
|      |                               |                     |                     |

| Date | Key Starting points of Lesson | Key Points Reviewed | Notes for next time |
|------|-------------------------------|---------------------|---------------------|
|      |                               |                     |                     |

Overall Notes:


Chart 17

# FUNDAMENTAL
# TEACHING SKILLS

*The Fundamental Teaching Skills, also the fundamental learning skills, combined with a working understanding of classical theory, provide the ability to adapt theory to fit the individual horse and rider.*

FUNDAMENTAL TEACHING SKILLS
- LESSON FRAMEWORK
- COMMUNICATION
- AWARENESS
- GOAL SETTING
- INSTRUCTOR'S TOOLBOX
- TEACHING A NEW SKILL
- COACHING

Well-qualified instructors have an excellent understanding of the classical theory of riding and knowledge of riding skills based in experience. You can only teach what you know well. To teach what you know as a rider, you must also know how to impart your technical knowledge in a variety of ways to meet the diversity of student needs. Four fundamental skills, in additional to sound technical knowledge of the sport, are needed to teach riding: **Lesson Structure**, **Communications**, **Awareness** and **Goal Setting**. Every instructor needs to effectively use these skills. The essential qualities of each of these four skill areas are covered in the following chapters. The information included is useful both as an introduction to these skills and as a periodic refresher for instructors already actively using this information in their teaching.

The **Instructor's Toolbox** includes proven teaching techniques that make teaching more successful. A review of these will help you enjoy more success with your students and greater satisfaction in your career.

Teaching riding is a combination of introducing new skills to the students and coaching the students as they practice the skills. The chapter on **Teaching a New Skill** gives a guideline of several methods for introducing a new skill. Once learned, it takes hours of practice to commit the skill to muscle memory. The **Coaching** chapter gives useful tips to use coaching during practice as well as for competitions.

When all of the **Fundamental Learning Skills** are combined with a sound technical knowledge and the desire to pass information on to your students, you will be able to fulfill your role as an educator of riders. With the information found in this section, instructors will have the tools needed for adapting and integrating the classical technical skills to meet the individual students' needs to learn new skills or retrain old ones.

# LESSON STRUCTURE

Following a consistent routine in the order of a lesson ensures that you present your information in a reliable way for both you and your students. By doing so, you are also modeling a useful routine for students to use when they train alone. While sticking to a routine lesson structure is valuable, instructors must teach students to be flexible based on the day's conditions. Ideally, the instructor enters the arena with a plan for each lesson, a plan to be followed unless circumstances suggest change.

The student's warm-up or information given during the greeting phase will help determine whether this plan can be followed or not.

The lesson structure suggested below is just one option. Some instructors already have developed one that works well. What is important is having a consistent structure that allows your students to know what to expect next. Consider comparing your own lesson structure with this one. You will want to make sure all elements, particularly confirming rider insights and lesson review, are present in whatever structure you use. Allowing time in each lesson after instruction is finished for the rider to practice new skills helps the rider confirm the lessons learned and helps the instructor confirm whether or not what has been taught has been learned. A brief overview of the lesson helps rider and instructor decide what to do next in practice and in subsequent lessons.

The time dedicated to each of the phases of any lesson depends on the needs of the student, the horse, the time allotted for the lesson, circumstances of the site, and the day's variables. The first lessons of a student new to an instructor often involve more time spent on pre-lesson observations, greetings,

---

**A good lesson in six orderly steps**

1. Pre-lesson observations
2. Greetings & update
3. Warm-up & warm-up review
4. Lesson
5. Confirmation of rider insights — (unaided and observed practice time)
6. Lesson review

Chart 18

---

81

and lesson review, steps 1, 2, and 6. Less time is spent on these steps as student and instructor have more experience working together. Once instructors have taught students to do a correct warm-up routine, the warm-up can be done before the actual lesson begins. Student and instructor can discuss the warm-up to determine the content of the lesson. If a student new to you is beyond Stage 1 in Rider Education (Basic position and control in the Mastery of Technical Skills), be prepared to take several lessons to teach the recommended warm-up routine and the significance of reporting to you their thoughts and feelings at the end of the warm-up. The time needed for the heart of the lesson and confirmation varies with the rider's stage of education. I always allow five minutes for the review; in my mind it is one of the most important parts of the lesson. To stay on time (a commitment of as much importance to students as to yourself), quickly evaluate the student's needs during warm-up and divide the time up as needed for each lesson step, setting a realistic goal for the lesson. Often, instructors feel that giving students more than their scheduled time is good. This can be done once in a while, but it is far better to learn to provide results in the time allotted out of respect for the horse's well-being, the rider's schedule, and your schedule for the rest of the day.

## STEP 1 – PRE-LESSON OBSERVATION

Take a little time to casually observe the student preparing for the lesson. This observation can give you insight into the state of mind of the horse and rider team without their feeling the pressure of performing for you. During this time, quickly evaluate their comfort levels, their responses to the environment (focus or distraction, level of confidence), the effectiveness of their preparations for the lesson, calmness, or excitement. For regular students who are able to warm-up on their own, see if they are using what they have been learning in previous lessons.

## STEP 2 – GREETINGS & UP-DATE

Your sincerity, tone of voice, and greeting set the stage for each lesson. Before you greet your students, make sure to take a moment to clear your mind of your preceding activities and gather your thoughts for the lesson ahead. Pausing briefly like this will help you give the students your undivided attention.

Just like your students, you will be receiving first impressions of each other in this early stage of the lesson. You will want to listen to your student's body language, choice and organization of words (positive or negative self-talk, organization of thinking, communication style), and to the horse's behavior. Inwardly, ask yourself if the student's words, goals, and actions match what you would like to hear or see from the student. If this is a regular student, you will want to be sure the following areas are covered in your update conversation. Prompt the student as needed with questions like these:

- Tell me, what has been going on since your last lesson?
- How have your rides been since your last lesson?
- How often have you been able to ride in the past two weeks?
- What are the highlights of your training sessions in the past week?
- What do you feel you want to work on today?

If your student does not have a horse, you can ask her how often she practiced whatever you gave her to practice, whether it was visualization, watching videos, or doing exercises.

Questions for first-time students:

- Can you tell me about your horse's background?
- Can you tell me about your background?
- Who have you been training with recently?
- How often do you ride your horses?
- How long is an average ride?

It is important to develop a dialog with your student so you can begin to get on the same page. 🐎

## STEP 3 – WARM-UP & REVIEW

Instructors will be part of the warm-up step of the lesson until students reach Stage 3 of Rider Education. Instructors will teach students how to do a proper warm-up and, once that is accomplished, turn responsibility for this phase over to the students. If students are in Stage 3 or above when they start with you, make certain the student can do a proper warm-up; if not, take time to teach the routine.

Instructors need to be aware that students warm-up correctly, even after they have been taught to do it. 🐎

The warm-up review is the second time instructors will have a chance to ask the students questions to help formulate the lesson. For students with whom you regularly work, the greeting and warm-up review may be done at the same time (unlike first-timer lessons, the warm-up will have been completed before the lesson formally begins). This is an ideal time to see if you and your student are on the same page. A beginner might be asked, "Describe what you liked about the way you used your leg during the warm-up?" Or, "Now that you are warmed up, what do you feel would be best to practice in the lesson?" For a more experienced student, "How did your position feel?" or "How did your horse feel?" or "What do you want to work on in this lesson?"

From the student's answers, you begin to see if your student is developing a sound sense of the program, the skills, and the feel you are instilling through the learning program. If the answers are not appropriate, listen even more carefully and, at the end of the student's update, let your student know in a positive way what you want to do and why. You must relate this to what the student felt and wanted to achieve. Clarifying and feedback are appropriate techniques in this case. If the answers are correct or close to your view, paraphrasing is an ideal way to acknowledge this. If you do not agree with your student's answers, come up with a plan to move from your student's concept toward your own. One carefully crafted sentence can often do this. Mary explained that her goal was to compete in a dressage show in six months at the 1$^{st}$ level. As I watched Mary's warm-up during her first lesson, I was concerned by her goal, because her horse had not accepted the aids, and she could not sit the trot. My carefully crafted sentence, "Mary, it is great that you have a goal; there is a lot to work on to prepare you for your show. First, we need to... Let us reevaluate where you are in four months and decide what level you are ready to show." The students need to know why your plan will help them move forward with their plans. (See chapter Active Listening in *Equestrian Instruction*)

From the warm-up review, a clear plan is developed with the instructor as a leader who is involving the student in the lesson itself. Over time, students begin to feel comfortable in the planning or goal setting part of each daily ride.

## STEP 4 – LESSON

The lesson begins with stating the clear purpose determined during warm-up review. As the lesson proceeds, it is important to stick to a simple, clear plan, making one to three points only. No matter what you are teaching, use a full communications cycle. Make sure exchanges with the student are simple and clear, whether you are teaching a new skill or practicing a known skill until it is confirmed. Simple, clear, easy-to-hear communications with quiet spaces in between allow students time to feel the interaction between themselves and their horses.

If a student is unable to follow your directions, simplify even more. Try another way to explain or return to something the student does well. It is essential that instructors remain flexible during lessons, making use of their various teaching tools to help the students experience success. Keeping lessons simple and clear is the best way to do this.

When things are going well, be careful not to get greedy and ask for more than horse and rider can give. It is better to allow more time for confirming rider insights and to quit as winners.

# STEP 5 – CONFIRMING RIDER INSIGHTS

When the students have accomplished the goal of the lesson, give them a little quiet time to enjoy the feel. Quiet time for horse and rider allows the rider to notice with body and mind what has been accomplished. Acknowledging the students' ability to recognize accomplishment is one more step toward creating independent riders who can reproduce what they learn when they are on their own. If students have *almost* met their goals, your assistance during this phase is helpful. Intermix widely spaced and positive phrases of encouragement with quiet time. If riders have not come close to meeting the goal of the lesson, this phase of the lesson is skipped. The riders have been working so hard, they probably will not even know you skipped it! As often as possible, your goal is to have the student feel and be able to duplicate the skill you have taught that day. More than your acknowledgement, the students need time to feel and experience the learned skill on their own terms.

# STEP 6 – REVIEW

The review of the lesson is the part of the lesson that is key to creating independent students. During this time, you ask them to clarify what they have learned. Monitor and inhibit wordiness. I begin this step by asking, "What are the three words you heard the most during the lesson?" This question helps forestall long-winded answers. Long, detailed explanations seem to delay progress for both student and instructor. A few suggested questions:

- What have you heard me say the most today?
- What was the most positive feeling you had during today's ride?
- What are the three things you want to practice between your lessons?

Again, listening to their answers gives you valuable feedback and insight into their minds and information on what you achieved together during the lesson. If you do not agree with their conclusions, ask more questions to try to get to the root of the misunderstanding. With this understanding, you can paraphrase, give feedback, or clarify the lesson points. When you need to clarify a point, it is important to explain why you are making the point, saying that it will help you get on the same page. All instructors will want to examine the situation carefully when they and their students are not on the same page. Self-examination is essential to be certain that you are on the right track in your lesson format and communication skills. Even when the lesson has gone well, it is ideal to do a quick review of the highlights and make note of possible improvements. This keeps you on top of your own teaching program and skills.

If you are a new instructor, I strongly recommend that you keep a journal. It can help you stay clear on each student's progress and help you easily remember from one lesson to the next the students' programs, their strong and weak points. I did this for the first five years of my teaching career and, as a result, I developed the ability to take mental notes. A mental journal replaced my written journal.

Consistent lesson structure, like the one presented in this chapter, is a key element in the success of the learning process. The time needed for each step and the order of the steps may vary with the student and the day. Many instructors have indicated that time is one of their biggest challenges. With experience, planning, and self-examination, you will soon be able to stay within the scheduled time frame, having allotted the approximate timefor each step based on the warm-up and goal of the day.

# COMMUNICATIONS

Communications are at the center of quality instruction. Communication between rider and instructor and horse and rider is central to all teaching and riding results. Essential components of skillful communication are a wise use of the power and tone of voice, the ability to listen, and consciousness of and completion of the cycle of communications.

effective listening builds confidence

When a message is conveyed clearly, using just a few, easy to understand words, the student is more likely to be able to listen without withdrawing attention from the horse. Body and mind need time to process what has been said and shown. The instructor's voice can help riders and horses relax and take appropriate action. While learning to use one's voice well takes practice, it is one of the easiest of the communication skills to acquire. Do your vocal skills need a tune-up? The answers to these questions can help you decide:

- Are you getting the responses you want from your student?

- Does the student ask you to repeat yourself?

- Does your videotape of a recent lesson match what you think you are saying and doing?

- How wordy are your explanations?

- Can you make your statements even clearer?

- Does your tone of voice change in the lesson to reward your student when you receive the response you want?

**Listening** carefully gives you a deeper understanding of how students learn, their most comfortable communication and learning styles,

| Communication Highlights |
|---|
| Effective Listening |
| Ask Appropriate Questions |
| Complete Cycle of Communications |
| •    Paraphrasing |
| •    Clarifying |
| •    Feedback |
| "Getting On Same Page" |
| Positive Attitude and Words |
| Chart 19A |

and their levels of confidence. I have learned that the most important communication skill I bring to the arena is listening.

Second to listening is **asking appropriate questions**. The answers indicate if my students and I are on the same page or not.

The third most important communication skill is the ability of the instructor to close the **cycle of communication**, leaving both instructor and student confident of mutual understanding. Paraphrasing, clarifying, and feedback are three common closure techniques.

**Paraphrasing** allows you to be certain you have understood fully what your student has said. Simple restatement can break down lots of communication blocks. Ways to start your paraphrase are:

- What I hear you saying is . . .
- In other words . . .
- Let's see if I understand. You said . . .
- Did I hear you correctly when you said . . . ?

**Clarifying** is used when you are not certain the student fully understands what you have said, or if you do not understand the student's answer. It is an unthreatening way to increase understanding. It is also a great opportunity to bring awareness in from another sense, such as feel. Consider starting a clarifying statement with:

- Super, what did that feel like?
- That is very interesting and I wonder if. . .
- Can we take a few more minutes with this? I'd like to ask you. . .
- Help me please. I am not certain I understand what you mean by. . .
- I'm glad you said that; it makes me want to know. . .
- I see. I notice that you are (physical observation) which makes me wonder. . .

**Feedback** is your verbal response to what you think you have heard. Ideally, feedback should be given in the order that is most likely to produce the results you are looking for. During Sabina's warm-up review, she wanted to improve her horse's rhythm, consistency, willingness to go forward, attention, and engagement. When I asked her what she would do first, she gave me a startled look and said, "I have no idea." I told her that I would suggest getting her horse's attention with the inside bend, getting her horse off her leg with transitions, and maintaining a consistent rhythm in the gait. The words used should be simple and, whenever possible, related to feel. Using feedback, you acknowledge what is correct, what has changed, and what could be corrected. All forms of feedback confirm the learning process for students, letting them know that you have noticed them doing something right. Essential to influential feedback is positive thinking, positive phrases, and simple, specific words. Feedback is short and to the point.

**"Getting on the same page"** with the student is one of the most valuable communication skills, a result of an instructor's acute listening. When instructors listen to their students carefully, withholding judgment for the time being, they gain insight into students' ways of thinking—noticing the words used and body language. Information we gain from asking about background, goals, and related information helps us determine if a student's goals and knowledge are realistic or not. If not, we must determine what needs to be changed for the student to be realistic? Before we start into a lesson, we need to be aware of the student's starting point. We must make a clear transition statement that connects the student's self-perception and our intentions to fill in the missing holes. Moving the student from his page to our page can take a sentence or several lessons. Little will be achieved until both student and instructor are on the same page. The same goes when it is time to move onto the next subject; when it is time to "turn the page."

The instructor's **positive attitude,** helpful communications, and clear thinking are invaluable resources for any student's progress. Most people who think and express themselves negatively do not realize it. How can you tell if your attitude is positive and helpful? Listen to what you say to yourself and to others. Core beliefs are reflected in self-talk and, ultimately, our communications with both humans and horses. Negative self-talk can arise from a lack of confidence, a deeply held negative attitude, or a need to protect one's self from failure. Do not despair further if you find yourself talking negatively. Almost everything that can be said in a negative way can be turned around and said from positive perspective. Here are a couple of examples:

- I can't sit the trot vs. I will work harder on sitting the trot.
- I hate that corner; my horse always shies in that corner vs. I am going to keep my horse's focus through that corner and turn his shying into forward energy.

To brighten up tarnished attitudes, instructors first of all must examine their core beliefs and habits of self-expression. Avoid common pitfalls. Instead of "do not", use "do." In almost any situation, except for perhaps the most grave, you can just as effectively tell someone what *to* do instead of what *not* to do. Even when someone realizes what should *not* be done, what should be done may still remain a mystery if you do not say what that is. Positive self-talk and expression start with you, the instructor, and then move with you into the arena to help your students toward positive results and habits.

You can get an idea of your students' attitudes by noticing positive or negative self-talk during the lessons. Do they use "I can't" or "I'll try, but . . ."? Store initial observations of negative or vague expressions in your memory bank. Give your students a little time to learn positive attitude formation from your example. If that fails, or if they are extremely negative, time must be taken to explain the disservice negative self-talk is doing themselves and their horses. 🐎

| Positive vs Negative Self Talk & Thoughts | | | |
|---|---|---|---|
| Thought ⟹ | Feeling | Thought ⟹ | Feeling |
| What am I going to do if I don't get the test right? | Worry Tension | I will do the best test I can. If I make a mistake, I will take what I learn and use it next time. | Ready Relaxed |
| Why did I think I could be a successful instructor? | Self-Doubt | How am I going to help this student? | Confident Curious |
| I never get a fair chance. If I just had half a chance, I'd show them. | Victimized | New judges, I will show them what I can do. | In charge Challenged |

Chart 19

Instructors who project confidence create relaxed, ready learners. One of the best ways to do this is to practice using a full communication cycle. This is always a three-part cycle, no matter who starts the cycle: instructor addresses student, student responds to instructor, instructor acknowledges student response, or the other way around. Communications between rider and horse also have three parts. The instructional technique called "half-halt" can be broken down into three parts. Rider prepares horse for a figure or transition, the horse responds, the rider acknowledges with release. A horse's difficulty can initiate the cycle. The horse gets out of balance, unsettling the rider. The rider responds with an appropriate use of aids, the horse responds, the rider acknowledges the response by returning to their relaxed consistent reference feel in seat, legs, and hands. The same is true of the preparatory half-halt; rider prepares horse with a push, slight hold, and then signal of what exercise the rider expects him to do. Instructors can take the mystery out of the half-halt by explaining that it is an adjustment based on the communication cycle. Make the communication cycle a reliable teaching tool by using it in all their communications.

This quick overview of communications has highlighted the most important points in the communication process. The more well-versed we are as communicators, the more effective our teaching becomes.

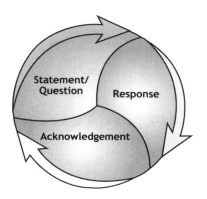

## communication cycle

| Communications Check List | | |
|---|---|---|
| | **Skill** | **I need to review & practice** |
| **Getting on the "Same Page"** | Vocabulary | |
| | Simple & short explanations | |
| | Acknowledge goals | |
| | Aware of self-talk | |
| | Aware of communication style | |
| | | |
| **Active Communication Techniques** | Paraphrasing for understanding | |
| | Clarifying | |
| | Thoughtful feedback | |
| | | |
| **Communications for building trust** | Listening with empathy | |
| | Listening with open mind | |
| | Listening with awareness | |
| | Listening with energy | |
| | Listening to horse | |
| | Listening with sincerity | |
| | | Chart 20 |

# DEVELOPING YOUR EYE:
## *Increasing Awareness through Observation*

Before you can be fully aware of your students and their needs, you must be able to observe yourself with positive honesty.

Observation is an essential skill for you as an instructor that includes being aware of who you are, your weaknesses and strengths, the limits and expansiveness of your technical knowledge, and your motivation and goals. It also includes a well-developed ability to be in the present moment, focused on what is happening in your vicinity.

WE FORGOT THE NET!!!!!!!

Entering the arena, focused in the present and leaving your personal mental baggage at the gate, puts you in a position to be acutely aware of your student. From the beginning to the end of a lesson, you will want to be actively using observation. The three main senses you use are vision, hearing and intuition. Being in the present, with a clear mind dedicated to the horse and rider in the arena, allows you to make the most accurate observations.

*As an instructor it is not enough to be aware of your students and their horses, you must also be aware of yourself.*

One of the first observations to be made as a student enters the ring relates to safety. There are eight critical points to notice immediately.

Initial observations are made before the lesson formally begins. In those first moments, see how effectively the students are communicating with their horses, their awareness of the environment, the correctness of their positions, and the responses of the horses. During the exchange of greetings, catch a glimpse of the effectiveness and style of their communications with the instructor, their grasps of technical skills,

92

the clarity of their thinking and their levels of relaxation. While the instructor learns the most in the first few lessons with a student, each lesson provides an opportunity for life or environment to interfere, so instructors must always remain alert to these qualities and to the student's state of mind and mood. Observations continue in the warm-up phase of the lesson. The warm-up review phase provides a more complete overview of horse and rider, their goals, the harmony between the two and their performance.

Throughout all interactions with students, instructors will want to remain keenly aware of the students' level of technical knowledge and their mental attitude to see if they match what the students are showing and saying. Instructor sensitivity to these issues is instrumental to educational success. The more we teach with awareness, the more we will expand our observation, listening and intuitive abilities. Increasing skills of observation is one of the most enjoyable on-going challenges in teaching.

Another key area of awareness addresses the level of mental and physical relaxation in the horse and rider. Mental discomfort can result from confusion, worry, fear or anxiety. It is the instructor's job to notice and address the discomfort in a way that will help the student find a comfort zone that enables productive work. Physical tightness, more easily detectible, needs to be dealt with as well. It is almost impossible to teach a tense rider because tension blocks learning. Instructors can pick up clues from either horse or rider that point to the source of the problem. Any clue can help the instructor trace the problem back to the source and begin to find solutions. The task is first to notice the symptom, find the difficulty, then plot a course for change.

There is no right or wrong way to make observations. It does not matter whether the eye is drawn first to rider or first to horse. Ultimately the goal is to be able to see the level of harmony in the partnership as well as to notice the state of each of the partners. Once the instructor can see the good points and the amount of harmony, we can see where the team is blocked or stuck. From there we can match what we see with what we know. During this phase we quickly decide where the team fits in the Stages of Rider Education. It is the process of matching the observation with the student's skill level that determines where we start in each lesson.

The main issues that interfere with performance are poor rider position, unbalanced horse, tension or stiffness in horse and/or rider, poorly educated horse, inadequate technical knowledge and obstructive rider attitude. When instructors recognize the presence of any of these, we know our original lesson plan is not producing effective results. Once we accept this, we offer a fresh explanation of what we want or ask the student to try something less complicated or more basic. Our intention is to do so as a way to build rather than destroy confidence. In this process we are aware of what we are asking, what we want the students to accomplish and if their performance is staying the same, improving or

| SYMPTOMS OF DISCOMFORT | |
| --- | --- |
| **Rider Symptoms** | **Horse Symptoms** |
| Crookedness | Stiff or uneven gaits |
| Uneven leg length | General lack of energy |
| Inability to focus | Inability to focus |
| Frequent requests to walk | Excessive sweating or mouth foam |
| Shortness of breath | Quickened breathing |
| | Jigging |
| | Shying |

Chart 22

| DIAGNOSING DISCOMFORT | |
| --- | --- |
| **Bridle to Horse's Mouth** | **Saddle to Horse's Back** |
| Ears pinned back | Ears pinned back |
| Tongue over bit | Running from aids |
| Tilting head | Refusing or running out at jumps |
| Repeatedly opening mouth | Refusing to pick up leads |
| Mouthing bit constantly | Hollowing back |
| Bracing against bit | Short, choppy gaits |
| Refusal to stop or turn | Refusal to stop or turn |
| Tail wringing | Tail wringing |
| Head shaking or tossing | Unwillingness to go forward |
| Abnormal head carriage | Resistance to being mounted |
| | Resistance to bending |
| | Bucking or humping back after mounted |
| | Unhappy about being tacked up |

Chart 23

deteriorating. Our observations then indicate whether or not we are on the correct path or if we need to make a change.

The Warm Up Check List, Chart 24 provides a quick guide to use to help develop your eye.

## WARM UP CHECK LIST

A great tool for warm-up to develop the habit of organized awareness. You can mark x in what you feel needs work, and then prioritize them. First do your safety check, and then follow this list. After practicing using this list, it will become an automatic way for you to observe.

| Skill | Points | Priority | Notes |
|---|---|---|---|
| Goals | Well thought out | | |
| | Need more thought | | |
| | Too high | | |
| | Too low | | |
| Position | Good | | |
| | Elbow to bit | | |
| | Ear-shoulder-hip-heel | | |
| | Elasticity | | |
| | Depth | | |
| | Physical tension | | |
| Mind | Relaxed but alert | | |
| | Good focus | | |
| | Too concentrated | | |
| | Distracted | | |
| | Lack of confidence | | |
| | Worry | | |
| | Fear | | |
| | Technical knowledge | | |
| | Effective riding plan | | |
| Communication | Effective | | |
| | Indecisive | | |
| | Negative | | |
| | Inattentive | | |
| | Aggressive | | |
| Control | Horse response to leg | | |
| | Horse response to rein | | |
| | Horse response to seat | | |
| | Horse relaxation | | |
| | Horse straightness | | |
| | Horse rhythm | | |

**Additional Notes:**

Chart 24

Developing awareness is a process that continues throughout your professional life. At different times, the instructor's awareness will shift between one's self, the student, the horse and the horse/rider partnership. Awareness brings our attention to each aspect of the teaching environment. The more we observe, the more aware we become. The more aware we become, the better teachers we become.

# GOAL SETTING

**Professionalism:
Setting our course**

Planning and setting goals are vital strategies that instructors use both before and during each lesson. It is a good idea to approach students indirectly with goal setting. Many are afraid that a set goal will add unproductive pressure or stress. Since it is an essential skill for progress in day to day riding, as well as for the development of independent learning, goal setting or planning must be taught to riding students. Fortunately, it is easy to teach indirectly. Using a consistent lesson format that makes a simple plan between the warm-up and the lesson, followed with a review to create a plan for rides between lessons establishes the groundwork for students to learn to use goal setting in a non-threatening way.

When an instructor first begins to work with new students, two important pieces of information needed for goal setting must be gathered. They have a powerful effect on planning the progression of learning.

- What motivates the students to ride?

- Why are they taking lessons?

- What are their dreams?

- What do they want to achieve most with their horses or their riding?

The answers to these questions lay the groundwork for all planning. This information helps the instructor create the learning program for each student.

When this information is combined with the instructor's technical expertise in the skills of riding and an assessment of the student's technical skills, the intermediate plan is created. The intermediate plan includes the steps needed to work toward the student's long-term goal. The plan is filed in the instructor's teaching journal to be referred to as the plan is put into action. The overview of the intermediate goal is discussed with the student at the beginning of the first lesson. It is important to keep students up-to-date on the plan of action because the plan can change. The goal can change when the student learns a new skills or returns to a previous step to fill in a 'hole' that has shown itself. Involve the student in the process so they will be aware of the steps they are making toward their intermediate goal, which is vital to your teaching program. It is important to map out the plans according to your student's stress levels. Some students thrive on planning well in advance, while others prefer to take small steps.

 Be careful when you create goal deadlines to take into account each student's way of dealing with stress. (see Tapping Into Your Student's Motivation in Professional Development) ⚞

 Many instructors find it beneficial to have students complete a goals summary sheet once or twice a year that prompts them to look at their goals, dreams, and limitations or problems. This is an excellent way to find out if instructor and student are on the same page, as long as there have been regular discussions on the need for flexibility and revision of goals. ⚞

As close to the first lesson as possible, the instructor and student discuss the student's long-term goal or dream. From this, instructors help the student devise a plan to reach that goal, creating the intermediate goals that will lead to the final goal. The emphasis of each ride's plan is on an intermediate goal. The instructor and student adjust the plan for each lesson based on performance during warm-up as it compares to the previous lesson or ride. This ground-level planning is the most important step in teaching short-term goal setting. Learning to set and work with goals is embedded in the overall learning process, not something taught directly and separately. By asking students to give an overview of their performance between lessons, followed with an overview of their warm-up as compared to their last warm-up, instructors provide students an avenue to develop awareness of their own learning processes and a way to collect the information needed to make a plan. Evaluating the plan in the review at the lesson's end and collecting from the review an idea of what to practice between lessons is another step in planning. With a few months practice of this process, students usually learn how to set goals without ever actually having to formally learn goal setting.

Karen is a prime **example** of how much goal setting can help. Shortly after a career change Karen, who had a world-class educational background, came for lessons. She knew what she wanted her horse to do in the training program. Most of the time in the first few lessons was spent evaluating her young horse's training and creating a plan with exercises to advance him. After each lesson Karen was directed and consistent with a plan. By the fourth lesson her progress was not continuing as expected, so I asked her to give me her training goals since her last lesson. Despite a long explanation, she never gave a clear plan. I then asked her to evaluate her warm-up and give me the plan for the day. Karen was able to identify what was good and what needed work, but she was unable to organize  a plan that would benefit her horse. By now we knew each other well enough that I decided to suggest that our lesson needed to focus on developing a monthly training plan. We discussed the factors Karen needed to consider to create order in her mind. We then put the plan into action daily after the warm-up review. The next month Karen arrived having made progress and thanked me for pointing out her need to organize her knowledge and riding time.

Karen, who thrives under pressure, *can* work more directly with goal setting related to organizing her time and creating a deadline. She thrives on pressure and goals, thus as she learned to use them she fulfilled another need of hers, action and results. She reported that her training sessions are finished in thirty to forty minutes instead of an hour and a half. However, many students need an indirect method of goal setting. Setting up a calendar-based plan for meeting specific goals can add performance pressure. The indirect method of involving students in the process of learning a skill often works most effectively. Roy is one of these people. He is timid and lacks self-confidence. He prefers to know what to do, and to make a plan based on achieving the skill. He does like to be tied to a time deadline. As we get to know our students, we learn how they deal with stress and pressure. This then tells us how best to deal with goal setting within each lesson. Riding is an activity that has a steep learning curve, so students must learn to be flexible in their training expectations, and they must accept the need to review, when necessary, skills already learned. No matter how much planning is in place, the fundamental skills of learning are never bypassed.

Once students are comfortable with goal-setting, they can be asked to keep  personal goal journals. The discipline of keeping a journal helps turn the learning and evaluating process over to the student. Based on student requests, the pocket-sized *My Riding Goals JOURNAL* was written for riders to fill out soon after a lesson or a ride, and for review beforehand. This little book is easy to use and helps riders direct their own goal-planning processes.

# INSTRUCTOR'S TOOLBOX

The following is an overview of some of the most effective and useful teaching techniques and tools for instructors; tools essential for your professional success. They have been adapted from the field of education.

## INVOLVE AND ENGAGE THE STUDENT

Involving students in the learning process encourages them to own the skills, thus becoming more and more independent from the teacher. This philosophy is the backbone of this book; to create an independently thinking and acting student. Involving the student in the process is one of the most successful ways to do this. An involved student helps the teacher feel successful because learning can continue moving forward.

When you ask students questions, you are engaging them in the process, and their answers give valuable insight into their communication style, state of mind, attitude, and understanding of the skill being taught. A delicate balance must be found for how often and when to use this tool based on the student's skill, aptitude, and level. A shy student lacking in confidence needs to be slowly engaged in communication. Common sense will indicate how much or how little to engage the student. There are two key times in every lesson that you conversationally engage the riding student: at the beginning when you review the warm-up and at the end when you review the whole lesson.

## WORKING TOGETHER:
## GETTING ON THE SAME PAGE

Getting on the same page, a skill covered in the communication chapter, is the primary tool used to get the student involved in the lesson. It is a discussion that brings student and teacher to a common understanding of what they are trying to accomplish together in that lesson, as well as a shared starting point. Getting on the same page goes beyond involving and engaging the student. This key communication skill can unlock the door to the rider's mind and provide the necessary information on which to build a lesson framework. When students feel their instructor is recognizing and validating their input, the greatest results can be achieved. Often, what we as instructors would like to accomplish differs from what students would like to work on. We must recognize their desires, express our own, and build a bridge between the two standpoints in order to have a successful learning experience. No amount of questioning or listening to students will be successful if they do not understand why we want to do something.

Once the instructor recognizes what the student wants to do and what the student already understands, the instructor will know what needs to be taught. As the instructor, you will need to build a bridge between what you know is needed and what the student thinks is needed. It is helpful to frame a sentence to clarify the revised goal. This one sentence can include why you want the student to learn this particular skill and how it fits into the student's goals.

## SIMPLICITY OF STRUCTURE

Riders can mentally process more information at one time than a horse can, but not as much as they might think! Keeping it simple involves the number of words said, the number of actions performed at one time, the reach of the goal for the lesson, and all the expectations. This principle, simplicity, holds true from start to finish in the lesson, homework, and intermediate planning.

Keeping in the forefront of our minds the need to move forward one step at a time, we must consider the horse's simplicity first. When our students understand this, they will give themselves permission to keep their riding simple. We, as instructors, must also suppress our desire to give out too much information at one time. Our students will come away with more concrete skills and solid learning if we focus on one or two elements rather than on giving them as much information as possible. If we throw out lots of different ideas hoping to give them their money's worth, but do not allow them time to really own the skills, we are actually slowing down the learning process. This principle applies to explanations and corrections, as well as to the major points. In the arena, use as few words as possible. Conversation, either talking or listening, interferes with feel.

Another area where simplicity is essential is in the number of words used. Fewer words are better. Clear, concise words travel from riders' ears through their bodies to their seats much more quickly—the source of "feel." Figuring out which words to choose for simplicity's sake is part of your task as the teacher. Because you are involving your student in the lesson process, one of the areas of your student's learning style that your well-asked questions will call forth are the words your student uses to describe feelings. Catching these words and using them gives you another way to get together on the same page and to speed up learning. A few words, drawn from the student's vocabulary, will make learning all the more valuable to the student.

Keeping lessons simple and systematic are two of the most important tools to implement to enhance the education of the rider.

 Keep the lesson's purpose to one to three points.

## FLEXIBILITY OF APPROACH, PLAN, AND EXPLANATIONS

Many instructors create a plan with their students at the beginning of each lesson, but what if the plan is not working? Two to five minutes is a long time if something is not improving. Any more time opens the door for frustration to enter. The astute instructor can see within a matter of seconds if what is being asked for is producing a response. For each action instructors have requested, there should be a response. The response from either horse or rider gives the feedback we need in order to know if we are on track or not. What we do next depends upon the response:

- Positive response leads to positive acknowledgement.

- Negative response leads to creative correction.

- No response leads to positive questions to the student to uncover why.

 Notice the smallest change in horse and/or rider.

If the first words used elicit no response, try a few others, one at a time so you know what works.

If a change in words is not working, reexamine the points of the plan.

Celebrate active response in your response.

Be patient. Notice and appreciate small steps forward.

Make changes as quickly as possible when the need for change is seen.

## CONSISTENCY

How can we be flexible yet consistent in our teaching? Instructors need to be consistent in plans for skill development and for lesson structure, as well as in their expectations of student and horse responses. The plan we come into the arena with is a starting point. How we go about realizing the day's goals must change with regard to the day's conditions. Mary offers a good example. She was learning how to deepen her seat at the sitting trot. She had been working on this for many weeks and was close to being able to sit for the entire lesson. At one lesson she arrived stiff and tight. During the greeting phase of the lesson, Mary told me that she had slipped and twisted her ankle earlier that week. She proudly told me that, nevertheless, she had continued her practice. After watching her a few minutes, it was clear that the pain in her ankle was stiffening her body and consequently her horse. I congratulated her on having the mental discipline to keep practicing and then drew her attention to her horse's compensating response. Mary was quick to ask, "How can my ankle affect him? It is so far from my seat!" This opened the opportunity for me to go more deeply into an explanation of the physiology of horse and rider and how this affects balance and movement.

Mary furthered her goal of riding the sitting trot with a deeper understanding. We can remain flexible in our presentation and implementations as we follow the system of rider education presented in "Technical Mastery" later on in this book.

We must also be flexible in our explanations. If a student does not understand an explanation, we must try another. If Mary had not understood my explanation, it would be my job to try another one.

Whenever we teach a new skill and find students falling short in something we have already taught and they have confirmed, we need to let the students know that regressing in this way is natural, expected, and temporary. Help them let go of any concern about it and reassure them that we will refresh the old skills, if needed, once the new skills are confirmed. We must be flexible enough to return to past lesson skills when necessary.

Consistency is the backbone principle of Equestrian Education Systems, the German Scale of Education, and the personal program of any professional trainer/instructor. Consistency helps valuable habits develop in body and mind, laying the groundwork for natural actions and well-trained responses.

- Horses are more comfortable and better trained if ridden with consistent aids.
- Horses have more muscle and fitness with a consistent work schedule.
- Riders become more consistent in performance if instructors follow a standard lesson structure and develop a consistent state of awareness of themselves and their horses.

## CONCENTRATION AND FOCUS

Instructors are challenged to enter each lesson focused attentively on the horses and riders in the arena. Full attention to the students, coupled with a persistent awareness of what else is going on in the arena, is important for safety and for results. Nothing is more distracting to a student than an instructor who is talking to the audience, talking on the phone, or watching other activities while they are teaching. We must set an example of what we expect in focus from our students, and what our students can expect from their horses. First and foremost, horse and rider need to have a relaxed focus on the subject at hand. Instructors must insist that students keep their horses' attention for safety's sake. Beyond safety, focus is necessary for good communications.

Some students are either too easily distracted or too concentrated. When these extremes occur, instructors need to redirect the rider's focus before moving forward in the lesson. For students who are easily distracted, suggest a mental focal point, such as each corner. Ask riders who are too concentrated to look out at something specific in the arena.

Once horse and rider are both appropriately focused on the task at hand, the instructor can alternately direct and redirect attention between the horse, the activities in the arena, and following the instructor's directions. Concentration is a continuum most instructors work with quite naturally, but it can be helpful to divide it into four parts for purposes of discussion and understanding. Understanding these four states of concentration, all of which may be used in each lesson, is essential to instructors.

### Four types of focus

- Broad External

  Broad External focus: observing what is going on around you
  - Initial observations of your student and horse, the weather,    and other activities or riders in the arena.

- Broad Internal

  Broad Internal focus: collected knowledge on a given subject
  - At the beginning of each lesson, combining what you see and hear with what you already know to form a plan for the day

- Narrow External

  Narrow External focus: focusing on a result or action
  - Helping each student in the practice of a new skill

- Narrow Internal

  Narrow Internal focus: thinking of the detail that needs to go into a skill
  - Mentally organizing in order to explain in a simple, clear, concise way how to do something

Some riders must use Narrow Internal focus before using Narrow External focus to understand the details before they try the new movement. It is important to train such students to return to the Narrow External without using Narrow Internal thinking. The amount of mental detail in Narrow Internal blocks the sense of feel. For instructors, teaching the shift back to feel is one of the most difficult but necessary challenges in helping students learn. ⚞

## CONFIDENCE

Your confidence as an instructor is a result of practical knowledge that has produced successful results for yourself or your students. A finely developed, positive self-awareness confirms the correctness of your own knowledge and success. Positive feedback from students and horses is another confidence builder.

---

### 12 CONFIDENCE BUILDERS

1.  Safety first; knowing you are attentive to this is the foundation of confidence.

2.  Goals are to direct; help students set realistic goals and meet them!

3.  Once students understand a new skill, give them the opportunity to work with it on their own under your watchful eye. Reward positives.

4.  Add challenges carefully, enabling them to experience success.

5.  Encourage students to make their own plan and decisions; give them permission to make mistakes.

6.  Be aware of a student's response to your comments. A few ill-timed comments can deplete confidence. Respect the student's competence. Sensitivity to style builds confidence.

7.  Lavish well-timed praise on students who are showing positive change.

8.  Help students recognize what they have achieved and enjoy with them the satisfaction of achievement.

9.  Reinforce a positive "I can" attitude with realistic parameters. Reality permits success, and success builds confidence.

10. Encourage physical fitness; a well-tuned body builds self-confidence.

11. Train your students to focus on the present as they keep in mind the intended outcome.

12. Encourage self-evaluation, insisting on the positives as well as the changes the student wishes to make.

Chart 25

---

We project confidence through self-carriage, body language, manners and grooming, tone of voice, responsiveness, and the ability to make decisions and follow through. It is important to maintain a balance between confidence and humility. To get another opinion if we have tipped the scale to one side too far, we can ask another instructor or seek an outside evaluation. If we are open-minded and can self-evaluate, a video review is another way we can check up on our skills.

Instructors who build confidence in their students create thinking, independent students who can make the decisions that are essential to safety and performance. The first step in developing confidence is to develop a relationship of trust with the student. Setting a good example is important. Creating successful educational experiences builds confidence. Instructors who remain acutely aware of their students and their horses as a whole during the lesson have the opportunity to create confidence-building successes in each lesson.

Regular review of the essential tools can present useful reminders to all instructors. These tools will help you feel you are operating to the best of your ability. When you encounter a challenge, check back with these tools and find something that might be of help to you.

**INSTRUCTOR'S TOOLBOX**
- INVOLVE & ENGAGE
- GET ON THE SAME PAGE
- SIMPLICITY
- FLEXIBILITY
- CONSISTENCY
- CONCENTRATION & FOCUS
- CONFIDENCE

# Teaching a New Skill

Whether you are teaching a new skill to a beginner or to an advanced rider, the process is the same. Students will be able to properly and efficiently learn the new skill if certain steps are taken. First, be sure that all the foundation skills needed for the new skill are in place. You will know when students are ready to move on when they can perform a skill smoothly without hesitation or much thought. A good test for using a confirmed skill is to intentionally divert the students as they ride with talk about some other fun subject. If their performance remains the same, they are ready to add a new skill.

## STEPS IN TEACHING A NEW SKILL

There are three basic methods to introducing a new skill; explanation followed with practice, practice followed by explanation, and demonstration. The most common way to introduce a new skill is to explain it, then let the students try it and make corrections as they do so. If the student has a basic understanding of the new skill, we can ask them to show us what they understand and discuss the theory of it later. Using this method students are asked to try the new skill and *then* discuss it with the instructor. For visual learners the ideal method is demonstration, theory and then practice. The decision on which method to use is made based on to whether or not the student has some understanding of the skill being introduced and the students best learning style.

### Explanation followed with Practice

Use this method when students are relatively unfamiliar with the new skill or with the language of the discipline.

    1. Fully explain the new skill (or movement) to the students. Tell the students why they are ready to learn the skill and how it fits into their learning program.

       a. Keep it as simple as possible.

b. Use a mixture of fact and feel words.

c. Confirm riders' understandings.

2. Let the students try the new skill and, as they experiment, help them get the desired result by making simple corrections.

a. Make clear, simple corrections aimed at the core of the difficulty.

b. Confirm riders' understanding.

3. Once the students have achieved the desired result or any piece of it, acknowledge their success, and help them attach a sense of feel to it.

a. Reward students with prompt, behaviorally specific acknowledgments. Let them know when and what they have done right.

b. Allow students some quiet time to pay attention to feel when they are performing the skill correctly.

## Practice followed with Explanation

Use this method when students have a basic understanding or some experience in the skill or discipline being introduced.

1. Ask students who have a good feel for and a solid foundation of the preliminary skills needed for the new skill, ask them if they understand a particular move such as "leg yield" for example. Ask them to describe the movement's route, bend and essential elements. If their explanations are clear, go to the next step; if not, offer additional information.

2. Ask the students to perform the movement using any aids they feel are necessary. When they are finished, comment on what they did well.

3. Ask them to do it again, and then ask what they liked and anything they might want to correct. Comment on their responses`.

## Demonstration

After you have explained something new, get on a horse to demonstrate as you explain or ask another student to give a demonstration. A video can be used along with discussion. Finish up with a question and answer session to make sure you and your student are on the same page.

A natural part of learning is the destabilization of a recently learned skill when a student is under stress. Stress can come from adding something new such as information from a riding lesson from another instructor, being in a competition, or simply normal pressures of life. Once a new skill is learned, jump back into coaching mode and help the student stabilize the old skills while practicing the new one. A classic example is when a student who is riding a beautifully positioned sitting trot is asked to do a leg yield, and soon is either crooked or leaning forward. Many instructors would be inclined to suggest corrections to the position; however, unless the position is interfering with the execution of the new skill, it is best to let the student continue with the leg yield. Once the aids feel coordinated, the instructor can focus attention on improving position. If, however, the position is interfering with the leg yield, correct it as simply as possible while the student continues to explore the aids to leg yield. What the student is learning will determine the number of practice sessions required until the skill is confirmed. Repetition is a tried-and-true tool for learning. Students need to repeatedly use a new skill until it is committed to feel before being introduced to another new skill.

## CHECKING FOR CONFIRMATION OF A NEW SKILL

The creation of an independent, confirmed skill is done in steps. Once students correctly accomplish a new skill and you feel it is confirmed, it is time to expect the student to use the skill without mentally focusing on it. One good way to test for confirmation is to have a discussion with your students about feel and details of the skill while they are doing it. The third step to independence includes turning the new skill's execution over to the student completely, while remaining alert to their success as they continue to perform the skill. Remember that attention to yet another new skill is likely to erode recently acquired skills.

Even after we have passed a responsibility over to the students, they often forget to take time to prepare themselves properly, so we must remain observant. With each lesson, we must make certain students are practicing new skills using *all* the steps without leaving out what we have already taught them. When a step is omitted, it is often because the instructor has not provided enough repeated opportunity to practice the new skill to confirm the habit, or has not kept an observant eye on the student once the skill is taught, or the rider has become careless. The remedy is simple. First ask students if they are aware of what they have omitted. If they know, a reminder of what is missing is often enough when combined with a few repetitions of the movement with all the steps. If they do not know which step is missing, we must review the movement or skill process to re-establish in the student's mind each step in the correct order.

It is the rare student who feels that practicing a new skill is a way to make progress. Students often feel they are making progress only when they are learning new skills. Yet instructors spend most of the lesson time coaching; refining and developing the new skill and encouraging enough practice for the new skill to become a habit for the student. It is the instructor's challenge to keep the lesson interesting while avoiding distracting the student who needs to focus on the skill being learned. During this time, instructors must remain mindful about giving the students permission to take whatever time is needed to confirm a skill. Rider confirmation of new skills is essential to the development of a solid foundation for further learning and performance.

# Coaching

*. . . to improve reflection, competitive performance, & confidence*

BY NICHOLAS FOWLER

During any lesson, we balance at least two roles and perspectives - instructor and coach. While the coaching role has been demonstrated throughout this book, it is useful to focus on it here. What are the important differences between instructing and coaching? Why do we need to be aware of them? How does each role generate a different relationship with our student? What are some differences in coaching, and under what circumstances would we want to think of ourselves as 'coach'?

The instructor role is usually focused most on imparting specific knowledge that the student does not yet know. The instructor is explaining, advocating, and theorizing in order to impart special information. The student in this relationship is dependent upon the instructor for this information. The student is on the receiving end, listening to the information provided by the instructor, applying it, and feeling the horse's response. As the process is in practice, the instructor makes suggestions and corrections. This role is most valuable during the early phases of learning, but continues as an integral part throughout the learning experience.

On the other hand, the coach's role focuses on the student's reflection and awareness to integrate new information. The coach is providing feedback, as a mirror, to allow the student to make adjustments in a new behavior or skill. In this relationship, the coach plays a supportive role; the student has the primary responsibility to guide the learning. Through the coaching phase of the relationship, the student becomes less dependent upon the coach, learning through her own self-reflection.

A coach's communications will have a greater percentage of questions, helping the rider reflect on what she is doing and feeling and the

110

consequences of these actions. With this perspective, the rider can retain responsibility for what to try next, in this particular moment and with this particular horse. The coach's reflection is clear in that it is non-judgmental, just factual. This is particularly important as it encourages experimenting with a range of options and observing the results, leading to a deeper understanding of the riding art than simply perfecting a particular position, approach, or skill. For example, I can perfect my hand position through the constant feedback from my instructor telling me how it should be, or I can learn at a deeper level how the position of my hands affects the feeling of my ride, and how my overall position looks in the mirror, or as reflected by my coach.

When we ride past the mirror, what do we see? The mirror provides an immediate snapshot, or 'video-clip' of our position. When we correlate that with how our horse feels and the change we are trying to make, we can see if what we are trying is actually working, and perhaps if it is not, some reasons why. A good coach can help the rider to do that throughout the lesson. If the rider and coach have a thoroughly shared understanding of the goal being sought, and of the approaches being tried, the coach is in a good position to give not only a clear reflection, but also some further correlation with an outside perspective that is not available to the rider.

There are so many factors that contribute to a successful working relationship between horse and rider. The most successful riders have learned to balance all of these factors simultaneously. As a student, the rider will be focused on a few of these factors, but cannot hold all of them at the same time. With the coach's support, the rider will be able to hold and work with a greater number of factors. It is in the dialogue before the ride (greetings & update) that the focus of attention is set up as the rider shares her intentions for this lesson. It is in the dialogue during the ride that the factors are shared back and forth, and new understanding is sought and found. It is in the dialogue after the ride (confirming rider insights & review) that learning is cemented and experiences during the ride are checked out and confirmed. Thus, the coach enables the rider to 'see' beyond the limitations of either a mirror or the feelings and thinking obtained through one's self-reflection.

When we were children, we learned to walk through direct experience of the results of our attempts. No one told us the detailed intermediate muscle movements required to balance and move a foot forward. We lose the opportunities to learn this way when we get to school and everything becomes so intellectual. We can get some of this learning back in a coaching relationship in which there is no advocacy for a certain approach in training a new technique. This gives the rider an opportunity to learn and grow simply through a more thorough experience of his own actions and their results.

Coaching can be very powerful, but it requires a great generosity on the coach's part - to give of one-self purely through observations, void of the intellectual content upon which we may pride ourselves. This points to one of the challenging aspects of coaching; honestly and deeply knowing your-self. Effective coaches must be able to let go of their own psychological needs, such as 'being loved' or 'being appreciated for our knowledge or our brilliant suggestions'. We must be careful that our own unmet or unconscious needs do not interfere with our abilities to be entirely open and available to support the needs of those we coach.

An effective coaching relationship asks more of our relating skills. How aware are you of the relationship between you and your rider, between rider and horse, between horse and other horses and the arena, between your rider and the ghosts of the day that he brings to his ride?

Coaching requires a higher level of maturity and deeper sense of taking personal responsibility on the part of rider and coach. Thus, a very young, immature, or beginning rider may need a higher proportion of instruction vs. coaching. Coaching is the technique used throughout teaching to give a student more responsibility in the learning

*Ask yourself what percentage of your statements to your student are either telling her what to do, or advocating for a particular approach?*

process; it allows the student to become more confident of her own skills. As an instructor, we can begin early to prepare our students for the responsibilities required of a good student such as taking full responsibility for what happens during the ride, taking the time to reflect to gain fuller understanding, and knowing and asking for what is needed. If we are not aware of these, we may never begin this process, but stay caught in giving our student the quick answer he seeks, keeping him forever dependent upon us and closed to all the other potential sources of learning.

A good coach usually brings a deep understanding of personal change and can help the rider reflect on those factors that are working against the change. Coaching encourages the student to seek experiments and trials to overcome these factors and clearly see and feel the results. In the same sense, a coach helps the rider reflect on factors working for the desired changes and acknowledge the positive results.

Much of this book has been about awareness. Awareness is a primary theme of coaching. We believe that the peak riding experience for horse and rider requires a level of awareness not common in our culture today. We spend so much of our lives in unconscious states experiencing shame or remorse for the past, or worry about the future, or concern about finances, or fear of how people perceive us. There is so much we could learn from our horse who lives almost purely in the present. Perhaps we need a section called 'Horse as Coach', but we leave that as an exercise, a fun reflection for you and your student.

As a coach, you can go beyond the mirrors to encourage your students' awareness of their current emotions, honoring their real feelings without judgment. Help them become aware of their own energy levels and those of their horse and the real benefits of working with the currently available energy.

---

### Integration Questions

1. An earlier tip was to "encourage the rider to keep each ride simple and think through problems, but not think too much - convert thinking to feeling."
   - How does this apply to you as an instructor and to your function?

2. When does too much 'thinking' get in the way of your intuitive connection with your student where they are - physically, emotionally, energetically, spiritually?

3. How can we encourage the rider to reflect on her role as her horse's coach?

4. How can we encourage the rider to listen to her horse's coaching?

5. How am I different when I wear my coach's hat? How are my clients different? Do they have different expectations of me? Do they have different expectations of themselves? How do I clarify this in my implicit contract with my clients?

6. How do I assure that I integrate this role into my lessons? When do I wear this coach's hat? For what type of student and at what stage will it work well? How do I know when to switch back to my instructor hat?

Chart 27

Competent riding instructors will find that coaching and teaching are very interrelated. Teaching is required to help the student gain a new skill. Coaching and teaching begin to intermix as the new skill is learned. Once the new skill is learned, coaching is used to confirm it into efficient usefulness, allowing the student to use the skill without thinking about the technical aspects of the process. An additional benefit of thinking of ourselves (instructors and riders) as coaches is that we can learn from the advances in other apparently unrelated disciplines and areas of life such as organization development, psychology, spiritual paths, consulting, and executive coaching. The references listed in the Appendix will help you discover principles and ideas that can apply in your riding and instructing.

# STAGES OF RIDER EDUCATION
## An American System of Learning

*EES is committed to the development of independent, thinking and feeling students who are well grounded in a classical approach to equestrian training.*

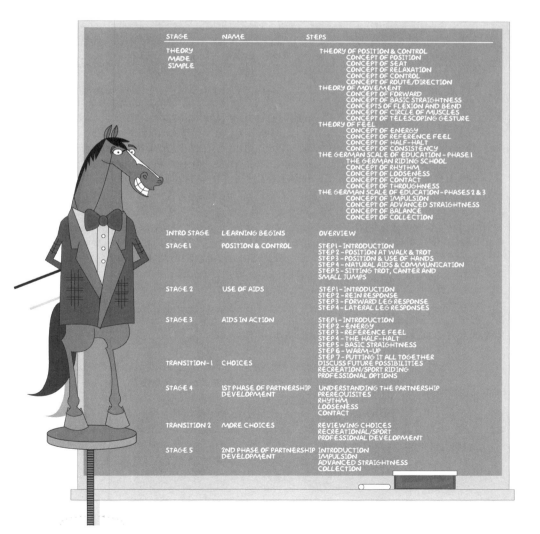

| STAGE | NAME | STEPS |
|---|---|---|
| THEORY MADE SIMPLE | | THEORY OF POSITION & CONTROL<br>CONCEPT OF POSITION<br>CONCEPT OF SEAT<br>CONCEPT OF RELAXATION<br>CONCEPT OF CONTROL<br>CONCEPT OF ROUTE/DIRECTION<br>THEORY OF MOVEMENT<br>CONCEPT OF FORWARD<br>CONCEPT OF BASIC STRAIGHTNESS<br>CONCEPTS OF FLEXION AND BEND<br>CONCEPT OF CIRCLE OF MUSCLES<br>CONCEPT OF TELESCOPING GESTURE<br>THEORY OF FEEL<br>CONCEPT OF ENERGY<br>CONCEPT OF REFERENCE FEEL<br>CONCEPT OF HALF-HALT<br>CONCEPT OF CONSISTENCY<br>THE GERMAN SCALE OF EDUCATION - PHASE I<br>THE GERMAN RIDING SCHOOL<br>CONCEPT OF RHYTHM<br>CONCEPT OF LOOSENESS<br>CONCEPT OF CONTACT<br>CONCEPT OF THROUGHNESS<br>THE GERMAN SCALE OF EDUCATION - PHASES 2 & 3<br>CONCEPT OF IMPULSION<br>CONCEPT OF ADVANCED STRAIGHTNESS<br>CONCEPT OF BALANCE<br>CONCEPT OF COLLECTION |
| INTRO STAGE | LEARNING BEGINS | OVERVIEW |
| STAGE 1 | POSITION & CONTROL | STEP 1 - INTRODUCTION<br>STEP 2 - POSITION AT WALK & TROT<br>STEP 3 - POSITION & USE OF HANDS<br>STEP 4 - NATURAL AIDS & COMMUNICATION<br>STEP 5 - SITTING TROT, CANTER AND SMALL JUMPS |
| STAGE 2 | USE OF AIDS | STEP 1 - INTRODUCTION<br>STEP 2 - REIN RESPONSE<br>STEP 3 - FORWARD LEG RESPONSE<br>STEP 4 - LATERAL LEG RESPONSES |
| STAGE 3 | AIDS IN ACTION | STEP 1 - INTRODUCTION<br>STEP 2 - ENERGY<br>STEP 3 - REFERENCE FEEL<br>STEP 4 - THE HALF-HALT<br>STEP 5 - BASIC STRAIGHTNESS<br>STEP 6 - WARM-UP<br>STEP 7 - PUTTING IT ALL TOGETHER |
| TRANSITION - 1 | CHOICES | DISCUSS FUTURE POSSIBILITIES<br>RECREATION/SPORT RIDING<br>PROFESSIONAL OPTIONS |
| STAGE 4 | 1ST PHASE OF PARTNERSHIP DEVELOPMENT | UNDERSTANDING THE PARTNERSHIP<br>PREREQUISITES<br>RHYTHM<br>LOOSENESS<br>CONTACT |
| TRANSITION 2 | MORE CHOICES | REVIEWING CHOICES<br>RECREATIONAL/SPORT<br>PROFESSIONAL DEVELOPMENT |
| STAGE 5 | 2ND PHASE OF PARTNERSHIP DEVELOPMENT | INTRODUCTION<br>IMPULSION<br>ADVANCED STRAIGHTNESS<br>COLLECTION |

# Why a "new" system of Rider Education?

One of the major differences between learning to ride in the USA and Europe is the presence of a 'system' in Europe. Most European students have the opportunity to learn from a consistent program, with well-educated horses. This is made easy because almost all the small villages have a riding hall staffed by professionally educated instructors where riders can get started correctly. Moving from one level to another in order to gain permission to compete is controlled by a testing procedure. While the lack of such a formal procedure allows the riding in the United States to be much freer, the foundation of riders here is much weaker. This is because the country is quite large and, without a consistent system, few instructors and horses are formally educated to become teachers. The remedy to this situation is not simply for America to import the European system to the USA. Given the unique set of circumstances, expectations, and needs associated with the American rider today, the "ideal" European system is often not a viable option. To address the specialized circumstances of the American rider Equestrian Education Systems has incorporated years of personal experience with a variety of different programs, such as the German Scale of Education, the USDF and USCTA training levels, and the United States Pony Club rating system; and integrated these with new and creative approaches to teaching and learning. The result is the ***Stages of Rider Education – An American System of Learning*** — that can work in our country. We hope to provide riders and instructors with a teaching framework that supports the wonderful variety of talents, skills, interests, and horses that characterize equestrian sport in the United States today.

It is important for instructors to respect and match the variety of interests and commitment levels of the American rider.

### How does this "American System" work?
The Stages of Rider Education provides instructors and students with a framework that clearly outlines the skills and steps needed to master each progressive stage. Ideally, riders will follow these steps in

an orderly fashion, progressing from one stage to another. However, in the "real world" this ideal way of learning seldom happens. Instead, many riders and horses begin their careers without a system, so they have significant gaps in their educations. As a result, instructors frequently find themselves in the position of having to teach riders skills from an earlier stage, while working on more advanced skills in a later stage. To deal with this reality the Stages of Rider Education are presented as a wheel composed of two interconnected circles. The inner circle of stages can turn within the outer circle of stages, allowing riders to access more than one stage at once. This more accurately reflects the "real world" situation than a system that is linear in nature.

Flexible American System of Rider Education

Depending upon what skill or step is missed, instructors may find themselves working in Stage 3 and Stage 1 at the same time, or maybe Stage 4 and Stage 2! The following scenario is a common example. A rider is competing at the Training Level in Eventing on a horse that is stiff and relatively uneducated. The rider, because of the horse's poor quality of response to her aids, is constantly holding onto her horse's mouth. As the instructor, your eye is drawn to the rider's holding, backward hands so you decide to focus on correcting this bad habit. However, when you ask the student to relax and have contact, the horse runs. Even though this rider is in Stage 3 in many areas of her education, you are faced with a need to return to Stage 2 and get this horse and rider team to understand the correct 'rein response' so that the education process can continue. It is hoped that by providing instructors with a flexible system that allows them to move easily in and out of the different stages, EES can offer them new and unique ways to teach students when presented with these challenges, while still holding to the standards of the classical riding system.

 Instructors should have experience at least two stages above the riders they are teaching.

## TRANSITION STAGES

In the United States, riders seek out equestrian instruction for many different reasons. Some want to enjoy the simple pleasures of the occasional trail ride, others aspire to the elite levels of a particular competitive sport, and many fall somewhere in between! Therefore, not all riding instruction is designed to meet the same goal. The first three stages of EES's Stages of Rider Education (the Introductory Stage and Stages 1 & 2) are the fundamental skills every rider is expected to achieve in order to be safe, to protect the horse, and to experience a lifetime of pleasure from the sport. Given the diverse goals of American riders, it becomes necessary to talk about the points at which riders may seek to "opt out" of the training process. Some riders may choose to stop at Stage 2, having met their basic goals, and continue to ride for pleasure. Others may choose to progress through Stage 3, which requires considerable riding hours as well as additional 'horse-related education' experiences both in and outside of the riding arena. In America many riders stop their upward advancements at this stage and decide to enjoy their horses for recreation or low levels of competition. Still others may choose to go on towards Stages 4 and 5, which require extensive training and education, leading to professional opportunities in the equestrian riding and training industry. As a result of all these options, EES's American System of Learning includes two transition stages that are strategically placed between Stages 3 & 4 and 4 & 5. The goal of these important stages is to assist instructors in helping their students reevaluate their goals and expectations in regard to their riding educations. During these transition stages instructors can address such important topics as riders' hopes, dreams, experience, time, talent, money and desire (among others) in order to help plan the next realistic step (or steps) for each student.

 Instructors need to take into account the roles of aptitude, attitude, talent and the horses available in calculating the average learning hours required in each stage of learning.

Theory is the backbone of any good system, so this section begins with a chapter called **Theory Made Simple.** In this section we provide instructors with explanations and overviews of the important concepts behind classical riding and horse training. After theory we go into the **Stages of Rider Education,** a systematic progression of the technical skills needed to develop a classically trained rider. Each stage has six sections:

**Goal(s) of the Stage:** The main focuses or topics to be learned for each stage.

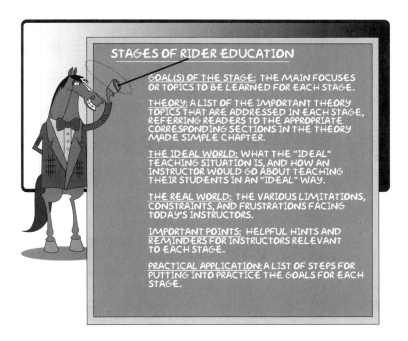

STAGES OF RIDER EDUCATION

GOAL(S) OF THE STAGE: THE MAIN FOCUSES OR TOPICS TO BE LEARNED FOR EACH STAGE.

THEORY: A LIST OF THE IMPORTANT THEORY TOPICS THAT ARE ADDRESSED IN EACH STAGE, REFERRING READERS TO THE APPROPRIATE CORRESPONDING SECTIONS IN THE THEORY MADE SIMPLE CHAPTER.

THE IDEAL WORLD: WHAT THE "IDEAL" TEACHING SITUATION IS, AND HOW AN INSTRUCTOR WOULD GO ABOUT TEACHING THEIR STUDENTS IN AN "IDEAL" WAY.

THE REAL WORLD: THE VARIOUS LIMITATIONS, CONSTRAINTS, AND FRUSTRATIONS FACING TODAY'S INSTRUCTORS.

IMPORTANT POINTS: HELPFUL HINTS AND REMINDERS FOR INSTRUCTORS RELEVANT TO EACH STAGE.

PRACTICAL APPLICATION: A LIST OF STEPS FOR PUTTING INTO PRACTICE THE GOALS FOR EACH STAGE.

**Theory:** A list of the important theory topics that are addressed in each stage, referring readers to the appropriate corresponding sections in the Theory Made Simple chapter.

**The Ideal World:** What the "ideal" teaching situation is, and how an instructor would go about teaching their students in an "ideal" way.

**The Real World:** The various limitations, constraints, and frustrations facing today's instructors.

**Important Points:** Helpful hints and reminders for instructors relevant to each stage.

**Practical Application:** A list of steps for putting into practice the goals for each stage.

EACH STEP INCLUDES THE FOLLOWING:

OBJECTIVE: WHAT THE STEP IS GOING TO TEACH.

THEORY OF STEP: REASONS BEHIND EACH STEP.

IMPORTANT POINTS: GENERAL HINTS AND REMINDERS FOR THE STEP

TOOLKIT: CONCRETE SKILLS, TECHNIQUES, EXERCISES, ETC., TO USE WHEN TEACHING THE STEP.

TEST: SUGGESTIONS TO USE TO EVALUATE WHETHER THE RIDER IS READY TO MOVE TO THE NEXT STEP OR STAGE.

Each step includes the following:

**Objective:** What the step is going to teach.

**Theory of Step:** Reasons behind each step.

**Important Points:** General hints and reminders for the step.

**Toolkit:** Concrete skills, techniques, exercises, etc., to use when teaching the step.

**Test:** Suggestions to use to evaluate whether the rider is ready to move to the next step or stage.

The Stages of Rider Education — An American System of Learning, is designed to provide instructors with new ideas, guidance, structure, and support when teaching a classical equestrian approach to American riders. The wealth of diversity that is America shows itself not only in the vast array of horses and sports seen in today's equestrian world, but also in each rider's physical, mental, emotional, financial, and philosophical mindset towards his or her personal riding education. As a result, instructors are called upon to deal with a mind-numbing variety of situations and circumstances in a competent and professional manner. It is our hope that this book will not only help instructors through this process, but will also inspire them to continue to develop, personally and professionally, by studying and building on their already considerable knowledge bases. Clinics, workshops, magazine articles, conferences and books are all wonderful ways to continue this development. Our wish is that instructors everywhere will continue to enjoy, and be enjoyed by, those riders that they have the wonderful opportunity to come into contact with – their students.

This book is focused on mounted Equestrian Education, and as such, does not include the unmounted aspects of horsemanship such as knowledge about horse care, nutrition, conformation, lameness, etc. Instructors are strongly encouraged to supplement their students' riding educations with unmounted lessons in horsemanship. A true horseman is well-rounded and is equally at home in the barn or on the back of a horse! ⚞

Riding education is a constant mixture of teaching students a new skill, supervising as students practice using the new skill, and then assisting them to integrate the new skill into their existing skills, goals and development. ⚞

| LEVEL COMPARISONS in USA | | | |
|---|---|---|---|
| **Stage** | **UPSC** | **USDF** | **USCTA** |
| Stage 1 – Position & Control | D1 & D2 | | |
| Stage 2 – Use of Aids | D3 & C1 | Intro test | Pre novice |
| Stage 3 – Aids in Action | C2 & C3 | Training | Novice |
| Stage 4 – 1st Phase of Partnership Development | B | 1st Level | Training |
| Stage 5 – 2nd Phase of Partnership Development | A | 2nd & 3rd Level | Preliminary |
| Specialization | | 4th Level Trainer/Instructor | Intermediate & Advanced |
| | | | Chart 29 |

# THEORY MADE SIMPLE

Behind every good system lies good theory. Behind Equestrian Education System's Stages of Rider Education lies the classical theory of the German educational system for horses and riders. In this book, we hope to provide instructors with a basic understanding of the important concepts associated with this classical approach. The information presented here is not meant to be exhaustive, as there are many fine books that provide in-depth instruction in classical riding and education (see Appendix). Rather, the theory included in this chapter is designed to provide instructors with easily understandable descriptions, definitions, and illustrations of the core concepts. By knowing the theory behind EES's Stages of Rider Education – An American System of Learning, we believe that instructors can be more flexible in their use of the system, and thus more effective as teachers.

This chapter is divided into sections based on five theories. The theoretical concepts are introduced as they are relevant to the topics and are developed through the stages. We hope you find this information beneficial, not only to your students, but also for your own education.

## THEORY OF POSITION AND CONTROL

### The Concept of POSITION

All formal equestrian instruction starts, and ends, with position. In fact, position holds such exalted status within the equestrian community that "equitation" classes are included at nearly every horse show across all disciplines. Yet it is not uncommon

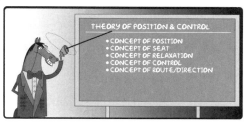

for instructors to field questions from beginning students, parents, and self-described "cowboys" questioning the wisdom of spending so much time on position. They suggest that it is best to let the rider figure out how to ride just by riding! On the surface, these people have a good point. Why don't we let our beginning riders learn how to stay on a horse naturally? This is an excellent question. The response is twofold:

1. The "classically correct" position has been established over hundreds of years of trial and error, across many different countries. Throughout the world, there is little disagreement over what constitutes the correct way for a rider to sit; it is the position that minimizes the stress and strain on both horse and rider. The differences among the various equestrian schools across the globe are seen in the small stylistic variations in position and in the philosophy of horse training, not in the descriptions of how a rider should correctly sit on a horse. As a result, a classically correct position is a well-established expectation and goal of educated equestrians worldwide. However, it takes proper instruction and a lot of practice to perfect this position. Today, especially in America, the classically educated seat is seen less and less frequently.

2. The "classically correct" position is important because it has been found to be essential for the rider's and the horse's safety, balance, and control. Perhaps the best way to explain this is to describe what can happen when riders are self-taught, or learn the natural way. On the plus side, these natural riders often develop a wonderful sense of feel and balance on a horse. The down side is that the feel and balance that the rider acquires is developed for the comfort of the rider, not the horse. What feels "natural" for most riders to do when riding a horse can be quite uncom-

fortable for the horse and can make it difficult for the horse to perform correctly. Here are three common **examples:**

- When riders begin riding on their own (and even under instruction sometimes), they quickly learn that the easiest way to stay on a horse when trotting, cantering, or jumping is to grip with their knees. This increases a rider's security on the horse by limiting the movement the rider is making (minimizes the bouncing), which makes it easier to stay on. The problem with this technique is threefold: 1) It severely limits the flexibility of the rider's pelvis, preventing riders from moving their seats with their horses in a relaxed and harmonious way, and ever developing independent seats and hands;  2) Stiff, tight seats create discomfort for the horse. The horse responds to the tightness of the rider's seat by tensing up and becoming "hollow" in his back. This leads to tenderness and soreness underneath and behind the saddle. Riders with stiff, uneducated seats can be one of the root causes of some of the back troubles that horses have today;   3) Gripping with the knees confuses horses since they tend to slow down or speed up when this pressure is applied.

- A second example is seen in riders who learn without the benefit of formal instruction and have a hard time applying the aids correctly and precisely because they have not trained their bodies to be under their voluntary control. When these riders ask their horses to do something they put their bodies in a position that feels right to them, but causes unintentional consequences. Asking the horse to canter is a good example - the "natural" thing to do is to lean forward and slightly to the inside. This brings the rider's weight onto the front, inside part of the horse's shoulder, which encourages him to run faster (ending up in canter!), and to pop his shoulder to the inside (which is why the horse tends to pick up the inside lead!). But by being forward and leaning on the horse's shoulder, the rider unbalances the horse. The horse cannot ever learn to balance himself if the rider is leaning forward, keeping the horse unbalanced. When leaning forward the rider's legs also tend to slip slightly backwards, causing the horse to respond to leg aids the rider did not necessarily intend to give. The rider may feel like he or she is not doing anything or asking the horse anything, yet wonder why the horse keeps speeding up!

- A third example is the self-taught rider's way of asking for a leg-yield. The natural thing to do is to lean towards the wall, using an inside, indirect rein. This causes the rider to drop the inside hip and shoulder and push the horse's weight to the outside shoulder and outside hind leg. This unwittingly forces the horse to pop his outside shoulder and become crooked! The rider then tries to correct the horse's perceived crookedness when it is actually caused by the rider's incorrect position and use of aids. This negative cycle is seen so frequently in riding that it almost is the norm.

When riders take the time to learn the classically correct position, they are surprised to find that they feel much more balanced, secure, and comfortable when riding. As in most sports, there are rules that must be followed, and riders need to train their bodies to become familiar and natural in this new and seemingly unnatural (at first) position.

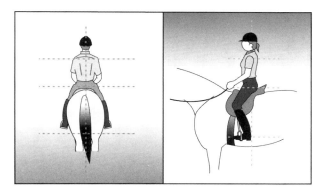

**Straight Lines of a Correct Position**

The classically correct position is designed to maximize the horse's ability to both carry the rider and perform the movements asked with the least amount of stress and strain on rider and horse. It is the rider's responsibility to learn how to sit on a horse at all three gaits and over fences in such a way that not only does not hinder the horse in his attempts to do what the rider asks of him, but also makes it comfortable and easy for him.

INSTRUCTOR'S
REMINDER

American instructors face the challenge of needing to have an additional set of skills in their toolkits in order to teach the typical American student. American culture today is a "fast food society," where people have limited time, seek instant gratification, and want quick results. Instructors need to be prepared to meet and work with the set of challenges this mentality produces. This usually means finding a balance between meeting the realistic needs of your students and convincing them of the value of a few "full-course meals." 🐎

## The Concept of SEAT

A correct seat is the foundation of all classical riding. This section discusses the classically correct seat for both flat work and over fences.

### THE CORRECT SEAT ON THE FLAT

The most critical part of a good position is the SEAT. A correct seat is one that stays in the center of the saddle with the thighs hanging quietly elongated off the sides, and the weight of the rider's body falling softly into the rider's heels. No grip is needed because the rider stays on using the balancing motion of the pelvis, which moves with the motion of the horse's back. The upper body remains centered and tall with the legs on either side of the saddle acting as counterweights for the pelvis. This prevents the rider from sliding off the saddle. As you can imagine, this takes some time to learn and perfect. Hence, the importance of a good school horse!

 A sign of a truly beautiful seat is when one cannot tell where the horse's back ends and the rider's seat begins – in other words, horse and rider are "dancing" together seamlessly, in fluid motion.

To understand what the seat is exactly it helps to know a little about the human pelvis, which makes up what we call a rider's "seat." The bones of the pelvis and the sacrum are fused together to make one big joint that must learn to move with the horse's back in order to keep the rider safely and comfortably in the saddle. The bottom of the pelvis (i.e., the rider's seat bones) can be described as similar to the runners of a rocking chair, with the front and back parts of the pelvis lifting up slightly in a gentle curve. It is helpful to teach riders to feel the difference between sitting in the center versus the front or back of their "rocking chairs" or seats (see Stage 1 for specific exercises). Riders trying to find a comfortable and safe place on the horse's back that minimizes the bouncing often use the front and back positions of the seat, but they are incorrect and largely ineffective.

When students begin to learn to sit the trot and canter they may try to force their seats down into the saddle by leaning back in the "chair seat." Others try to avoid the whole sitting trot problem by "perching" onto the front of their seats. Some try to force their seats from front to back, like they are polishing the saddle with their seats; this too is incorrect. Allowing the seat

to move with the horse as his back rises and lowers, while sitting in the center of one's "rocking chair," is the correct action of the seat movement. Some riders describe the feeling of their seats moving with the horse as like "the motion of a swing."

Those lucky riders taught to sit the horse correctly from the beginning will learn to develop balanced, deep, elastic, feeling and functional seats. From this foundation these riders can move forward in their training. They can learn to use their seats as a powerful communication tool between themselves and their horses. Without correct seats, riders are limited to being like passengers in a car – they can go along for the ride, but are unable to really dictate much about how to get somewhere! Without educated seats, riders are not able to influence the horse to perform to his fullest potential.

Each rider's goal needs to be the development of a truly independent seat. An independent seat is a seat that is educated enough so that the rider's pelvis can follow the motion of the horse at all three gaits without the rider's having to resort to gripping anywhere (especially with thighs or arms) to stay balanced and still. This allows the rider's hands and legs to be under the rider's voluntary control. The rider can then apply the aids for such important tasks as influ-encing the horse's direction/route and speed. If a rider wishes to become a true partner with the horse, the rider's seat needs to be classically correct and educated enough to move "as one" with the horse.

> *Each rider's goal needs to be the development of a truly independent seat. An independent seat is a seat that is educated enough so that the rider's pelvis can follow the motion of the horse at all three gaits without the rider's having to resort to gripping anywhere (especially with thighs or arms) to stay balanced and still. This allows the rider's hands and legs to be under the rider's voluntary control. The rider can then apply the aids for such important tasks as influencing the horse's direction/route and speed.*

## THE CORRECT SEAT OVER FENCES

In Stage 1, riders are introduced to the concept of the half-seat. The half-seat, also called "two-point position," is used for riding over fences. At times, riders (and instructors) may refer to this position as the "galloping position," but that is not truly correct. The galloping position is a modified form of the half-seat, designed for galloping at speed. The half-seat position is used to help the rider stay over the horse's center of gravity when jumping. In jumping, the center of gravity shifts slightly forward, ahead of the pommel of the saddle, which is why a seat variation is necessary. However, used as a beginner exercise, the half-seat promotes a deep seat and improves rider balance. It is developed into the true jumping position in later stages.

During Stage 1, the half-seat is initially used on the flat, building to use over ground poles as the rider develops balance and confidence. When doing the half-seat position, the rider's seat lifts slightly out of the saddle, but *equal tension remains throughout the rider's thigh, inner knee, and calf.* Riders need to take care not to grip too much in any one of these three spots. In order to remain in balance with the movement of the horse, riders must be encouraged to stretch their weight downwards as they lighten the seat, rather than gripping with the knees or pushing up off the back of the horse. The action is one of stretching downwards as the seat lightens, and results in a stronger, more secure lower leg, and a deeper seat.

The rider also maintains a straight line from the hip through the heel, but bends ever so slightly forward from the hip, maintaining the straightness of the back. Sometimes it is helpful to tell the rider to post the trot, then "freeze" the posting trot in the 'up' position. The goal is for the rider to stay as tall and straight as possible. Beginning riders tend to make the mistake of leaning too far forward, as this makes it easier to stay up out of the saddle. A correctly performed half-seat will work a rider's back and upper thigh muscles, as they will quickly inform you! It is important that students adjust their stirrups shorter for the half-seat, as this makes it easier to get the seat out of the saddle, allowing the weight of the rider to softly fall into their heels. The starting point for determining the correct shortened stirrup length is to adjust the leathers so that the stirrup falls about 1 inch above the ankle when the leg is hanging naturally. This can be adjusted depending on the rider's (and the horse's) conformation and saddle fit. The knee should end up being in a 45-degree angle when sitting.

1/2 SEAT POSITION

The rider's hip moves with the motion of the horse when in half-seat the same way as it does when sitting. Ideally, the lower leg and upper body stay quiet and balanced over the horse's center, and the pelvis takes on the responsibility of moving with the horse.

The challenge for instructors in teaching correct position is that there are two moving entities — one on top of the other! You can empathize with the dilemma beginning riders face. They are struggling to first FIND their balance, then they need to find their horses' balance, and then they are told to get, and keep, the two balances together! It takes a lot of practice before a new rider starts to feel safe or comfortable in the "correct" position at all three gaits. 🐎

## The Concept of RIDER RELAXATION

Instructors and riders alike espouse the virtues of the concept of rider relaxation. However, once a rider mounts up, relaxation of the rider tends to take a back seat to the much more fun and exciting stuff associated with riding like cantering, jumping, learning fun new movements, etc. Things like "deep breathing" or learning the difference between muscle tone and muscle tension do not have much popularity when there is so much fun and excitement going on. However, if you could ask the horses what they most want their riders to work on, many would probably say something like, "Get this person to relax, would you? My back is killing me!!"

Seriously, relaxation is a critical and often overlooked component of a rider's education. There are two kinds of relaxation, mental and physical. In the ideal state of mental relaxation for the rider, the mind is on the subject at hand, free of clutter, able to enjoy the present. Bodily relaxation is a physical state where the joints move free of tension and the muscles are toned to be used effectively as needed. Each individual rider has a degree of natural relaxation. This is determined by various factors, such as an individual's disposition as well as environmental and life circumstances. Because relaxation is a state of the body and the mind, the mind can influence the body and the body can influence the mind. Riders with a relaxed body and mind are in a better position to send and receive information from their horses. This is the all-important "feel" that is constantly sought by instructors for their riders. There are many books and articles that outline techniques and exercises, both on and off the horse, to help riders supple their minds and bodies. Over the past decade riders have embraced a variety of different approaches to help them relax and supple themselves such as yoga, t'ai chi, Pilates, and many others. See Appendix for a list of good books on this subject.

## The Concept of CONTROL

The concept of control is included in Stage 1 with almost as much emphasis and importance as position. The following modified version of a famous saying helps explain why control is treated as importantly as position.

**For want of control, relaxation is lost. For want of relaxation, position is lost. And for want of position, all is lost!**

While this may not be exactly as Shakespeare said it, it imparts important truths about riding. Control leads to safe, confident riders who can relax and maintain a correct position. When riders do not feel in control, survival mode kicks into gear and all thoughts are on staying alive – no matter how much the instructor tries to override this mindset. This situation is demonstrated with riders who come into the ring with every contraption known to man on their horses. Or in riders who stay at the walk or trot FOREVER! Remember, control is a perception. What feels "in control" to some riders may feel out of control to others (or to those watching!). "Look Mom! No hands!" is an example. Clearly, control is limited under these circumstances, yet many eager and brave young riders will gladly drop their reins and never feel as if control is an issue. At the other end of the spectrum, there are riders who feel out of control as soon as the horse moves. And of course there are those situations where the rider's perceptions and the reality DO match. The rider really has no control! It is the latter two situations that require the instructor to attend to control issues FIRST. Until the rider feels some semblance of control, learning will take a back seat to survival. This is simply human nature, and part of what allowed us to survive as long as we have! Position and Control really do act in a circular fashion. Control allows students to improve their positions, and correct positions lead to better control!

 Students started on the lunge line must trust the instructor's ability to control the horse. Students started off the lunge line need a very trustworthy horse that responds to their uneducated communications. 🐎

An **example** of the importance of control is Susanna, who had been trying to learn to canter for two years, but could not do it. Her instructor became frustrated, not knowing what to do, so asked for a consultation. Through observation and discussion with Susanna, it became apparent that the problem was lack of control. Susanna did not feel that she could control the horse's direction, and so was scared to go faster. Her fear came through in her body language, thus preventing the horse from cantering. Once Susanna learned to consistently control the direction of the horse, she felt secure and was able to canter.

## The Concept of ROUTE/DIRECTION

The concept of route, or direction, is one of the most important concepts in riding. Route refers to where the horse puts his hooves when in motion. In order for riders to try to remain in balance and feel safe, they need to feel in control of the route at all times. For riders, this means developing the mental discipline of always knowing where they want to go and the physical discipline to precisely follow their plan. This is not easy to do! Many riders, beginners through advanced, fall into the trap of just riding around, without a real plan or sense of direction. This is similar to what it would be like to get into a car, start the engine, and begin driving without giving much thought as to where one is going! The ability to stay "on route" gives beginning riders the confidence associated with being in control. This allows them to relax and then they have their minds free to think about improving their positions. As riders advance, staying "on-route" gives them the criteria needed to adjust rhythm and straightness via 'feel.' An unclear route easily masks rhythm and straightness.

## THEORY OF MOVEMENT
### The Concept of FORWARD

Introduced with the leg response in Stage 2, and developed more in each successive stage.

"Forward" is one of those riding concepts that is surprisingly difficult to grasp. Although it is a pretty straightforward (no pun intended) word, it is hard to pin down its exact meaning. For many riders (and their instructors), this term is spoken of with great importance and reverence, yet a clear definition is rare. For example, in the following situation two riders are watching a horse and rider perform a dressage test:

> 1st rider: "That is a nice leg yield, but the horse isn't forward."
>
> 2nd rider: (Nodding appreciatively) "No, he isn't, is he? This rider would score much higher if only she could get her horse to move more forward."

The Webster dictionary defines "forward" as: towards a place in front; onwards in time; in a progressive or conspicuous way.

*The United States Pony Club manual (3rd book- Advanced Horsemanship) defines forward as: "Moving forward with powerful strides from the hindquarters (Not to be confused with speed or quickening the tempo!)"*

*A "forward" horse needs to meet two criteria. He must move with:*

*1) Energy, which means activity and enthusiasm, NOT dull or lazy, and*
*2) Engagement, which means the ability of the horse to bring his hind legs far up towards the front of his body.*

According to this definition, it seems that all horses moving in the direction of their front ends are moving "forward" no matter what level of energy they are exerting. While this is technically true, this is not what riders mean by the term "forward."

Maybe the best way to define "forward" is to describe exactly what we want horses to do with their bodies (especially their legs) when they are and are not going forward.

This means that a forward horse moves actively by taking as long a step behind as possible, not by speeding up, jigging or changing gait.

A horse **IS NOT forward** when he becomes energetic by taking quicker, shorter steps with the hind legs. This is what all horses want to do initially. The rider has to use the natural aids (seat, leg, hand, voice) to help the horse understand how to take long steps with the hind legs rather than short, quick ones.

### The Concept of BASIC STRAIGHTNESS

Most people intuitively understand what we mean by the word straightness. For example, when we ask riders to "sit up straight," they (hopefully) line up their bodies so that their heads sit on top of their necks, which sit on top of their shoulders, which align with their chests, and so on. With horses, the concept of straightness is slightly different. "Straightness" in its classical definition, means *that the horse must travel in such a way that the hind feet follow in the tracks of the front feet, no matter what shape or figure they are making* (see The Concept of ADVANCED STRAIGHTNESS, usually introduced in Stage 4, for a definition of straightness in lateral movements). When a horse does this, he is said to be traveling straight. This definition is the reason why, in riding arenas everywhere, instructors are telling their students to ride their horses "straight on a circle," much to the consternation and confusion of newcomers and spectators alike! In this section, we will discuss straightness in terms of a) how a horse naturally

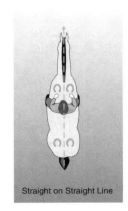
Straight on Straight Line

moves, and b) how horses have to adapt their movement, by becoming straight, under saddle.

Straightness and balance are intimately connected. Balance is frequently talked about at all levels but is a very difficult concept to understand. It is usually in Stage 5 where the concept of balance (natural, ridden, lateral and longitudinal) is more fully developed and linked to advanced straightness. ❧

### THE HORSE'S NATURAL WAY OF MOVING

Horses typically do not travel straight. Their natural way of traveling is to swing their hindquarters in one direction (usually to the inside) and their necks in the opposite direction (usually to the outside). This system for staying balanced works well for horses when they are out playing in the pasture, but not when riders climb on board. Riders disrupt this delicate "balancing act" by adding weight to the horse's back. In addition, when a horse continues to move in this way it is uncomfortable for a rider to sit and for the horse to carry! So riders must create a new way for the horse to balance himself with weight on his back; one that allows the horse to carry the rider comfortably and still perform the movements being asked. This means teaching the horse to move straight.

### HOW HORSES ADAPT THEIR NATURAL
### WAY OF MOVING UNDER SADDLE

When horses are first asked to travel straight, they initially want to swing their hindquarters to the side, or they try to shorten their steps behind, so that they do not step on their front feet. However, if riders can keep horses from being successful in this evasion, the horses will begin to travel straight. Once a horse begins to travel straight, he must make some changes in how he uses his body to stay upright (especially around

Straight on Curve

turns). Due to the limited flexibility in the horse's back, in order to keep the haunches and shoulders in a straight line the horse realizes that he needs to bring his hind legs forward and slightly in, towards his own center of gravity (which is right around the girth area). This is not natural for a horse to do! In turns and around corners especially, this maneuver forces the horse to increase the engagement of the inside hind leg by bringing it further up and under the stomach **without swinging the hindquarters to the outside.** For this reason, turning while staying straight is hard for horses to do (which is why circles must be used carefully, and why many students subconsciously avoid corners).

When turning while maintaining straightness, horses find themselves slightly stretching the outside of their bodies. This creates a small hollow on the inside of their bodies. One simple, easy to visualize term instructors can use to get this concept across is "hollow your horse on the inside." However, since 'hollow' is thought of in a negative sense related to the horse's back, make a clear explanation that this is a positive term related to staying on route. 🐎

---

**Straightness through the Stages**

**Basic straightness** (through 1st level) – the horse must travel in such a way that the hind feet follow in the tracks of the front feet, no matter what shape or figure they are making.

**Advanced straightness** (2nd level and above)- line of movement may differ from the line of route –the horse is straight when his weight is equally distributed on both sides of the imaginary line that goes from his tail to poll.

Whether one is talking about basic or advanced straightness, the horse must remain balanced on the line of the movement while remaining on the line of route.

Chart 30

---

## The Concepts of FLEXION and BEND

Bend and flexion are two terms that get mixed up, used interchangeably, and are frequently and generally confused with each other! In this section, we define flexion and bend; and then we identify overbending (what it is, what it is not) and how it differs from flexion and bend. We finish this section with a brief description of the anatomy of the horse's neck and its relationship to the "telescoping gesture," which is the movement the horse makes when properly bending and arching his neck.

**Flexion:** Flexion deals with the position of the horse's head only, not his neck. Flexion happens when the horse relaxes his jaw and gives a slight turn of the eye in the direction of the asking rein. The rider, in glancing down, can see the "inside" eye and edge of the "inside" nostril. Thus, flexion can be thought of as the positioning of the horse's jaw. Horses can turn their jaws side to side, or drop them down towards their chests (this is referred to as too much flexion – sometimes called "overbending"). Proper *flexion is the ultimate goal, not neck bending.* This is because a truly straight horse is straight hindquarter to poll, so that only the head is flexed in the direction of movement.

**Bend:** Bend is another term with numerous meanings. In classical terms, it refers to the degree of bend throughout the horse's entire body. To be "bent" means that the horse is supple enough when moving that the inside hind leg can engage deeply underneath him, causing a gentle curve in his body, which stretches the outside of his body on the line of travel. A correctly bent horse with an engaged inside hind leg is often described as supple. In the classical definition, bend and supple are interchangeable words.

Please note: The word 'bend' has many connotations in the horse world. People use this word to describe the suppleness of the horse's body (as in the above definition), the bending of the head and neck (as described in overbending below), and the degree of flexion (as described above).

**Overbending:** Yet another confusing term! In the classical definition, overbending is a basic suppling exercise where the rider **intentionally** moves the horse's neck side-to-side. The goal is to help teach the horse how to bend his neck and flex his jaw. But simply pulling the head to the side is not considered proper "overbending." In order for this exercise to reap its training benefits, care must be taken to keep the base of the neck positioned in the middle of the horse's chest, so that the horse "overbends" evenly from the base of his neck to his poll with a nice, gentle, banana-shaped curve. Ideally, the neck bends no more than one to four inches away from this "centerline." In no case should the rider bend the head and neck further than the line of the point of the shoulder in this "overbending" exercise. Overbending has benefits for the rider as well. It is a useful way to teach many riders the correct rein response, which then leads the way to learning the combination of leg and rein responses. Considerable detail is spent in Stage 2, step 2 (rein response) that will help teach the rider each step of the bending and flexion response. By learning the rein response systematically, through "feel," riders will find that they can quickly commit the correct feeling associated with bending and flexion to their muscle memories. As they advance, they will be able to call upon whatever step in the bending and flexing process they feel they need when asking for a half-halt.

Overbending is the foundation for flexing. Riders who learn this response will be able to flex their horses as needed in preparation for changes or for rebalancing. ⚞

All of this overbending is done with caution! Overbending is taught only to teach riders how to bend, and as a suppling exercise for the horse. Unintentional overbending, or overbending the neck with the nose in towards the chest, is a disobedience and can become a bad habit. ⚞

### The Concept of the CIRCLE OF MUSCLES

The circle of muscles is a term used to describe the horse's system of muscles that work when a horse moves. We have found it very helpful to introduce some of these basic truths about how a horse "works" to students as they are learning the use of aids in Stage 2. As we all know, aids work because of the law of 'cause and effect.' If students come to understand how interconnected their aids are with the horse's system of muscles, then the instructor's explanations about using the aids will make much more sense!

**INSTRUCTOR'S REMINDER**

Students learning the rein response in Stage 2, step 2; and students working on contact in Stage 3 will especially benefit from this concept. Understanding this principle will give instructors more tools to resource as they help students learn the use of their aids.

Circle of Muscles

The way the circle of muscles works:
1. The whole process starts in the HIND END **(the "engine")**. The rider uses the leg (or whip) to encourage the horse to move forward, taking long, active steps that bring the hind legs up as far under the horse's barrel as possible. *The further the horse's hind legs can step up under his barrel, the more the horse is said to be "engaging his hind end."*

2. Once the horse starts moving, two important sets of muscles are involved in helping the horse bring the hind legs underneath the barrel: a) The abdominal muscles help bring the hind legs forward by contracting in rhythm with the horse's stride, and b) the horse also brings the hind leg forward by flexing his loin muscles (these are around the lumbosacral joint- where the lumbar and sacral vertebrae meet at the top of the pelvis).

3. When the horse properly uses the abdominal and lumbar muscles, the back begins to take on a slightly rounded shape (which is what we are referring to when we say a horse's back is "round"). *The more the horse engages its hind legs, the more the horse's back will become round.* The rounder the horse's back becomes, the more he will develop a swinging motion behind the saddle. This is because the horse's pelvis works in a side-to-side motion as a result of the alternate moving of the legs. The more the horse swings his legs underneath himself, the more the horse's hips will swing, creating a nice feeling of relaxation and looseness. For the rider, this can be felt (and seen by observers) in the rising and dropping of the horse's hips during motion (especially at the trot).

4. A chain of muscles connects the horse's back to his poll. As a result, a horse working with his hind legs engaged will swing his pelvis, which lifts and round his back. In turn, the horse will make a "telescoping gesture" with his head and neck, where he stretches out and down, with a slight drop at the poll. This is the "training level frame" you see in the first stage of a horse's training. This frame is critical for a horse's muscle development, as it strengthens the horse's topline. The stronger a horse's topline, the easier it is for him to carry his rider.

5. Once a horse travels consistently "round," and maintains the tele-scoping gesture of the head and neck, he begins to strengthen a very important muscle in the base of the neck, which is called the scalenus muscle. This muscle is important to know about, as it is what allows a horse to **"lift"** *the neck, withers, and ultimately, the forehand* (See the Concept of the Telescoping Gesture).

Once a horse is moving forward (see forward energy) with a round back, and can flex and bend properly in both directions, the rider can then feel the energy that is coming from the horse's hind end, passing through the horse's back, and ending up in the rider's hand. When a horse "comes into a rider's hand" this means that the horse is stretching and arching his head and neck (because his back is round), which has the effect of the horse's offering his mouth and jaw to the rider's hand. At this point, the horse is re-laxed, supple, obedient, and can be said to be "on the bit."

## The Concept of the TELESCOPING GESTURE

It can be quite useful to know the basics about the anatomy of the horse's neck and the telescop-ing gesture in order to better understand bending and flexing. When riders and instructors under-stand the basic way the horse's neck works, they are in the position to know the difference between a horse that is correctly arching his neck and one that is carrying his head and neck in a "false frame."

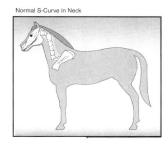

Normal S-Curve in Neck

Deep Lower Curve in Neck

### Basic Anatomy of the Horse's Neck

There are seven bones in every horse's neck, but they do not follow the shape of the neck as we see it from the outside. Instead, these bones form an S-shape.

The most important thing to know about this skeletal structure is the shape of the lower curve of the neck, near the base of the horse's neck. You want a horse to have a short and shallow lower curve, instead of a long, deep lower curve Why? It makes it easier for the horse to make what is called the "telescoping gesture." The telescoping gesture is the natural arching of a horse's neck that occurs when the horse is work-ing correctly through his back. The most no-ticeable sign of the telescoping gesture is that the muscles in the middle of the horse's neck

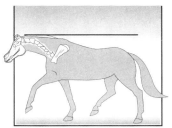

Telescoping Gesture Straightens the Lower Curve

(namely the complexus muscle) begin to bulge out. The muscles on the top of the neck are not seen to be bulging when the horse is using his neck correctly. These muscles bulge when the horse is "falsely" arching his neck. This typically happens when the horse is made to "set his head" without the prerequisites of an engaged hind end and soft, round back. When a horse is properly working his circle of muscles, he contracts a small muscle in the base of the neck called the scalenus muscle. This muscle straightens out the lower curve of the S shape of the horse's neck bones, which does three important things:

1. By straightening out the lower curve in the neck, the telescoping gesture raises the base of the neck, which **fills up the areas right in front of the withers** (fills in that dip or gap so many horses have from falsely arching their necks).

2. It lengthens the neck, so that the horse will want to bring his head away from his chest, and reach out and down, not curl in towards his chest.

3. The middle muscle of the neck (complexus muscle) will bulge (it is filling with blood), and by doing so, get stronger and bigger, which pushes up the crest muscles from the poll to the withers, creating a smooth, round topline.

There are two levels of the telescoping gesture: 1) The training telescoping gesture, where the horse stretches out and down with his head and neck, with only minimal elevation from the base of the neck. This is the frame that green horses are started in. As horses work in the training frame, they strengthen their scalenus muscles, which allows them to elevate their necks more as their educations progress; 2) The advanced telescoping gesture, where the horse, because of a stronger scalenus muscle, raises his neck upward as he stretches forward, creating a more pronounced arch to the neck. You see this frame when horses are asked to do collected work.

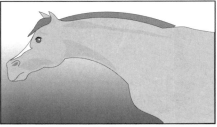

Elementary Telescoping Gesture

Instructors and riders use different terms to describe these telescoping gestures, including:

- Releasing the neck

- Yielding or flexing at the poll

- Reaching for the bit

- Coming into the rider's hand

- Accepting the bridle

- Being "on the bit"

Advanced Telescoping Gesture

# THEORY OF FEEL

## The Concept of ENERGY

Forward energy is one of the most difficult concepts to understand as well as to teach. Before students can understand receiving forward energy, they need to understand just what "energy" means. For instructors to teach it, they need to truly understand it! Begin with the definition of "forward" earlier in this chapter. Teaching forward energy and a receiving hand at the same time helps

prevent students from feeling they must hold a horse together, particularly in the more advanced stages of riding. It is also helpful to teach this in a group lesson so the forward energy can be demonstrated visually.

Forward movement creates and employs energy; this is a truism in riding. Managing this energy is the key to the safety, comfort, and ultimate success of any rider. Riders learn that they communicate with the horse through their aids to direct this energy. The goal for all riders is to direct this pushing energy, no matter how much or how little is available at any given moment, by responding to the horse correctly, making good decisions on a moment-to-moment basis, and having a clarity of purpose. Receiving the horse's impulsion and energy, allowing oneself the feeling of responding to the incoming energy with receptivity rather than resistance, and allowing an elastic, even rein contact are required for effective communication and maximum control.

The energy of the horse in motion starts in the driving hind leg, moves forward through the back under the rider's following, elastic, balanced seat, moves on to the horse's light shoulder (the one about to bear the weight), into a soft neck and jaw, and finally to the bit. Riders then feel the energy in their hands as they maintain a steady contact with the reins to the bit.

## The Concept of REFERENCE FEEL

A reference feel is that "ideal feeling" a rider gets when the horse is moving as well as can be expected, given his level of training. It is that moment when the rider feels "at one" with the horse. Having a reference feel allows riders to know when a half-halt (or adjustment) is needed. It is the rider's consistent awareness of the presence and absence of this ideal, desired feeling in the hands, seat, and legs that gives the cue that a half-halt (adjustment) is needed. Any change from the ideal alerts the rider to action. The sooner the rider feels the change and responds, the fewer aids are necessary, and the more easily the horse understands what is being asked. When the communication cycle is completed, the return of the established reference feel rewards horse and rider. It is a reward because the rider is no longer having to ask the horse for something, and thus "bother" him; the horse is moving comfortably in front of the rider's leg and the energy is freely moving forward to the rider's hand. The reference feel is an enjoyable state for horse and rider.

## The Concept of the HALF-HALT (Adjustment)

The half-halt is another one of those terms that is almost universally misunderstood. Riders describe the half-halt in many different ways such as a brake, a momentary pause, an "almost halt," and other assorted metaphors. In our experience, few riders really have a good grasp of the half-halt and how it is accomplished. We have found that riders better understand and ride the half-halt if they truly understand just what it is horses do with their bodies in response to the half-halt aids (see Stage 3, step 4 for specific exercises to help riders learn the half-halt). In brief, the half-halt is used as a form of "rider body to horse body" communication. Through the actions of the rider's physical body on the horse, the rider is telling the horse to do something - usually to slow down, engage the hind end, and rebalance. This works when the rider applies the leg aids in such a way that the horse tracks further under his body by taking longer, more engaged steps behind, and *at the same time* uses the seat (and hand) to prevent the horse from moving faster. In other words, the half-halt is when the rider slows the horse down while at the same time asks for more energy and engagement from behind. It is a fairly simple concept, but proper application is the problem! Some riders will say that the half-halt is when you "kick and pull" at the same time. Well, almost! From the horse's point of view, kicking and pulling is an insult. And, it doesn't work, as frustrated riders will gladly tell you. Riders need to learn how to use their bodies (especially the seat and hand) in such a way that the horse engages behind but stays at the same speed, or slower, while being relaxed and comfortable and using his back – all without any backward pull on the rein by the rider. You can feel the effect of the half-halt yourself if you try jogging around the ring. Push yourself more forward, but maintain the same speed and tempo. You will find yourself shifting your weight back slightly, and lifting your knees higher. Now try to do this while staying relaxed and comfortable. You can feel why horses

| Half-Halt (adjustment) --- 3 Steps & 3 Basic Uses | |
|---|---|
| **hold–push–release** | For horses who get strong in the hand |
| **push—hold—release** | To prepare a horse for a change in direction or gait |
| **push—hold—release** | To create more engagement |
| | Chart 44 |

might not be so willing to answer the half-half all the time – especially if they do not have the proper muscle development to carry themselves in such a fashion for long periods of time. It is demanding and difficult for the horse.

Once the horse and rider partnership forms to the point where there is body-to-body communication, and the half-halt is understood by both parties, it can then be used by the rider as a subtle adjustment to the horse's way of going. This can be done to create, or re-create, balance and engagement or to prepare the horse for a transition, ring figure, corner, or movement. All half-halts are accomplished in three steps, (push, hold, release) though the order may change (push, hold) depending on the purpose of the half-halt. Importantly, all half-halts end with a release, which is the rider's way of saying "thank you" to the horse.

The end result of a correctly executed half-halt is that the horse increases engagement of the hind end while maintaining a soft, round back. This in turn results in the horse's becoming lighter in the rein and more balanced at that moment. Riders will often ask for numerous half-halts in a given training session. What looks like a steady, consistent performance is the result of a constant sequence of half-halts to keep the horse appearing consistently steady and light. Students learning the half-halt tend to apply the aid after they feel the need for it. As they develop and advance in their skills, they will begin to develop an almost instinctive feel for applying half-halts before they are needed, making their performances even more smooth and seamless to watch.

**Half-Halt**

## The Concept of CONSISTENCY
(Introduced in Stage 2 and developed through subsequent stages)

**Consistency** is a concept that is highly valued in any kind of training program, whether it is with people, dogs, horses, or elephants! Consistency is what makes average riders good, and good riders better. It is the discipline of having clear expectations, good habits, and a compassionate heart. Instructors who teach students to be consistent in each day's ride will enable the three basics of rhythm, looseness and contact to work together most effectively to advance both the student's and the horse's education. Instructors teach not only the technical skills needed but also lay the foundation for consistency through the way they organize each lesson. (see Consistency in Instructor's Toolbox)

To be consistent each day's ride should include the following steps:

1. Loosening up – Preparing the horse to work, walking with light contact (outside the arena if possible) to get the muscles and joints working,

2. Warming up – Working at all three gaits with light contact, getting on the horse's page, evaluating how the horse feels compared to the previous ride's warm-up, and determining what goes into the training set ("Can I follow my training plan, or do I need to return to some basics based on what I am feeling?"),

3. Training sets – The continuum of the training program, done in one to three sets depending upon the horse's condition and response and the difficulty of the work being asked, and

4. Cool down – Walking on a long rein with light contact letting the muscles relax and return to normal.

The best riders are those who prepare themselves and their horses by paying close attention consistently to the important factors that influence themselves and their horses. It is the instructor's responsibility to teach students good habits by performing consistently day in and day out. The following list contains some of the critical elements that should be attended to on a regular basis:

- Rider maintains own balance, position and depth of seat
- Rider feels rhythm and follows with contact
- Rider maintains route
- Horse moves forward with
  Response to leg (softly and quickly)
  Response to hand
  Note: rider has a following seat, motion back to front
- Horse is easily able to bend/flex equally to both sides

# THE GERMAN SCALE OF EDUCATION – PHASE 1

## The Concept of the
## GERMAN RIDING SCHOOL

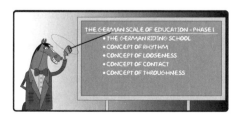

Instructors MUST be thoroughly grounded themselves, through understanding and experience, with the order and foundation of this classical information before teaching it to their students. Once instructors have the big picture clear in their own minds, they can be creative and flexible about how they intermix the teaching strategies of these stages to help their students reach their goals. It is when instructors are not clear about the big picture that the seeds of confusion, frustration, and incorrect riding are planted, fertilized and grown. ✦

## Short History of the German System
By Stephan Kiesewetter

The German Riding System is a wholistic system. The system involves all aspects of the horse and the rider; this includes the physical aspects as well as psychological aspects.

The German system is developed over more than 2000 years. The first roots of it are found in the work of the Greek philosopher Xenophon, called "Peri Hippekes," which means "About Horses." This work can be considered as the starting point of a systematical education of horses.

During the next 18 centuries this system developed, with lots of good as well as with a lot of curious and wrong developments. For example the Duke of Newcastle, who was the inventor of the draw reins and the most popular horse trainer of his time. He was able to educate a horse from a very beginner to an advanced horse within three months. Unfortunately most of his horses suffered ataxia when the education was finished.

Löhneisen edited the first written version of the German Riding System in the 18th century. During this same time Francois de la Gueriniere, one of the most successful horse trainers in all of Europe, invented the "coat feeling lower leg." This has had an incredibly positive impact on the development of riding. These two masters can be considered as the founding fathers of todays training system.

For a long time a written version did not exist, the knowledge was passed from generation to generation only by the spoken word.

In the beginning of the 20th century two important books built the base for our modern riding system: 1. The Gymnasium of the Horse
2. The Heeresdienstvorschrift Nr. 12 ( Military Manual for Using and Educating Horses)
The first one can be considered as the Bible of German horse trainers and professional riders. The problem is that it is very difficult to read and to understand, as the reader needs a detailed knowledge about horse anatomy and physiology. The second is the basic version of the "Principals of Riding" and the "Advanced Techniques of Riding."

The result of this 2000 year process of development is an educational system, which is based on the rider/trainer listening to the natural abilities, and the physical and psychological prerequisites of a horse.

Chart 31

"The German Riding System as it exists today is not simply a manual on how to ride a horse, but rather is a program of systematic physical education to gymnasticize the horse, with the goal of bringing each horse to his full potential given his natural physical and mental aptitudes. The soul of this system is the Scale of Education, which is interwoven through every part of the horse's education. The Scale of Education is not only a long-term educational plan for bringing a horse from its initial backing to becoming a schoolmaster; it is also a daily training plan. With an understanding of the Scale of Education, the rider is able to routinely test and check the quality of the horse's daily training.

None of the six steps in the Scale of Education can really be considered separately as all of them are intimately related to each other, yet they must be developed in a certain order. This applies both to the use of the scale for daily training as well as to the long-term view of training the horse.

The goal of the Scale of Education is 'letting the aids through,' which results in a horse that is a pleasure to ride because it is reacting to the 'whistling' aids of the rider. This goal can only be achieved by a systematic, daily training process." - Excerpted from Stephan Kiesewetter's lecture series.

We have included the information on the German System because it has a long history of producing well skilled riders. It is the basis of the Ideal World section in each stage. The Ideal World is very rare in America, thus we have created a system to be used in the Real World based on the conditions that most instructors face in America.

**The Scale of Education —**
**The Basics of Training for ALL Horses**

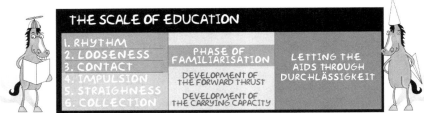

## The Concept of RHYTHM

Rhythm is the backbone of the entire training program. It is easy to understand for the musically inclined, but for many it must be learned. Rhythm is the regularity of the strides in each gait, covering equal distances and with equal duration. In all the phases of training rhythm is used as a criteria for when to use half-halts. Rhythm needs to be maintained during transitions, movements, turns and straight lines.

The correct way to begin each ride is for the rider to immediately establish contact with the horse through the leg to a light, receiving hand. With this light, consistent contact the rider walks the horse to loosen it up (see warm-up procedure). During the warm-up the rider feels the horse's rhythm and follows it. It is important that the rider also establish a mental connection with the horse, keeping the horse focused on the work being asked. In addition to acute awareness of the horse's natural rhythm, the rider must be alert to staying on a pre-determined route and must maintain the correct body position so as to be ready to communicate with the horse through the aids. Ideally riders should be aware of rhythm through every phase of the training session, and be comparing the current rhythm to what was felt in the last ride and to the capability of the horse at this stage of training as well as the ultimate desired end result.

## The Concept of LOOSENESS
**(often referred to as Relaxation or Suppleness)**

Looseness is a concept that is a bit elusive to grasp, as it does not simply mean relaxation or suppleness per se. Rather, the term looseness refers to the way a horse's whole circle of muscles works when he is traveling under saddle. Horses are considered to be moving with the quality of 'looseness' when they travel forward with energy while maintaining some degree of straightness and rhythm. Most importantly, a loose horse will move with muscles that are free of tension and joints that bend and straighten equally on each side of the body with each step. For a horse to be loose in the body, he needs to be focused on his rider. Distracted horses tighten their muscles. Riders of horses traveling with looseness describe the feeling as one where the horse is traveling "across the ground" smoothly and with little effort. Every horse has a capacity to travel with looseness, but the degree and quality of the looseness will depend on many factors, such as age, training, natural freedom of movement, length of step, degree of stiffness, and individual conformation/muscular traits. Stretching is essential to the concept of looseness, both as an exercise and as a test. As an exercise, horses that are asked to stretch become more longitudinally supple. As a test, once moving with looseness, horses will want to stretch (see Stage 4, step 4 for more details on stretching).

Indications of looseness are:

- A content, happy expression in eyes, ears and movements
- A rhythmically swinging back
- A closed but not immobile mouth
- A slightly lifted tail that swings with the horse's movement

## The Concept of CONTACT

Contact is a form of communication established through the physical connection between the rider's hands and the horse's mouth via the rein. The quality of this connection, or contact, depends on two factors: the rider's level of education, and the level of training of the horse. New riders tend to pick up contact with considerable awkwardness because their arms are no longer able to move anywhere or wherever they want for balance. Instead, riders are taught right away that their hands now "belong" to the horse, and therefore must stay steady, in front of the saddle (with a straight line from the elbow to the bit), quiet, and above all, "not bounce." Early efforts by riders to follow the movements of the horse's head and neck - while keeping their hands in the right position and trying to keep the rein steady - tend to be tight and stiff. Over time, and with experience (especially on a horse with a "trained mouth"), riders learn how to soften and relax their shoulders, arms, hands, and fingers to create a steady, elastic-like feel in the rein.

Similar to new riders, green or inexperienced horses tend to respond to their early experiences with contact with some anxiety. That is, these horses tend to get a bit tense and nervous when a rider first picks up the rein, leading them to stiffen up in their back, neck and jaw. This response, by the way, does not tend to produce a "soft, elastic-like feel" of the rein! With proper training, horses learn to respond correctly to a rider's hand by relaxing and softening in their back, neck, poll, and jaw (see Rein Response in Stage 2, step 2).

In the Stages of Rider Education, the order of progression of contact goes from light contact, to light contact with the horse's is being round, to a contact with a horse being truly "on the bit." "On the bit" is an expression that indicates a horse that is balanced, engaged from back to front, with his hind legs stepping well under his belly. When the horse has an established forward rhythm, he will

On the Bit

seek contact with the rider's hand, and the rider provides it. Contact continues to develop as training progresses. Just as looseness improves the quality and consistency of rhythm, contact improves the quality of both rhythm and looseness. Contact is never the result of a backward action by the rider's hands, but instead always results from forward action beginning with the horse's hind legs.

Over the course of a rider's education, their hands become trained to be independent from their seat. Only then are riders able to receive the energy of the horse. The term "light contact" means picking up the rein with minimal weight in the rein, much like what is required in hunter classes at horse shows. As riders progress in their educations, they learn to take more weight in their rein while maintaining the quality (elastic) of the connection. As well, riders develop the ability to use their contact in various ways, such as how to "hold," "resist," "stretch," and "soften," all of which require a great degree of tact, timing, and feel.

One of the most common rider faults is a lack of an "elastic-like feel" in the rein. This is often caused by the lack of a proper education in both rider and horse, so that they end up feeding off of one another in terms of stiffness. That is, neither party understands the proper response to the rein, which makes the stiffness in the horse create stiffness in the rider, which reinforces the stiffness in the horse! It is a negative cycle that is hard to break out of once in it. For this reason, it is helpful if riders can first learn on horses whose mouths are educated enough to teach the rider the proper "feel" in the rein. Likewise for the horse; the training goes faster and smoother when the rider can offer the horse a quality connection even when the horse makes doing so quite difficult.

### The Concept of THROUGHNESS

The goal of all training sessions is toward "throughness" (letting the aids through). Combining rhythm, looseness, and contact in that order of priority creates throughness. A "through" horse is easier to ride and stays sound longer.

Instructors develop their eyes to be able to recognize from the ground the signs of the throughness they 'feel' when mounted. The horse steps under with his hind legs, the muscles and joints are relaxed with appropriate tone and are in full use. The energy of the horse appears to be moving from the push of the hind leg into the bridle. The horse is arching his neck using the "telescoping gesture" which means that the complexus muscle (the middle neck muscle) is bulging. The rider appears to be part of this flowing energy.

## THE GERMAN SCALE OF EDUCATION—PHASES 2 & 3

### The Concept of IMPULSION

This concept, like those of "forward" and "engagement," is a source of much confusion. Instructors and riders alike have been heard to use these three terms interchangeably. Instructors may tell their students, "You need more

impulsion," when the students are trotting lazily around on training level horses. The problem with this statement is that a training level horse cannot yet work with true impulsion - but may indeed need more energy or engagement!

**Definition:** Impulsion is when a horse moves energetically from the hind end forward with power and thrust. Energy moves from the hind legs, over the back (which is round), up through the withers, neck, poll and into the rider's receiving hands.

One way to visualize the concept of impulsion is to think of the difference between walking energetically versus skipping. When walking, there is energy expended to move you forward. When skipping, energy is still expended to move you forward, but additional energy is needed to move you forward and "up." This is similar to how impulsion works for horses. To work with impulsion, horses have to increase their energy outputs in order to propel themselves forwards *and upwards* in their movement. You can see the results of this in the horse's increased flexion of their stifles and hocks. Horses have to build up the muscles in their backs, hindquarters, stifles, and gaskins to maintain working with impulsion. Think about how tired you would become if you skipped around the arena versus walking around the arena. Horses get tired too! This is why horses are often not worked for long hours at this level. Twenty minutes of doing exercises that demand increased impulsion may be all that is asked, followed by a cool down that allows the horse to finish with exercises that he can do easily, which maintains his self-confidence and enjoyment of his work.

## The Concept of Advanced STRAIGHTNESS

It is during Stage 5 that riders come to develop a more complex and in-depth awareness of the concept of "straightness." At this level, straightness takes on the added quality of the horse's weight distribution. Earlier in this chapter we talked about straightness in basic terms: keeping a horse's body parts lined up so that both the hind and front hoof prints follow the route that the horse is on. For example, if a horse is making a 20-meter circle, being "straight on that circle" means that the horse's hoof prints follow the bend of the 20-meter circle. Therefore, basic straightness can be described as when **the line of the horse's move-**

*The horse's body weight is evenly distributed laterally and longitudinally. The forehand is in line with the hindquarters and the hoof prints fall equally on both sides of the line of movement. The horse moves his center of gravity back through the increased use of his hind legs.*

*ment is the same as the line of the route.* An important note: if you were to draw an imaginary line down the center of the horse while on the 20-meter circle, the horse's hoof prints would fall equal distances on either side of that line.

Instructors of Stage 5 students are now ready to expand the students' perception of the term "riding straight." When talking about the more advanced concept of straightness, we must take into consideration those movements where the horse's line of travel (or route) is not straight in and of itself. For example, movements like the leg-yield, shoulder-in, travers, renvers, and half-pass require the horse to be moving in one direction but positioning his body in another. Defining straightness in these situations is a source for much confusion. When thinking about straightness during Stage 5, a rider needs to consider the movement he or she is asking the horse to perform. If the movement is a 3-track movement, the rider must focus on the new path of the foot falls. In the shoulder-in, for example, the inside hind foot is in line with the outside front foot, and the route is being determined by the inside hind leg. Straightness in this movement is determined by whether the horse's hind and front hoof prints are falling equally on either side of that imaginary line that dissects the horse straight down the middle, and if his weight is also equally distributed on both sides of the imaginary line. In other words, advanced straightness means that *the line of the movement may differ from the line of the route.*

In order to accomplish this task, riders have to "feel" if the horse is distributing his weight equally on both sides of this imaginary line. We now have entered the murky world of the concept of "balance." Straightness and balance are closely intertwined at this level of training.

---

### Straightness through the Stages

**Basic straightness** (through 1st level) — the horse must travel in such a way that the hind feet follow in the tracks of the front feet, no matter what shape or figure they are making.

**Advanced straightness** (2nd level and above)- line of movement may differ from the line of route —the horse is straight when his weight is equally distributed on both sides of the imaginary line that goes from his tail to poll.

Whether one is talking about basic or advanced straightness, the horse must remain balanced on the line of the movement while remaining on the line of route.

Chart 30

---

## The Concept of BALANCE

What exactly do horse people mean by "balance"? The confusion many equestrians feel about this topic is easy to understand. Just go into any riding ring around the country, and ask the horse people there to give you their definitions of balance. Most likely you will hear as many definitions as the number of people asked! One of the reasons the issue of balance confuses equestrians everywhere is that there are four distinct types of balance:

1. Natural Balance

2. Ridden Balance (under saddle)

3. Lateral Balance

4. Longitudinal Balance

To make matters worse, there are many factors that can influence a horse's balance (see chart 38). To help clear up the misunderstandings and confusion surrounding the concept of balance, we are going to provide a definition, and then discuss that definition for all four types of balance.

Definition: Balance can be defined as a horse's ever-changing attempts to move most efficiently for the work being required.

### NATURAL BALANCE

Natural balance can refer to two different scenarios.

1) The way horses travel naturally "in the wild" or out in the pasture.

2) The way horses travel naturally within their gaits.

| **Factors Influencing Balance** |
| --- |
| ▪ Conformation |
| ▪ Terrain and footing |
| ▪ Discipline or activity |
| ▪ Degree of difficulty of movement being performed |
| ▪ Level of training |
| ▪ Rider's position, seat & aids |
| ▪ Amount of forward energy |
| Chart 33 |

### In the Wild

As described in the concept of the circle of muscles, a horse "naturally" balances when running around in the pasture by using his head, neck, and hindquarters as counter-balance measures. Keeping his back fairly straight, the head and neck swings in one direction, while the hindquarters swing in the opposite direction. This method is quite effective for the horse under many circumstances. He can wheel quickly (as we probably all have personally experienced), run fast, and stop on a dime! The only problem with this method is that it does not work very well when a rider climbs on board. The rider's weight and center of gravity changes the horse's center of balance, making it difficult for the horse to use the counter-balance measures of the forehand and hindquarters; thus the horse's efficiency when moving is lost.

### Within Gaits

Horses that are described as "naturally balanced" are those whose conformation traits makes it easy for them to travel "level," in that they naturally want to travel with their weight fairly equally distributed on all four legs. This is often seen in the canter, when the horse seems to maintain a regular rhythm and pace; not rushing or falling back to the trot. There are many different conformation traits that contribute to a 'naturally balanced' individual. In general, these horses tend to be level across the croup to the wither, with middle to high set on necks. No one part of the horse tends to be grossly out of proportion, and they usually move softly and lightly across the ground. These few animals make the gifted athletes that can be trained most easily.

### RIDDEN BALANCE

Once the rider mounts the horse, his balance must change to carry the rider. The horse does not want to fall down or lose his balance, so he will move in such a way to remain upright with the rider on his back. The horse's balance is affected by the rider's degree of balance, suppleness, elasticity and education of seat. Instructors can tell a lot about the rider's relaxation and position by observing the reaction of the horse in route, rhythm and relaxation. Since the rider affects the horse and the horse can affect the rider, the instructor needs to develop a keen eye and skill for diagnosis to see the effects each member of the partnership has on the other's balance.

### LATERAL BALANCE

Lateral balance is when the horse maintains equal weight distribution on both sides of an imaginary line that dissects the middle of the horse from poll to tail.

Perhaps the best way to understand and "feel" what lateral balance means is to do the following exercise:

1. Fill up two buckets of water
2. Walk down your barn aisle carrying the two buckets of water without making an effort to be particularly straight.
3. Next, draw a straight line down the middle of the barn aisle
4. Now, try walking straight down the middle of that line while carrying the water buckets

What was the difference between your two walk attempts? When walking "normally" the weight of the buckets pulls most people side to side as they walk. That is, they do not travel very "straight"! When trying to follow the line (route), your job probably became a bit more difficult. In order to travel straight with those buckets, you were forced to shift (distribute) your weight *equally* from side to side as you walk. This is what horses must do in order to travel straight on a designated route. In other words, you "balanced" yourself when walking with those buckets just as a horse must "balance" himself when traveling straight on a line or route.

As students progress and learn new skills, they may also back-slide a little. This is not something to worry about, but as soon as the new skill is understood and the student is on the way to mastering it, remind the student to return and repair the skill that took a temporary backslide.

## LONGITUDINAL BALANCE

Longitudinal balance refers to the horse's ability to shift his weight from **back to front.** That is, a longitudinally balanced horse attempts to re-distribute the weight from his front end (where most horses "naturally" carry about 60% of their weight) to his hind end. It is important to realize that this weight distribution NEVER reaches a 50-50 split. At most, such as during the piaffe, the horse achieves a weight distribution of 55% to 45%, front to back.

> *The horse can only shift his weight from front to back when his back is round.*

A real world example is useful here. Kim was constantly complaining because her horse, King, was always in a hurry. He listened to adjustments only for a step or two at a time. The problem was that King was stiff and **not using his back,** thus was always running to keep up with his lack of longitudinal balance. It happened that his stiffness was in the shoulder area, and in particular his right shoulder was bearing more weight in each step then any other body part.

The rest of his body was trying to keep up with his right shoulder. Kim had to 'feel' this and know what to do. First we returned to Stage 2 flexing, and tested to see if King could flex equally to both sides. Kim quickly felt the difference in his two sides. Systematic exercises with flexion, keeping it simple for Kim and King, led to both gaining an understanding through feel. Kim was so excited as King now stopped running and required about 50% fewer adjustments. King was now able to **lift his back and use it.** In the process Kim learned a new way of adjusting King, thus expanding upon her control panel. Over the weekend clinic Kim added more and more exercises to King's program that would build up engagement with the flexion, and King's gaits started to become more and more beautiful with his back up and without running!

Horses often go off route because they have lost their lateral or longitudinal balance.

## The Concept of COLLECTION

Collection is the result of a straight, balanced horse now shifting his weight back while maintaining forward thrust and impulsion. The rider's hand receives the energy created from this process, making the horse more elastic, ready, and willing to perform with minimal aids from the rider. The hocks and stifle joints bend more and carry more weight. While the steps become shorter, they maintain energy, show more expression, and feel more powerful.

Example- Think about jogging down a hill with the same speed and tempo as on a flat surface. In order to accomplish this you will find your weight shifting back, and your strides becoming shorter yet having more energy (thrust). You will feel this in your thighs, which are acting in a similar way to how a horse uses his gaskins!

The Fundamental Teaching Skills section provides instructors with important tools to use in teaching their students the technical equitation skills. 🐎

# INTRODUCTORY STAGE

## GOALS OF INTRODUCTORY STAGE

Before taking up riding, it is important to have an introduction to the basics of horse care. This ignites a general awareness of what is involved in riding and working with horses. Horsemanship at this level is designed to begin the partnership between horse and rider with a foundation of basic knowledge. Good instructors will start teaching each student technical skills both on and off the horse, and an understanding of the horse as a loved, appreciated being.

## THEORY

Encourage ground time with horses. The emphasis of the first few lessons is on building a comfort level between the student and the horse while leading, grooming, and putting on the saddle and bridle. Allow the student time to enjoy and get to know the horse. Because the instructor is familiar with the experience of being around horses, it is easy to skip through this part quickly. The student must be given time to develop this familiarity. It is important to wait until the student has become comfortable and confident with these essential preliminaries before adding new information or skills. The student's time on the ground with the horse is well spent as it establishes a caring relationship between the horse and the rider, improves rider confidence, and demonstrates the necessity and pleasure of the non-riding parts of being involved with horses. Ground time with the horse gets the learning process off to a healthy start.

154

## IMPORTANT POINTS

1. This is an ideal time for instructors to begin building students' confidence by teaching safety around horses. Riders new to horses are often overwhelmed by the size of the animal and experience a natural fear. Helping the student understand the basics of horse psychology as they work around the horse will set the stage for a successful future.

2. Introduction to horses:
   - Safety around horses
   - How to lead
   - How to groom
   - How to tack up
   - How to mount and dismount correctly

## PRACTICAL APPLICATION

The practical application at this time requires a very well mannered, properly educated, forgiving horse with a quiet temperament. The role of the horse at this stage is to accept errors in the way the student handles them without putting the student in danger. It is good if the horse has enough personality to let the student know when they are making an error. Helping the new horseperson to notice and respond to the horse's reactions is a vital part of getting started 'right'. From this groundwork students can begin to develop awareness and the ability to 'feel'.

A good lesson plan is very important during this stage of instructing.

## STAGE 1
# POSITION AND CONTROL

*Students enter Stage 1 having basic ground experience with horses, a desire to learn and a variety of motivations and backgrounds.*

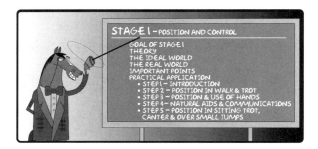

## GOALS OF STAGE 1

1. To teach students how to sit correctly on a moving horse demonstrating these four basics:

   • Straight-line perpendicular to the ground from ear to shoulder to hip to heel,

   • Deep seat with the rider's weight going down from the head through the body core and flowing out from the inside of the heels, with the heels being the lowest point of the foot,

   • Flexible and elastic joints, which act as shock absorbers; especially the lower back, hips, knees, and ankles,

   • Rider's weight balanced evenly on both sides of the horse.

2. To teach students how to gain basic control of a horse while maintaining the correct position in the three basic gaits and over small jumps, including:

   • Use of natural aids,

   • How to communicate via horse language,

   • Keeping the horse aware and listening to the rider.

**INSTRUCTOR'S REMINDER**

The goal of riders in Stage 1 is not to develop a perfect seat, but rather the development of a correct foundation so that the rider's seat does not interfere with the horse's comfort and has the potential to develop into a useful aid. Improving the seat is an ongoing process, culminating in the development of an independent seat by Stage 3. ⚞

## THEORY

The concepts that will be introduced and worked on throughout this stage are: Position, Seat, Relaxation, Route/Direction and Control. Instructors will find it helpful to review these sections in the Theory Made Simple chapter. Students will also be introduced to the use of the natural aids and basic communication with the horse.

## THE IDEAL WORLD

The BEST WAY for riders to develop a good seat is to:

1. Learn the correct position on the lunge line,

2. Progress to learning control off the lunge line on a quiet, well schooled horse.

A properly conducted lunge lesson is the safest way to start a new student. Riders started on the lunge line learn correct position faster because they are able to work on the control of their own bodies and their balance without worrying about controlling the horse. It is the ideal opportunity for riders to develop their seats and positions without the complication of what to do with their hands. The instructor can help students realize the benefits to be gained from lunge lessons by letting them know that all riders, including top professionals, use lunge lessons for continual seat development.

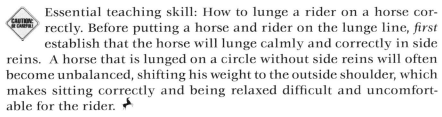

**Essential teaching skill:** How to lunge a rider on a horse correctly. Before putting a horse and rider on the lunge line, *first* establish that the horse will lunge calmly and correctly in side reins. A horse that is lunged on a circle without side reins will often become unbalanced, shifting his weight to the outside shoulder, which makes sitting correctly and being relaxed difficult and uncomfortable for the rider. ⚞

Ideally, a horse used for lunging should be balanced, sound, relaxed, and soft in his back. A horse that accepts side reins and correctly moves forward through his back will create comfortable gaits. It is also very important to use correctly fitting tack. If the saddle is not properly balanced on the horse, or is the wrong size for the rider, it will be impossible for the rider to find the correct balance and position. The lunging instructor must be aware of methods and exercises to help the rider develop an independent seat, muscle tone, coordination and feel.

Instructors must also know the proper techniques for lunging a horse. Spending time on this step in the beginning of the learning process will save considerable time later on.

Once students have gained control of their bodies and have a correct position at the walk and posting trot without using their hands for balance, it is time to add lessons off the lunge line. After body control and balance are sufficiently established, riders may pick up the reins and begin to learn how to control the horse by telling him to stop, go, and turn. In our experience, the most effective way to teach control is to focus on the following four points in this order:

1. Route: stay on the intended path,
2. Rate: maintain the desired pace,
3. Relaxation: of both horse and rider,
4. Position: maintain the correct position and balance.

If students are mounted on safe, well-schooled horses, focusing on route and rate ensure safety because riders feel that they are in basic control of their horses. Once students feel safe, they can check relaxation and position. Ideally the rider is able to maintain the position and relaxation gained on the lunge line as control is introduced. However, even in the ideal world, adding the four points of control often causes students to feel awkward again, as if they were learning to drive a car for the first time. At this point instructors need to focus on route and rate until those skills are firmly established and then return to reestablishing the position and relaxation the student had on the lunge line.

The combination of lessons on the lunge line and riding suitably trained and balanced horses provides the ideal setting for riders to develop careful, soft, independent hands. Students have the opportunity to learn a solid foundation without worrying about their hands or having to control their horses. They can concentrate on developing a correct seat and leg position before introducing the use of their hands. The natural tendency to use hands before legs is discouraged when the hand is not used from the very beginning.

Once control is introduced, most riders' positions are affected in one way or another due to the need to coordinate what the brain tells the body to do with what the limbs actually are able to do. Instructors must understand this and be willing to allow some "errors" in position while the student focuses on learning the skills of control (unless safety becomes an issue).

## THE REAL WORLD

In Stage 1, the real world poses two problems for instructors: 1) How to teach position when lunging is not available, and 2) How to deal with beginners who are mounted on inappropriate horses.

## PROBLEMS WITH TEACHING POSITION

Perhaps the biggest problem for instructors when teaching beginners is how to handle those situations when they do not have the "ideal world" of lunge line lessons available. This can occur for many reasons. The instructor may not be comfortable lunging, or does not have a horse that is safe for lunging; or there may not be any safe places to lunge a rider on a horse. If, for whatever reason, a student has to begin riding without lunge lessons, the instructor must find a safe way to begin the rider's learning experience of how to sit correctly on top of a horse. It is particularly helpful if the beginner horse is quiet, will stay on route, and maintain his tempo and rhythm when the rider drops the reins. Because most beginners have no understanding of how much their body positions and movements influence their horses, they can unintentionally send their horses forward. For this reason, it is important that instructors have other options "up their sleeve" in case the "ideal" lunging lesson is not available. Some ideas include:

- Using a quiet, safe school horse in a private lesson, with the instructor or an assistant leading the horse,

- Holding the lesson in a small area of the ring, so that the instructor is always close to both rider and horse,

- Group lessons on quiet, predictable school horses that politely follow the other horses around the ring despite the rider's unintentional leg aids to go faster.

 Instructors need to be aware of the challenges and differences between teaching children and teaching adults (see ISOYI – Stages of Life). 🐎

## PROBLEMS WITH TEACHING CONTROL

Often in the real world instructors find themselves in the unenviable position of dealing with beginner riders mounted on horses that are unsuitable. The horse may be beyond the rider's skill level, physically and/or mentally intimidating, unschooled, spoiled, fearful, or all of the above! Under these conditions, instructors have no choice but to attend to safety issues first, which typically means beginning with control. There are three possible options available to the instructor in this situation:

- Find a secure, safe area where the instructor can control the horse with his or her voice and body language to help the student,

- Teach the rider rudimentary horse control before focusing on the rider's body control and position,

- Put the horse in training until he is safe and steady enough for the rider to learn on. During this time, provide the student with a more suitable lesson horse.

In addition to safety concerns raised when beginning riders are mounted on unsuitable horses, there are important technical problems as well: it is human nature to tense up and freeze when anxious, nervous, or scared. When this happens learning takes a back seat to survival, and beginner riders mounted on horses that are unsuitable will be unable to "take in" the excellent information the instructor is providing! To keep riders from being distracted by survival issues, it may be necessary to focus on control issues first. Otherwise, students will stay distracted—their attention split between the instructor and the horse. If it is uncertain whether a particular rider can safely shift focus from survival to control, it is important for the instructor to either put that student on a lead line, walk with the student, or ride the horse to explain the facts about control to the confused horse. If tightness or a severe position problem shows itself, the instructor can make the necessary adjustments while continuing to work on control. As is true with teaching all new skills keep explanations and directions very simple and add the next skill when the current skill becomes second nature to the student.

*An unsuitable horse and rider combination can enter the ring at any stage. Control must be established before any other progress can be made.*

### THE CHALLENGE OF GROUP LESSONS

Sometimes instructors must start beginners in a group. There are pros and cons to the group format. While teaching multiple beginners at once can be a major challenge (since the riders have not learned control of their bodies or their horses!), the availability of honest, well-schooled, very quiet horses that "know the ropes" can help riders develop a sense of safety and security, even in a group. Group lessons offer the beginner a chance to learn visually by watching other riders, and to be exposed to more information and education in a shorter time period because of the presence of the other students in the ring. However, having only group lessons at Stage 1 may allow position faults to develop and become engrained if there is not enough individual attention. If the school horses are not quiet and well schooled, beginners are apt to learn incorrect responses and a wrong "feel" from their early efforts to sit correctly and use their aids. There are many good books available that discuss group teaching in considerable detail. A few of them are listed at the end of this chapter.

Many instructors mistakenly believe that all control issues will be resolved with a correct position. Instructors constantly face the challenge of deciding when to move on to another skill because it has been drilled into their heads that position is so important. While this is true, it helps to be flexible in one's approach to solving students' position problems. **Example:** Sally struggled with her position for years. She spent hours on the lunge line but remained very crooked on her horse. Approaching the problem from the perspective of control, she got her horse straight on the wall and through the turns, and her own crookedness disappeared. She was sitting crooked because she was balancing on a crooked horse! 🐎

The voice and body language of the instructor in combination with a quiet horse are very important aspects for developing a relaxed, confident rider. 🐎

## IMPORTANT POINTS

1. A rider's balance is intricately related to position! New riders need to learn how to feel securely balanced on the horse without gripping with their legs or pulling on the reins to stay on. Once riders develop the feeling of correct body alignment, they can practice relaxing in this position and will develop the strength needed to maintain that correct position.

2. Balance on a horse is a skill; it does not come overnight. All beginning riders feel the need to grip to stay on because they do not yet have enough balance – their bodies are on "red alert," and should be! There is a certain reality that comes from being a beginner – which makes the choice of horse so important. As the rider develops some comfort level and balance through exercises and practice, the instructor needs to use words that encourage the rider to relax and stay elastic in his/her position, not stiff and tight. With awareness and understanding, grip is released as balance is increased and muscle tone developed.

In order to follow the movement of the horse, riders need relaxation combined with muscle tone (or muscle tension), a correct position, a well-developed sense of feel, a clear understanding/ picture of a functional position, and a clear mind. 🐎

American instructors need to be flexible about moving back and forth between the following steps when teaching. 🐎

## PRACTICAL APPLICATION
### Step 1 – Introducing Position

*Objective:* Give the student a brief but clear explanation of the functional, correct balanced seat and half-seat positions.

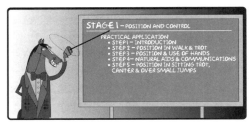

*Theory:* Explain the basic components of a balanced seat and half-seat, and the purpose of each. Review the concept of seat in the Theory Made Simple chapter.

**Toolkit**

- Use demonstration with explanation when possible.

- Watch an accomplished rider and talk with students about what they are seeing.

- Ride a horse and describe your position and aids as they are being used.

- Ask students to pick out some common position issues, themes, or similarities in different riders; they often pick up on the basics - straight back, perpendicular line, heels down, relaxed joints, etc.

 It is important to keep explanations simple and to the point so students are not overwhelmed with too much information. This is a time for action not talk. 🐎

- Ask your students questions in order to gain an understanding of how they think, what they see and how they process the information.

- Review and demonstrate half-seat position ridden with springy ankles and a relaxed leg, with the upper body in its appropriate line.

*Starting beginners can be one of the most reward-
ing aspects of teaching. For these new students, you
are opening the door to one of the most wondrous,
magical, and meaningful relationships they may
ever experience - true partnership with a horse.
With this opportunity comes the responsibility not
to skip important steps in your students' building
blocks.*

*Test to move to Step 2:* Ask students questions
to confirm their understanding, have them get
on a horse and demonstrate the correct position while standing still.

1/2 SEAT POSITION

### Step 2 – Position in Walk & Trot
*Objective:* Develop and practice the correct
basic position in walk and posting trot, and
the half-seat in walk and trot.

Students may be encouraged to put their hands on the pommel or
their hips. Timid or insecure riders may hold a neck strap or the
pommel. 🐎

*Theory:* The "correct" position is essential for the rider's and the horse's
safety, balance, and control. This position has been established over hundreds of years of trial and error in many different countries. As a result,
there is little disagreement throughout the world over what constitutes
the "correct" way for a rider to sit—it is the position that minimizes the
stress and strain on the horse from carrying a rider. Review the concepts
of position and seat in the Theory Made Simple chapter.

*Important Points*
1. Begin with a relaxed, centered seat and stretched leg with the
   heel under the hips, and then bring the shoulder and ear in alignment with the hip, while maintaining the leg position.

2. A brief description of the trot as a diagonally moving gait helps riders to understand posting. Help riders understand the posting movement and feel the rhythm of the horse's trot. Explain the purpose of the half-seat position, and most importantly work with the rider to develop the downward push of weight as the rider goes up in the post or half-seat position.

3. This is an important time to involve the student in their own learning process by asking them to provide their own descriptive word for describing how his or her body feels when balanced and relaxed...a few examples from riders: springy, elastic, loose, soft, jelly-like, relaxed. Most students will try to describe their feeling in a sentence or more; help them simplify by paraphrasing or picking out a few of their words, or ask them another question to find the 'right' word for them. Once the word is established, the instructor can use it to help students maintain that feeling. Sometimes it is humorous and fun! One adult beginner said, "I am embarrassed to tell you what I feel like, but I will; I feel like jello!" When he began to lose his balance, I would say, "Remember the jello!"

 Keep students moving - even while talking. ⚘

**Toolkit**

⚘ Feel the Position Exercise

First, have the rider feel the incorrect position.

- Have the rider imagine the bottom of their pelvis to be like the runners of a rocking chair, rising up slightly in the front and back. Then, ask the rider to rock forward on to the front of their "rocking chair." This is called "perching." This lifts the seat bones slightly off the back of the saddle and hollows the rider's back.

- Next have the rider rock back on to the back of their rocking chair. "This is the classic "chair seat." When the rider tilts too far forward or backward, the pelvis loses its flexibility, effectively becoming "locked" and stiff. This position encourages the rider to grip upwards with their thighs and knees to stop from moving too much, creating a negative cycle that becomes hard to break out off.

Now have rider feel the effective and correct position.

- Have the rider sit in the middle of their "rocking chair," and feel what his/her seat bones. It is this position that allows the most freedom of movement in the pelvis to move with the horse.

- Create exercises to focus on the student's lower body and leg, aligning the hip and heel, with the student's weight going down through the center of the body. This requires balance, relaxation (mental and physical) and muscle tone.
  - Games, such as "around the world" or touching the toes of one leg while keeping the opposite leg in the correct position
  - Exercises to develop heel awareness and suppling the ankle, such as lifting heels up as high as possible, then stretching them back down
  - Exercises to develop seat movement; rock the pelvis ("rocking chair") from front through center to back, walking with one leg held up by hand, knees pulled up so the legs are over the front of the saddle while walking
- Create exercises to focus on the student's torso, aligning the shoulder over the hip. This is done once the seat and legs are able to maintain their alignment.
  - Post at the walk, without hands, staying in balance, with heels going down as rider goes up
  - Half-seat position with springy ankle
  - Half-seat and posting position touching parts of horse, own toes and doing arm and hand exercises
- Create exercises to focus on the student's whole body; the alignment of ear, shoulder, hip and heel with the student's weight going down equally on both sides through the center of the body with elastic joints, thus forming a balanced, deep seat.
  - Visualize body weight; start with the weight of the head (about 20 lbs) gaining weight as it goes down the center of the body, through the spine to the crotch and dividing between the two legs, traveling equally through a soft thigh, a springy knee, a relaxed calf, an elastic ankle and out a springy heel

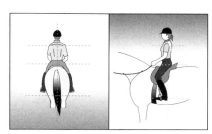

Straight Lines of a Correct Position

  - Close eyes and answer a few easy 'feel' questions about the body
  - Posting at trot with attention to heels going down as rider goes up
  - Go from half-seat to posting to sitting, or any combination of these—great ways to gain body control with elastic legs and balanced upper body
  - Go over a few ground poles maintaining half-seat position

- Begin with short sets so student does not get fatigued
- Use hands as needed to help balance by holding saddle, mane, or neck strap
- Remind student to keep ankles elastic and springy

*Test to move to Step 3:* Riders can maintain basic position and half-seat position at the walk and trot while going around the circle on a lunge line one time without using their hands for balance, or something similar if lunging is not possible. An essential part of this test is making sure that the students' heels go down as they rise in the post.

---

### Keep Lessons FUN, INTERESTING and EDUCATIONAL
### While Developing Balance and Confidence at the Same Time!

- Walking around off the lunge line either inside the arena or outside the arena. This enables riders to develop a feel for free movement. Without a learning agenda, their minds are free to focus on the environment, allowing their natural balance to take over. Remain very aware of safety issues, making sure you are close enough to help if help is needed, reassuring both horse and rider by your continued presence and attention.
- Ride bareback, vault, go out on trails; do fun things to learn the combination of the correct seat with development of "feel."
- As soon as a student has basic control, cavalletti can be introduced to provide variety and another opportunity to improve balance.

Chart 34

---

## Step 3 - Position & Use of Hands

*Objective:* Allow hands to follow the motion of the horse's head, and to become aware of the straight line from the elbow, through the hand, to the bit.

*Theory:* The rider's ability to follow the motion of the horse's head without restricting it lays the foundation for developing correctly feeling hands. Riders who master this step are more easily able to later develop the contact needed to receive energy from the horse's hind leg and help a horse move rhythmically with looseness and relaxation.

*Important Points:*

1. With the body lined up correctly and the rider more able to control his or her limbs, it is now a good time to point out the sensitivity of the horse's soft mouth. Unless the horse has a very comfortable canter, control at walk and trot are learned before a student canters. Speed often frightens new riders. Explain how and why to use the hand and the effect of the hand on the horse's perfor-

mance. This is included as part of the BIG PICTURE, but must be kept simple at this stage. Explain how the horse uses his head and neck and demonstrate the role of following hands.

 This is a complex step and instructors must encourage riders to be patient with themselves. ⚞

## Toolkit

⚞• Exercises for hands: As riders try to keep their hands steady while their bodies continue to move, the importance of flexible elbows and shoulders becomes apparent.

- • Hold hands at shoulder height for few strides, then straight above head and then in front, parallel with ground

- • Pat head and rub belly

- • Move extended arms slowly clockwise and counter clockwise with the thumb touching the middle finger and all other fingers extended

- • Hold reins correctly, drop and pick up; once this is easy, repeat in the half-seat position

- • Braid a rope while riding

- • Have students hold their hands in a position like they are reading a book. You can expand this exercise to include "tell me a story," which has the student "reading" out loud their pretend story. This gets their minds off thinking, and allows relaxation to happen. Students often laugh as they try to tell you their story, which requires relaxing!

COMFORTABLE YET?

- • Have students pretend to serve a platter of appetizers

⚞• Practice holding the reins, but without contact, and follow the motion of the horse's head

*Test to move to Step 4:* Riders can walk and trot around the ring (ideally still on the lunge line) holding the reins correctly and following the horse's head and neck, without holding themselves on the horse with their hands.

| COMMON RIDING MISTAKES in Stage 1 | |
|---|---|
| Gripping with legs to stay on (knee is most common, then thigh, and calf) | This is a normal, natural early response to the body's feelings of danger and unbalance. Riders need to be educated NOT to do this, and the best way is lunge line lessons on a safe, reliable horse. Unsuitable horses MAKE riders grip out of necessity- because they are automatically in "survival mode." |
| Using stirrups as a "floor" | This keeps the foot either level, toe down, or heel up, all of which are dangerous and are ABSOLUTELY incorrect positions for the foot. Without the heel being down (in a relaxed, not forced, way) the ankle cannot absorb the shock of the horse's movement, so other parts of the body have to respond to the shock (example: gripping leg; stiff, tight back). |
| Sitting too far back, or perched too far forward in saddle | Sitting back is usually an attempt by riders to keep their seats in the saddle during bouncy trot work rather than teaching their pelvises to move with the horse's movement. Perching forward is also the result of stiff, untrained hips; but here the rider chooses to literally "get out of a bad situation!" |
| Slouching the back, dropping the neck (Sometimes called "chicken neck") | This is also a result of a stiff pelvis and lower back. By slouching, the rider tries to absorb the movement of the horse in the abdominal section. The problem with this (besides looking funny!) is that the hips stay locked, and do not learn the flexibility necessary for developing a good seat. |
| Rocking the upper body or lower legs with the motion of the horse | This is especially seen in canter. The root cause is the same for both problems - a locked, stiff pelvis (starting to see a pattern?). The human body HAS to move with the horse somehow. If the pelvis is locked, then the upper body or lower legs (often both!) pick up the slack. Ideally, the upper body and lower legs stay quiet and still, and the rider's midsection (hips) absorbs the movement. The problem with this fault is the same answer as above - the rider does not learn how to develop a following seat - which severely limits what the rider can ask of, and do on, a horse. |
| Hanging on the reins for balance | This is a cardinal sin that is seen all too often today. It can be extreme, but typically riders who use the reins for balance do not look like they are doing this at first glance. However, it quickly becomes clear when riders are asked to relax their arms or soften the reins after a request. When riders do try to relax and soften, they become more unbalanced and may start bouncing, which is uncomfortable for them. Again, as their hips learn to become flexible and move with the horse, riders will find their own balance, and will no longer need to "borrow" their balance from their horse's reins (or their sensitive mouths!). |

Chart 35

Common Instructor Mistakes in Stage 1

• **Too much theory:** Since everything is new to the beginning student, it is easy to want to teach too much theory (strongly cognitive instructors will be especially tempted to do this – it is their own comfort zone). Talking interferes with the rider's ability to learn to feel movement. Even with adults who tend to want to learn cognitively first, theory needs to be kept brief and simple. Kids do better without theory or with as little as possible. If they ask questions, then share simple, brief, and clear explanations - even if they are not "classically correct" in their simplicity. Kids want the basic idea, and then they want to "get on with it"- to ride! How much theory is needed and when is the appropriate time to discuss it are decisions for each instructor to make, remembering that the more people think, the less they feel.

• **Too much too soon:** Doing too much in one lesson. Often instructors think that beginners might be bored because what they are learning is so basic, so instructors try to teach too much, too fast. Remember that for beginners everything is new and exciting, so teach only one or two skills at a time.

• **Too boring:** Since so much repetition is needed, instructors need to be active, enthusiastic and creative to make practicing the same skill over and over again interesting.

 Important teaching techniques that will help students have a fun and successful learning experience include: using an orderly approach when introducing a new skill, being certain that one skill is well learned before adding another, and repeating corrections as frequently as needed in a kind, clear, but definite voice. Sometimes it may be tempting to skip steps, especially in certain situations (for example: bored students, naturally gifted riders, pressure from a student or a parent to move up faster, etc.), but skipping steps does a disservice to the rider in the long term.

## Step 4 – Natural Aids and Communication

*Objective:* To help riders a) understand what parts of the rider's body control the various parts of the horse, and b) see that their positions can be maintained while using the aids. There are three specific goals to teach the rider at this step:

• The use of the natural aids.

• How to understand and communicate in horse language so the student can communicate most effectively with the horse.

• How to keep the horse aware of and listening to the rider.

*Theory:* The relationship between controlling route/direction and the rider's balance and ability to stay on the horse is important. Being in control allows relaxation and builds confidence in both horse and rider. The natural aids are the most important methods for communicating with and controlling the horse, so a correct understanding in this stage will benefit the rider throughout all the subsequent stages.

*Important Points:*
Explain the basics of control as indicated in chart 36 below.

### THE USE OF THE NATURAL AIDS

Describe the role of the hand, leg, voice and seat (at this point, insist that riders simply continue to follow the horse's motion with the seat, learning to use the other natural aids without changing the seat).

| NATURAL AIDS & ELEMENTARY CONTROL | | | |
|---|---|---|---|
| First introduction to aids is simple and basic | | | |
| Aid | Communicates via | Controls | Explanation |
| Hand | Reins | Direction & Speed | **Child**: Like steering and stopping on your bicycle |
| | | | **Adult**: Like driving a car on "automatic" |
| Leg | Being used on & behind the girth | Creates power & energy | **Child**: This is the "on button" |
| | | | **Adult**: Legs create energy like the gas pedal creates energy for your car |
| Seat | Seat motion | Allows forward energy by following | **Child**: Follows like on a swing |
| | | | **Adult**: Follows like the runners on a rocking chair |
| Voice | Mouth | Helps other aids | **Child**: Like talking to your dog |
| | | | **Adult**: Same explanation as child |

Chart 36

During this step students must understand the BIG PICTURE. They also must know why they are being taught to maintain a light contact with their natural aids now, and that they will be building on this contact throughout their learning experiences. Make it clear that adding too much or incorrect contact too soon will interfere with the rider's control by confusing the horse.

### HOW TO COMMUNICATE VIA HORSE LANGUAGE

Briefly discuss the basic concepts of horse communication – that horses naturally seek a pressure-free and pain-free state, have simple minds and are innately lazy, and above all seek comfort. The horse therefore understands the following cycle of communication from the rider:

the rider applies pressure, the horse yields, and the rider releases the pressure! Simple!

**The communication cycle (PARR):**

- **P**repare the horse
- **A**sk
- **R**esponse by the horse
- **R**eward the horse's response

### KEEPING THE HORSE AWARE AND LISTENING TO HIS RIDER

Understanding the communication cycle and teaching the rider the importance of controlling route/direction are two of the most essential skills for safe and effective riding. Teach them correctly from the very beginning by insisting that the student prepare the horse for a change, ask for it, expect the horse to make a timely response and *reward* the horse for answering! The consistent use of this cycle of communication facilitates balance and control of the horse. It may seem like this is an abundance of information for the novice rider, but it is not. It is a fairly simple sequence of events: prepare, ask, response, reward (PARR), that quickly can become a habit, even for young riders. An understanding of the communication cycle will enable the student to understand the role of the aids and better feel the results. The instructor's repetition of each step of a command will help the student learn to coordinate the aids and complete the communication cycle for that command while maintaining relaxation and a correct position. The horse's correct response to the rider's actions will give the rider confidence in the control panel.

*The three elements that work together to stay on route, thus develop confidence are:*
*1) PARR,*
*2) Use of natural aids and*
*3) A clear intent of mind.*

The second confidence builder related to control is insisting that the rider direct the horse on route around the arena. Under all conditions the horse must go 'on the route' the riders expects. During this Stage keep the route simple and easy to follow. The rider's balance and relaxation improve when riders learn to feel that they are in control.

**Toolkit**

Demonstrate with explanation: Make it clear that the more relaxed the rider, the more quickly and accurately the horse will respond. It is helpful to give an overview demonstration of the communication cycle in action. This gives the student an overall picture of the objective.

🐎 Exercises to practice the communication cycle (using this format when teaching beginners a new skill ensures the development of a valuable habit that carries over into all interactions with horses)
  • Action: Go from halt to walk

    Communication cycle between instructor, rider, and horse:

    Prepare:      Instructor asks student to prepare the horse to walk
                  Rider shortens reins and gives initial squeeze with
                      leg

    Ask:          Instructor asks student, "Ask horse to trot by tap-
                      ping your leg on his side."
                  Student does so

    Response:     Horse walks
                  Instructor asks rider to reward horse

    Reward:       Rider follows with arms
                      Stops tapping with legs
                      Release squeeze of legs
                      Maybe pat horse!

🐎 Walk around the perimeter of arena. While maintaining position, the rider learns to walk around the ring, staying on route, practicing the different exercises used on the lunge line. Here, the rider is encouraged to be careful with the horse's mouth. The communication cycle is used to keep the horse on the perimeter.

🐎 Practice figures at the walk – turns, diagonals and large circles – while using the communication cycle to guide the horse where the rider wants him to go.

🐎 Trot around arena – add exercises used on the lunge line at the trot.

🐎 Perform walk–trot–walk transitions using the communication cycle.

🐎 Ride into the corners. Once the student can stay on route, have the student give with the inside hand for one to two steps in the corner (remember to give a simple explanation to help the student understand how to get the horse into the corner).

🐎 Ride ring figures at walk and trot. Ideal order: diagonals, circles, figure eights & serpentines.

🐎 Maintain an even rhythm at the trot.

🐎 Ride in the half-seat position over caveletti and small jumps.

🐎 Giving with one hand and regaining contact without disturbing the horse's route or rhythm

🐎 Practice going from long rein to light contact.

🐎 "Me and my shadow" – this is a common exercise, good to use when teaching the rider the proper "feel" of the contact. Have the rider and instructor hold a rope or rein between them (on the horse and off). Have the rider move his or her arms around, giving the instructor a chance to demonstrate how to create an elastic-like feeling in the rein. In other words, the instructor will successfully shadow every movement the rider makes, without tension or restricting in any way. Then switch, and have the rider try to do this while the instructor is the one to move. This is also a great exercise to do when you can pair up students.

---

**Keep lessons safe, interesting, fun, and educational, but also challenging .**
*Here are some suggestions for how to do this:*

- Trail ride
- Exercises while mounted
- If a student usually has private lessons, add some group riding
- Have students try a new discipline once or twice – jumping for the dressage rider, western for the hunt seat rider, etc.
- Have students ride different horses

Chart 37

---

*Test to move to Step 5:* The horse willingly and comfortably walks and trots when and where the rider asks while the rider maintains a correct and relaxed position. Ask questions until students can readily describe what parts of their bodies control what parts of the horse's body as they continue to demonstrate. The student must maintain a following, non-interfering hand at the walk and posting trot, while retaining a correct position with a happy, willing horse.

| SUPPORT the LEARNING PROCESS | | |
|---|---|---|
| Astute, aware instructors can suggest non-riding skills to enhance riding education | | |
| **Supplement Skill** | **Age** | **Benefit** |
| Relaxation | Adult | Helpful for students who are nervous, timid, stiff, or afraid without an obvious cause |
| Goal Setting | All | Creates plan for progress |
| Visualization | All | Promotes positive learning |
| Positive responses/self-talk | All | Helpful when students reveal negative self-talk or doubts |
| Exercise | Adult | Create body awareness & flexibility |

Chart 38

## Step 5 – Position in Sitting Trot, Canter and Over Small Jumps

*Objective:* Maintain the correct position at the sitting trot, canter and over small jumps while retaining body balance and control without interfering with the horse.

*Theory:* Movement and flexibility of the hips is a key point for being able to sit the trot and canter, and staying with the horse over jumps. Jumping exercises are most helpful in creating hip flexibility, suppleness and usefulness. Pivoting at the hip while maintaining the lower body depth and upper body relaxation allows the rider to absorb the horse's forward thrust over the jump so the horse can jump without interference.

### Toolkit

- Explain the mechanics of hip movement and demonstrate it for visual learners.

- Alternate between posting trot, half-seat, and sitting trot with about 6 steps in each, while maintaining the horse's rhythm.

- Transitions between walk and sitting trot, 10-20 steps in each.

- Trot without stirrups, with the toe hanging loose and the seat following the motion of horse, thus promoting balance.

- Canter, first in half-seat position, building to sitting in the saddle in the canter

- The exercise of leaning forward to touch the chin on the horse's crest and then leaning back from the lower hip joint while keeping the lower legs in position is excellent for helping riders feel their hips open and close, as well as suppling the hip joint. It is important to keep the chest open and up, and the lower leg maintaining the correct position.

- Observation: have student watch a horse and rider over a jump while pointing out the action of the horse and then the rider.

- Practice the release to be used over the jump first at the walk and trot, then progress to ground poles and caveletti, and finally to grids and small jumps.

- Jump small fences at the trot.

*Test to move to Stage 2:* Rider can perform at walk, trot, canter, and over cavalletti and small jumps while maintaining a correct position on a comfortable and willing horse who follows the rider's instructions for direction (route) and speed.

After each step ask, "Can the rider maintain the correct position with elastic joints, weight going down through the heels, steady hands, and an even pace while completing the exercises?" If "Yes," then continue with the sequence.

**INSTRUCTOR'S REMINDER**

Prompt students to stay in the "now" so that as they develop their riding skills, they become automatically aware of their bodies' balance and relaxation, their horses' direction, relaxation, route, and speed, and thus the team's overall balance. Keeping awareness of the body is an important part of developing a rider's automatic muscle response from the very beginning. **A body that KNOWS from experience what to do (rather than simply a brain that THINKS it knows) is the goal of our teaching.**

Once students have completed the tests at this stage they are ready for more advanced topics. Moving to Stage 2 of Rider Education can be celebrated as a big step for students. Ideas: Certificates, a free lesson, student's name on the bulletin board, or acknowledgment by a barn party. Be innovative!

## STAGE 2
# USE OF AIDS

*Stage 1 of Rider Education helped students develop a balanced position and elementary control of the horse.*

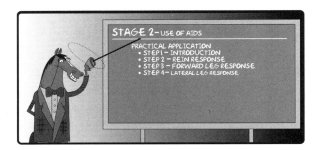

### GOALS OF STAGE 2

There are four goals specific to this stage in a rider's education. They are to:

1. Teach riders how to apply the basic rein and leg aids correctly, while maintaining correct position at all three gaits.

2. Help students continue to develop their physical balance and coordination at all three gaits and over small fences.

3. Introduce the student to the concept of "riding by feel" by emphasizing body awareness and horse response, instead of memorization, when applying the aids.

4. Help students use the proper rein and leg aids over small fences and between jumps when riding courses.

### THEORY

In order to teach the basic aids to students in Stage 2, instructors need to be well versed in the following concepts: Forward Energy, Basic Straightness, Bend and Flexion, and Circle of Muscles. Riders learn and understand the effects of the aids on the horse most efficiently when they have an ***elementary*** knowledge of the mechanics of a horse's movement.

 Because the instructor's understanding of theory is more thorough (and needs to be), care needs to be taken not to overwhelm students with all theory's details and nuances. Teach the basic, underlying principles so that the student understands "why," but no more! Simple language is best, with clear, practical examples. Sophistication in the understanding of theory develops gradually. 🦌

## THE IDEAL WORLD

Under ideal circumstances, riders would progress from Stage 1 having developed basic body balance and elementary control

*"If a rider initially learns the wrong things concerning the feeling of the aids or the horse's body (or if an instructor teaches the wrong things at this stage), it will become necessary to correct such problems later in the rider's education, where it can be frustrating and time consuming for both riders and instructors."*

— Stephan Kiesewetter

on a horse that is safe and appropriate for beginners. These riders' education can then progress onwards to Stage 2, where they learn to further refine their use of the natural aids. In this ideal world, riders at Stage 2 of their education begin to learn the "correct feel" of a horse's response to their aids while continuing to improve and refine their body balance on the flat and over small fences. For such important and correct learning to take place, the rider needs a horse that is properly trained, and responds immediately and correctly to all appropriately applied aids, yet lets the rider know when the aids are improperly applied. At this stage, it is important that the rider perceives the horse to be safe and trustworthy. Under such ideal conditions, riders learn quickly and efficiently, as they are guided by the instruction and feedback of both the instructor and the horse. The ***horse should be a major part of the learning process, and will be IF it is well schooled, safe, and can be considered a school master for the rider.*** At times, riders may need a different horse for Stage 2 than was ideal for Stage 1, as the skills needed to be a good lunge line horse may not be the same skills needed to respond sensitively and correctly to the application of the aids. In this ideal world, riders do not become overly attached or bonded to horses that are inappropriate for them at this stage in their riding, and are willing to listen to the advice of their instructors before purchasing their own horses.

Beginner horses are worth their weight in gold, and in the perfect scenario, the rider agrees to lease or borrow one of these "saints."

## THE REAL WORLD

In the United States today, many riders begin riding without learning the correct, classic position. These riders have learned to use their aids from a faulty base of support. Unfortunately, with much practice, these riders can get quite "good" at what they do! In addition, muscle memory kicks in, and these incorrect position faults become habits, which are then hard to change. As well, many riders enter Stage 2 with continuing horse control problems, usually stemming from problems in the rider's position, greenness of the horse, or, far too often, both! A common way to spot these riders is to observe their efforts to seek out all the new methods and techniques for controlling the horse, in what appears to be a desperate attempt to bring about a missing sense of safety to their riding. In other situations control may be sought through the rider's misguided efforts to 'train' the horse. These riders are quick to latch onto the newest training "miracles," such as different bits, artificial aids, and unique training methods. These riders are full of enthusiasm and healthy curiosity, and they hope for positive results. Frequently, these riders are in a hurry to move forward, and can be quite a challenge to educate about the importance of the basics of position and balance. They want to be "there" right now! However, when these methods do not bring about the immediate results they were searching for these riders can become quite teachable, if not eager, students.

Instructors today are only one of the groups that are dealing with the consequences of the past decade's shift away from teaching the classical, correct position. Judges, clinicians, show managers, and many others are on the front line of today's reality in America. Many of our riders are coming up through their riding educations without a firm training in the basic, balanced position, resulting all too often in disastrous results for both horses and riders.

---

**Some of the Common Problems Instructors See**

- Using reins to balance
- Using reins to "set" the horse's head
- Using reins to slow the horse down
- Gripping incorrectly with the legs (thigh, knee, calf, or all three!)
- Riding horses that are too green for rider's skill level and therefore do not respond to the aids properly (may not respond to aids at all!)
- Riding horses who are too "hot" and high-spirited for rider's skill level
- Riding horses who are stiff, sullen, or spoiled
- Riding horses who are frightened and tense

Chart 39

---

## IMPORTANT POINTS

1. It is the instructor's challenge to a) assess the situation, b) diagnose the problem, and c) find a solution that intermixes the remedial work with the progressive work. This only happens when the instructor is well educated in the classic, correct position and its relationship to issues of control, and the theory behind both of these concepts. For example, many problems that occur in horse and rider combinations today stem from the fact that the rider is hanging on the reins too much. The fix is not just to tell the rider to stop pulling or hanging on the reins (which is seen so often!). For some students, the issue will be a combination of horse problems related to a lack of training, and rider problems, related to the lack of a sufficiently balanced and educated seat. If this is the case, the instructor must identify the problem (s), teach the student how to correct the problem(s) using exercises to fix it, and move on.

2. A balance must be sought between fixing the missing piece in the rider's education and continuing with the education in Stage 2. Many riders have mastered almost all of the Stage 1 skills but may be missing one or two key ingredients.

During this process of learning it is important to work towards making the student aware of what is happening through feel rather than through thought.

3. It is important to help riders understand and feel the influence of each individual aid so that their muscle memories are on the 'same page' as their knowledge.

4. Correct position remains at the forefront of the rider's awareness during this stage. Ideally instructors have riders review their positions during the warm-up so that students will be well prepared to begin adding a new skill. It would be nice to think that once a correct position has been established, it will never change; but even the best foundations are affected when students begin to make demands upon their bodies to influence the moving animal.

5. Create an awareness of route/direction, rhythm and straightness via the corrections we make throughout the lesson.

One of the reasons that so many riders show stiffness and a general lack of motion or tightness in their seats is because the rider wants to hold the correct position and stay "still." Instructors be aware to help riders understand that a fixed position prevents the horse from moving with any freedom and either dulls the horse's response to the aids or chases the horse away from the aids. Riders must move in order to be still on a moving horse.

*Stage 2: Use of Aids*   179

# PRACTICAL APPLICATION
## Step 1- Introduction to the Use of the Aids

*Objective:* To take what students have already learned in Stage 1 about the use of their legs and hands for basic control and to develop this further into a more comprehensive understanding of what the aids are, how they work, and the proper order to learn their use.

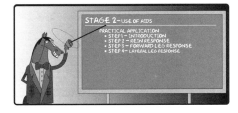

*Theory:* The rider's aids are basically used for control; in this stage students learn the basic understanding that their aids, working together, will control the route (direction), speed (rhythm & pace) and straightness (hind feet are traveling in the same track as the front feet) of the horse. These will continue to be developed through the stages to become the more finely tuned skills of rhythm (from speed), balance (from straightness) and throughness (from roundness).

The use of the natural aids; hands, legs, seat (sometimes called weight), and voice are:

Hands—regulate speed, route and position of head,

Legs—dictate speed, influence balance and route,

Seat—follows rhythm of horse (later it plays a much larger role),

Voice—used to assist other aids.

### AIDS AND THEIR ACTIONS

| Rider Part | Action | Horse Part | Communication effect |
|---|---|---|---|
| Hand | Fingers | Jaw, Poll, Neck | Direction, Speed, Flexion, Roundness |
| | Outside hand | Outside jaw & poll | Degree of roundness, pace, receiver of energy |
| | Inside hand | Inside jaw & poll | Neck flexion |
| Leg | Thigh with hand | Shoulder | Lightness, balance & direction of shoulder |
| | Calf at girth | Shoulder, front leg | Lighten shoulder, move forehand |
| | Calf behind girth | Hind leg | Forward energy of hind leg & engagement |
| Seat | Motion | Back & hind leg | Energy |
| Shoulders | Balanced | Shoulders | |
| Hips | Motion | Hips | |
| Eyes | Direction | Whole horse | Weight distribution & direction |
| | | | Chart 40 |

Time needs to be spent teaching the students what the natural aids are used for in addition to which parts of the student's body controls each part of the horse's body.

*Important Points*

1. Tie in the horse communication skills from Stage 1 with the use of aids in Stage 2, and be prepared to continue to remind students to use them as they learn the steps in Stage 2.

There are a lot of new ideas in Stage 2, and instructors are cautioned to introduce the overview as simply as possible and to refer back to the appropriate theory as a student develops through the Stage.

**Toolkit**

- Instructor and student discuss the theory behind the use of rein aids.
- Have student watch the use of aids in action by either watching the instructor ride and describe what is happening, or by observing an experienced rider demonstrate the use of aids.
- Have the rider or instructor explain what is going on, moment to moment.
- Have the student explain, in their own words, the BIG PICTURE behind the use of aids.

*Test to move to Step 2:* Ask questions to evaluate the student's understanding of what each aid is used for and how it is used. Discuss some specific skills exemplified during the demonstration. Have the student ride around the ring demonstrating what was learned about the aids in Stage 1, and connect it to what will be added in Stage 2.

Instructors may find themselves demonstrating and discussing frequently throughout this step.

## Step 2 - Rein Response

*Objective:* Develop contact and "educated hands," which can maintain a consistent feel in the reins and receive the energy coming (however little to begin with) from the hind leg through the back into an elastic even contact.

*Theory:* Without understanding the concept of the rein aids and the ability to feel the response of the horse when an aid is given, a rider has no alternative to pulling and holding on the horse's mouth. This is why rein response is introduced before leg response in this stage. By following the steps to learning rein response, students develop confidence and feel as they begin to ride their horses with even contact FROM the horses' hind legs TO the hand.

This step is the appropriate time to explain the theory behind flexion and bending, and the physiology of the circle of muscles (see theory chapter). This may help the mature rider better understand how bending actually works. This step on rein response is more detailed than most of the other steps. I include the detail because it may save you the two years it took me to experiment with it. Because the theory and application of the eight Rein Responses is new, the detailed theory is included in this step, rather than in our theory section.

*Using too much forward leg aid before the rein aid is understood and can be used effectively causes holding because the rider does not have the knowledge and skill to correctly receive and direct the energy created by the leg.*

Basic rules to impart:
• Use only one aid at a time
• Expect an immediate response to any request made with hand or leg
• Expect light, consistent responses to all aids

*Background:* I learned an exercise from John Lyons in 1996, and while what he taught made sense, I was worried that it placed too much emphasis on the hands to the neglect of the leg aids. I discovered through experimentation that teaching his eight-step rein response provided unexpected positive results. It took me another two years of interacting with my students to learn why it worked so well. Students told me that learning the rein response enabled them to feel more in control, thus they could relax their arms and hands and stop holding or pulling. They gained confidence and feel by learning this rein response. Before the rein response is taught riders must be comfortable enough not to use their hands for balance or for staying on the horse. By teaching the individual rein responses, the student feels the response, and when it is time to move the horse from the inside leg to the outside hand, the rider can feel it because of the muscle memory achieved in these exercises. Sue and her big warmblood mare are a good **example.** Sue came into the ring with her mare's head straight up and her own arms tight and holding. While Sue's basic position was very good, she was stiff in her seat as well as her arms. Sue had been told by a professional to never use one rein apart from the other, but instead to hold onto both reins and drive her horse forward from her legs. The good student that she was, she had been practicing this even hold for months. Her horse tuned her out and continued to work hollow every day for at least forty minutes. Sue spent most of her lesson walking and working to get the mare to respond to a neck bend on each side. Sue had to learn to be strong with her hand at times, while remaining relaxed in her joints and using her leg to get the mare to release in the shoulder. The mare was very responsive to the leg, so each time Sue used her leg she trotted. We decided to use the counter bend and let the wall help. Sue was a quick-minded teenager, and was able to hold her bending hand still, while using her leg on the girth. When the mare trotted, Sue told her to walk with the non-bending hand. Once the mare responded, Sue gained confidence and was able to give the necessary release. The second day Sue thought we had performed a miracle, as she was able to walk and trot with control, keeping the mare round. She was even able to ride straight into both hands for short intervals, and we added some canter. One month later Sue reported that she was able to walk, trot and canter with the mare going forward to her hands with rhythm!

The Eight Rein Responses teach the rider about rein aids. Taking the time to teach these responses ensures students can use their hands correctly as they progress through the stages.

---

**The 8 Rein Responses**

Response 1 - Small give (basis of next 7 steps)
Response 2 - Horse moves head slightly in direction of rein aid
Response 3 - Long muscle in neck relaxes
Response 4 - Poll is within 4" of the centerline, not more, and there is a
             uniform arc in neck from poll to withers
Response 5 - Bit is under eye
Response 6 - Wrinkles in horse's shoulder joint
Response 7 - Lower shoulder muscles begin to relax
Response 8 - A spot about 4" below withers on shoulder begins to lighten

Chart 41

---

**The Eight Rein Responses:** To progress from the "small give" to the creation of a soft joint in the horse's shoulder, the following responses need to be taught to get the feel of effective signal-responses. With each of the Eight Responses there is an explanation and a toolkit.

### RESPONSE 1
*Small Give (the horse responds to the rein by moving at least 1 inch)*
This exercise is used to teach: (1) an inexperienced horse to respond to the rein, (2) a somewhat experienced rider to learn to use the fingers separately from the whole arm, or (3) a combination of the first two. The need to teach both horse and rider arises fairly often since most horses and riders have yet to learn this properly. The "small give"

is instrumental in teaching the "soft" hands needed to receive the energy from the horse and to literally leave the lines open for communication. Once the "small give" is learned, it can be used for suppling, training, and rebalancing.

To get the "small give" the rider neither pulls on the reins nor allows the horse to pull away from the direction of the bit. Instead, the rider closes his or her fingers on the rein on the side the horse is to give towards, allowing the horse to move only his head and neck in the direction of that rein (at this stage, the amount does not matter). The goal is for the horse to give correctly to the fingers and not pull his head away from the aid. While learning this response, the horse may try to pull against the rider's hand. If this occurs, the rider continues to steadily hold the hand position, and if the horse pulls very strongly, the rider may stabilize the hand position by pressing the knuckles against the horse's withers or the saddle to prevent the horse from pulling through. A rider never needs to pull back against a horse that is pulling, but rather should simply hold the rein position steady. Once the horse gives, then the rider immediately releases, as a reward for the correct response.

When the horse gives, the give will have energy. The energy comes from the jawbone moving with lightness and ease in the direction corresponding to the rein. The jawbone "comes alive" when the horse gives an immediate response to the rider. The rider acknowledges the release with a pat, expecting the horse to keep the "small give." The horse must learn to maintain the give until the rider asks the horse to straighten his neck and head. The rider needs to repeat this frequently to confirm it to muscle memory. (John Lyons said 10,000 repeats to commit to memory, but I have discovered a new skill can be confirmed in far less repetitions!)

Most trainers automatically use flexion and bending as needed; these rein responses are a way to break it down so the student knows what goes into the use of the hand.

### RESPONSE 2

*The horse's head moves one to four inches in response to the "small give" rein aid.*

Once the horse learns the small give, the rider must be careful to communicate clearly in this next response by asking for an equal number of inches of bend to each side.

Often the horse will give one or more responses at the same time. After Response 1, the small give, the order of the response varies with each horse. The order listed is the most common order of response. Most important is for the instructor to draw the students' attention to each response, so they can gain positive muscle memory and connect it to their rein actions (and often the corresponding leg action). ⚐

## RESPONSE 3

*Long muscle in the horse's neck relaxes and becomes unblocked. (See 7A)*

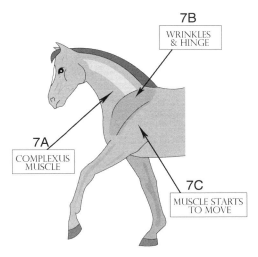

7B
WRINKLES & HINGE

7A
COMPLEXUS MUSCLE

7C
MUSCLE STARTS TO MOVE

## RESPONSE 4

*The poll of the horse can move anywhere between 4" above and 4" below the elevation of the withers (students must be taught to notice the most comfortable response from their horse) with a nice arc and banana shaped curve in the neck, beginning about a quarter of the way up the crest and going to the ears. The base of the neck remains in the center of the chest.*

## RESPONSE 5

*The horse begins to bring his nose toward the base of the neck, in line with the point of the shoulder; the bit is directly under the eye.*

## RESPONSE 6

*Wrinkles begin to develop in the base of the neck.*

The muscle at the base of the neck begins to relax and soften. The horse begins to use this portion of his neck to help carry his body. This is a correct result of properly using the previous responses, and is something we want students to recognize and feel.

## RESPONSE 7

*Lower shoulder muscle begins to work and become more flexible and responsive.*

## RESPONSE 8

*An area about four inches below the withers lightens on the side of the asking rein.*

---

**IMPORTANT RULES TO ESTABLISH WITH STUDENT**
**The simple rules that accompany the goal to get a "banana-like bend"**

- Base of the horse's neck stays in the center of the chest and the neck begins to bend about a quarter of the way up the crest.
- Horse keeps his body straight from withers to tail.
- Horse remains on route as much as possible (in responses 1 & 2 there are occasions when the horse will deviate from the route until the horse responds correctly to the small give.
- Horse maintains the same rhythm (again while responses 1 & 2 are practiced, rhythm may be lost, however, before moving to response 3, route and rhythm need to be reestablished).

Chart 41A

---

*Important Points*

1. Keep a careful eye on students to help them learn the feel of a correct give. The rider needs to develop increased sensitivity to small changes in the horse following a slight release in the aid called a "small give."

2. Riders often automatically use their legs to help get the response from the rein. This can be encouraged without detail and with attention drawn to feel to benefit muscle memory.

3. It must be clear to the student that the holding required to initially get this response on the average horse is in the HAND ONLY, while all other joints must remain as relaxed as possible. As soon as the horse responds the student must release by changing the holding hand into a soft hand. For riders in the early stages of learning this skill (and when working with stiff horses), the horse seldom maintains the bend after the release. The rider feels this and has the natural desire to hold it. Teach the student that it is OK to ask again when the horse loses the bend. With consistent repetition, the horse learns that it is to hold the bend until the rider asks the horse to straighten the neck and head. The RELEASE is the most important part of the response as it is the reward.

Instructors need to take whatever time is necessary for the student to feel the individual response. Each feel needs to be confirmed. ➤

---

## Questions Most Frequently Asked While Learning Correct Rein Response

**Q. Why is it so important to use only one rein at a time while learning?**
*A. It helps the horse and rider to develop independent responses in individual body parts. Before the reins can be used together, they must be able to be used separately. Both reins used simultaneously can block the energy or the horse's desire to move from back to front.*

**Q. When can the other rein be used during this learning process?**
*A. Use the non-bending rein and appropriate leg for only a split second when it is needed to:*

- *Help the horse stay on route,*
- *Correct over-bending,*
- *Control speed.*

**Q. How is a correct response rewarded?**
*A. As soon as the horse correctly gives and lightens to the bending rein, then a pat is given with the bending rein. At this point, the horse has correctly accepted the outside (non-bending) rein.*

**Q. How is the bending exercise correctly completed?**
*A. When the rider has finished with the bend, the bending rein is released as the opposite rein and leg is used to communicate the plan to return to the straight-ahead position.*

**Q. Why is staying on route so important during the bending process?**
*A. If the horse is allowed to deviate from the rider's desired route or if the horse changes the bend in another part of his body, it is an evasion.*

Chart 42

---

**Toolkit**

➤ Explain the eight rein responses with primary focus first on the 'small give.'

➤ Help students feel how to use their fingers while allowing their arms and joints to remain elastic and relaxed. Often riders are tense in their arms, preventing the use of their fingers alone without elbow, wrist or shoulder involvement. To remedy this there are two actions that work well:

- **Hand & Elbow:** When horses are not responding, have the rider stop and ask permission to feel his or her hand and elbow. With one hand gently hold the student's elbow, and hold your other hand over the student's hand that is holding the rein. Have the rider ask the horse for a "small give." You will feel the area of tightness that is causing the horse to resist. Now you can explain and demonstrate this to the student. With your hand still over his or her hand, ask the horse to give and your student will feel your elastic wrist and elbow but strong use of your fingers. Follow this by asking the student to repeat the exercise until you think that the student can get the result alone.

- **Lead line:** Get a long lead or lunge line. Hold the horse, and ask the student to throw one end of the line out onto the ground and then pull it back in using just the fingers. Ask the student to describe how it feels compared holding the rein. This helps a student to develop feel, but only for riders who are not locking their joints.

Teach the student to ask the horse for a "small give." Once the rider consistently receives the give requested on both reins independently at the walk, the exercise may be done at the trot. Introduce the 'small give' using the counter bend to introduce the 'small give.' This exercise makes bending easier through using the walls of the arena to help keep the horse on route. The purpose of this exercise is to have both horse and rider learn to feel a response to one rein only. Some helpful hits as you use this exercise: 1) begin at the walk first—movement is helpful in obtaining the proper release, 2) the non-bending hand remains uninvolved except to give occasional directions related to route and speed, 3) teach the student the correct aids to straighten the horse after bending so as not to allow the horse to just fall out of the bend.

Stiff, resistant horses with well-coordinated riders often benefit from beginning this exercise at the trot while extremely stubborn and pulling horses, or riders with fear are better off beginning in halt.

Develop awareness in your student by asking them to have their horse respond with equal lightness and number of inches of bend on each side. 1) Ask the student to bend the horse a specific number of inches. Determine the number of inches to ask for by how far the horse can bend to his stiffest side (note, no part of the horse's body is allowed to bend other than the neck and head), 2) when the horse responds to a rein message correctly, ask the student to pat the horse with the bending hand, keeping the rein in her hand. This rewards the behavior and builds trust between the horse and rider. Help the student understand and practice maintaining the consistent bend and returning to straightness at the rider's request to straighten his neck.

🐎Continue to ask for accurate small gives, help the student notice (you are teaching awareness to your student) the signs of relaxation in the horse's neck and ask a few simple 'feel' questions:
- Muscles begin to relax and bounce as horse moves.
- Neck begins to develop a nice arc or curve. Where the neck arches and curves is critical, as is the bulging of the complexus muscle, otherwise, the arch or curve can be "false."

🐎Ask the student to bring the horse's bit under the eye. Bring the student's attention to the horse's reaction of stretching his nose out and down. The rider feels that the horse wants to get more elastic in the hand and stretch. It is important to maintain the contact with this feeling, and not let the horse stretch down more than the rider asks for (maximum is 4" downward stretch).

- Exercise to help riders understand how this feels to the horse Get down on all fours.
  First, hollow your back. What does your neck want to do?

  (Answer = Come up, invert, raises head upwards)

  Next, arch your back - make your back "round." What does your neck want to do?

  (Answer = Arch, curl, bring head slightly forward and downward)

  Can you feel the pull at the base of your neck? Can you also feel that as you round your back more and more, you want to raise your head while your head is down? This is what happens to the horse! The first feeling is the long and low stretching movement seen in the early stages of training. As the horse increases engagement and energy, the back becomes rounder, which lifts the neck, and the horse now makes the "telescoping gesture."

🐎Draw rider's attention to the feel when the neck to shoulder joint begins to show its hinge. This can happen at any time. (See 7B page 185)

The key to getting the correct response is to make certain the rider has elastic joints and is using a steady hand, with only the fingers providing the pressure on the reins, while the wrist, elbow, and shoulder remain relaxed. Tight, rigid wrists and forearms (the most common reining interferences) reduce the ability of a rider to feel the energy and respond appropriately (see earlier exercise Hand & Arm & Lead line). 🐎

🐎Begin more complex exercises while continuing to practice the correct small give.

- **Bend to the inside:** The goal for this exercise is to add the inside leg to the bending rein aid in a non-threatening way. This exercise is more challenging, as most horses will move in the direction of the applied rein. Without the help of an arena wall, the rider must learn to use the inside leg to help keep the horse on route. The non-bending rein can also be used to help stay on route if it is needed. Practice bending and straightening until it becomes easy, being careful to maintain a minimum of six steps in each position, bent and straight. NEVER GO FROM ONE BEND TO THE OTHER without completely straightening the horse in between. NEVER SEESAW the bit.

- **Change of direction maintaining exactly the same bend:** The goal is for the rider to feel the role of the inside leg in maintaining the bend, while the focus remains on keeping the same contact with the bending rein. The outside rein is used only as needed.

As you recognize the horse responding correctly ask your student to notice: 1)that both the muscle on the upper inside of the neck and the lower muscle on the outside of the neck begin to enlarge. The strengthening of this portion of the neck (the scalenus muscle) through training allows the horse's front end to lift, transferring weight to the horse's hind end, which in turn gets stronger and results in a horse that is more evenly balanced through his back. 2)Notice that on the side of the horse where the rider has picked up the rein the lower shoulder muscle ripples. This shoulder weight shifts in the opposite direction from the asking rein(the horse does not change route/direction). The shoulder muscles give to the inside rein and inside leg (which the rider must use to stay on route while maintaining the bend). (See 7C page 185) 3)Notice this area below the withers as it lightens and moves in the opposite direction from the asking rein, and is lifted slightly.

Once the student learns the eight rein responses, one by one, and practices them consistently and correctly, the response will become automatic and later will develop into part of the half-halt. Teach each step thoroughly until the student feels the desired response. ⚞

*Most common evasions:*

- Maintain the desired route and speed while changing both bend and direction.

- Bend the horse equally to each side.

- Do not allow the horse and rider to change the bend without having a few straight steps in between.

Often riders mix this response with a horse going long and low and gladly allow the horse to stretch down. It is great for the student to NOTICE the response, but not let the horse stretch until he is asked by the rider. This is a good feeling to be combined with asking the horse to stretch long and low.

*Test to move to Step 3:* Ask the rider to demonstrate bending the horse through the rein responses to each side while staying on route. Watch that there is no backward action on the reins, and that the horse remains straight through his body, withers to tail, with the same rhythm and on route.

During lessons and training students frequently need to be reminded to maintain responsiveness to the aids. Checking the horse's responsiveness is also a part of each day's warm up.

## Step 3 – Forward Leg Response

*Objective:* To teach the student how to use the leg aid correctly to get timely and correct forward responses from the horse. Clarify the difference between a leg used at the girth and a leg used behind the girth.

*Theory:* Definition of forward = A horse that moves with a combination of energy and engagement.

Energy = activity, enthusiasm, NOT dull or lazy.

Engagement = the ability of the horse to bring his hind legs far up towards the front of his body.

This means that a forward horse moves actively, but does so by taking as long a step behind as possible; not by speeding up, jigging or changing gait. In this stage, the rider begins to learn about the concept of forward and lateral energy being created by the leg aids. Both horse and rider need to recognize the feeling of a small response from the horse for either going forward or moving laterally when the leg is applied. Initially the rider trains a forward response to the leg. Review the concepts of position, seat, and the circle of muscles (see theory chapter) in order to help students understand how the leg aids function and why the horse responds the way he does when the leg is applied.

*Important Points*

1. "No engine, no ride," as the saying goes. The horse is the power source, and if a rider is unable to initiate a response with as little effort as one uses to turn the key in the ignition of a car, the end result is an unresponsive, dull horse. If beginning riders are put

on non- or incorrectly responsive horses they may become tight, busy, or harsh in using the aids. To prevent these faults the school horse must learn to respond to a simple pressure from the leg.

2. Likewise riders must understand that their horses need the consistency of a leg that is softly on the horse's sides at all times. Just as gripping with the calf can drive horses forward, so can taking the leg away from the horse. Riders on horses that want to go too fast need to learn to keep their legs softly on the horses. Instructors need to create exercises for these riders and their horses to help them gain confidence while the leg remains on the horse. If a rider's legs are not resting quietly on the horse's sides, when the rider wants to use the leg, the movement required to put the leg into position can disrupt the horse. Again, this is related to control. Riders need to feel in control while their legs are on the horse, and they need to recognize that the action of the leg both creates the forward motion and relaxes the horse.

3. **One-Two-Three Rule:** There are three consistent, sequential actions to develop effective responses by the horse to communication through the rider's leg. First, the rider applies a leg aid with a light squeeze of the calf. If the horse does not respond by moving forward immediately, the rider gives a quick kick with the leg. If the horse still does not respond, the rider delivers a quick, firm tap with the whip or crop behind the leg at the same time that the leg is used. This last combination

> *The rider's mind needs to focus on the desired result, not how to do it. THINK IT, BELIEVE IT!*

should be firm enough to make the horse really jump forward. Reward the horse when it responds (even if it goes more forward than you originally wanted), and go back to the first light aid again.

4. Before actually applying the forward leg aid:
   - The student's leg must be lying softly on the side of the horse, as gently as a boot touches the leg it covers.
   - The rider must understand the subtle communication of asking (versus gripping) with the leg.
   - The rider's body weight must be traveling down the inside of the leg and out the heel to ensure a firm, deep leg.
   - The rider needs to know how important the placement of the leg is. When not giving an aid, it is to remain in the correct

position. To ask for forward motion or to move one of the horse's hind legs, the rider's leg moves slightly back (1-2").

- Riders must understand that their weight travels from the center of their body through their seat and out their heels, and that their seat follows the motion of energy that begins in the hind leg and travels through the back of the horse, the riders seat to the bit.

Upward transitions between gaits with an immediate response to the leg. For riders at this level, it is best to keep the transitions between the halt, walk, and trot. Canter transitions should be done only when the instructor feels that the student's balance, position, and security are strong enough that the student can mentally attend to the exercise, and not "survival" issues.

- Halt-to-walk: How fast does the horse respond? What does the rider need to do to get that response? Does the horse walk off energetically, or break into trot rather than move actively forward at the walk? Can the rider tell the difference between an active walk and a lazy walk?
- Walk-to-trot: What happens to the rider's position when the horse jumps into trot? Does the rider get "scared" or backed off by the energy of a forward response to the leg aid? How much effort does it take for the horse to respect the rider's leg? Why?

Jumping exercises: To help riders learn how to use their leg aids, it can be fun to do exercises over fences that encourage the correct leg aids from the rider. Some examples:

- Put several jumps in the ring and create a variety of exercises using counter bend and correct bend, transitions in the bend while trotting over small cavaletti and jumps. This will encourage the rider to continue using the leg and rein responses while jumping. Many horses get "wired" when they jump and the rider's tendency is to remove the leg connection rather than support the horse.
- To develop confidence in the use of the leg aid, have the student do fewer fences with more quiet transitions in between, keeping the leg steadily on the horse.

*Test to move to Step 4:* Horse responds immediately by moving forward from the hind leg when the rider asks with a light aid, and the rider's hand position remains the same while the rider's body follows the motion of the horse.

Instructors need to remind students to check this response in each day's warm-up and maintain it through their training sessions.

## Step 4 –Lateral Leg Response

*Objective:* To introduce the theory and feel of a lateral response to the leg aids and to practice receiving timely, consistent and accurate responses.

*Theory:* Horses can move sideways off the rider's leg aids as well as forward. The relationship between the rider's leg, hand, and intent is expressed through a combination of leg aids and rein aids.

*Important Points*

1. In previous steps riders learned to flex the horse solely through the use of the rein aids. This step helps students make the transition from flexing the horse only through using the rein aids to learning that the leg aids actually create the flexion and the hand simply assists the leg.
2. It is ideal if the rider can correctly maintain the use of the rein aid, but instructors must remember that riders need to learn each individual feel and response before they can put it all together. A slight deviation from the ideal hand use may be necessary and if this is the case, it is important to return to a loose rein while learning the leg aid responses.
3. Once the rider can get a consistent leg response, it is time to put the leg and rein aids together.

### Toolkit

- Have student repeat the exercise of **changing direction while maintaining the same bend** with awareness now placed on the bend throughout the horse's body (that is being created by the rider's leg)
- **Change direction and change the bend** using the new combination of inside leg and inside hand.
- Have student perform transitions with the new awareness of the inside bend created by the leg aids in combination with the rein aids.
- Teach students the turn on the forehand in order to help them coordinate their hand and leg aids

*Test to move to Stage 3:* Riders are able to walk, trot, canter and do a small course of jumps while getting correct responses to their aids for flexion and immediate answers to their leg aids. Have riders demonstrate turn on the forehand on the flat and between small jumps. Riders maintain the correct body position and are able to change the direction and bend of the horse at will, with light aids, staying on a planned route and with consistent speed. The horse should willingly and comfortably respond to the rider's aids.

Students who have the responses to their aids engrained in muscle memory will find it easier to move to Stage 3, where these responses are combined with developing energy and feel, and used to begin performing more advanced movements and jumping courses.

## STAGE 3
# AIDS IN ACTION

*Stage 2 in the Stages of Rider Education focused on teaching the student to apply the basic natural aids while maintaining proper position. Beginning work was started in developing the student's sense of "feel" as he or she learned how to communicate with, and respond to, the horse.*

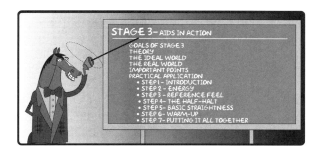

### GOALS OF STAGE 3

There are five main goals for this stage.

1. To further develop rider's hand and leg aid coordination,
2. To introduce the use of the half-halt (adjustment),
3. To help riders identify a "reference feel" and teach them how to use half-halts (adjustments) to maintain that "feel,"
4. To teach riders how to ride a correct warm-up,
5. Continue to develop jumping skills both in the ring and cross-country.

### THEORY

The concepts that are important to review in Stage 3 are Forward Energy and Basic Straightness, which were introduced in Stage 2 and are developed further here. New concepts that are introduced include Reference Feel and Half Halt (Adjustment). The concepts of Consistency and

Rhythm may also be introduced, as they are applicable. Please review the appropriate sections from the Theory Made Simple chapter.

## THE IDEAL WORLD

In the ideal world, students enter Stage 3 by progressing properly through Stage 2. They have practiced using their aids on safe, appropriate horses trained for that level. On these horses riders arrive at Stage 3 having learned the correct horse response for each individual aid as well as having made the initial efforts to use the aids all together. Ideally, Stage 3 students are again mounted on appropriate horses. By riding horses that are well schooled, loose, and sensitive enough to respond correctly to the aids, students are able to identify what a "good" feeling is (reference feel), and learn to use adjustments to get back to that good feeling when it is lost. Students' initial efforts to learn these rather complex and vague concepts are often awkward and slow. Having a horse that is well trained and sensitive enough to respond correctly to these early efforts ensures that the student is rewarded immediately for a correct attempt, despite any awkwardness. This sequence of cause and effect speeds up the learning process because students put together the proper mind and body connections from the beginning. They develop the proper muscle memory, habits, and feel, and do so fairly quickly.  If students can experience an "ideal" learning situation during Stage 3, they will progress onward, in a relatively short time, to Stage 4, the partnership stage.

## THE REAL WORLD

While some instructors may have the wonderful situation of teaching under ideal conditions, many instructors today are faced with students and horses that arrive at Stage 3 with "less than the ideal" background education. These horse and rider combinations often have some combination of rider position issues and horse training problems that make the instructor's job quite challenging. To start with, the horses may not have had the benefit of a consistent training program. They may even have been exposed to an incorrect or harmful training program that has left them confused, frustrated, scared, and/or in pain. For whatever reason, these horses have significant 'holes' in their educations. They do not know how to respond to the rider, and even if they begin to understand their riders, they are often stiff. Riders can enter Stage 3 with incorrect position habits that are well learned, but be filled with a desire and enthusiasm to move forward in their educations. These riders are finally in the position of working on their horses, and they do not want to "go backwards" by revisiting position work!  In addition, these riders' understandings of training theory are often flawed, or incomplete. Therefore, many instructors are faced with the formidable challenge of having to educate the horse and rider at the same time. While this can be difficult and time consuming, it is possible! It is very useful to take the horse and rider back to Stage 2 and teach the horse the correct leg and rein responses. From this understanding, many horses are able to make progress with their inexperienced riders as they gain confidence in their own bodies. The rein response from Stage 2, combined with careful regular work, builds the horse's confidence in his ability to use his body and respond to the rider. For riders who feel stuck, it is often the skills from Stage 2 that helps both horse and rider to fill in their education holes so that they can be prepared to move on with training.

## IMPORTANT POINTS

1. It is important for instructors to maintain a sense of moving forward with students in Stage 3, despite the existence of rider and/or horse problems. Students can often become discouraged when they realize that they have previously been on the "wrong track," and they need the instructor to "hold the hope" for them when they cannot see the forest for the trees (See Psychology Chapters in Professional Development).

2. In order to "sell" the importance of filling in the gaps of your student's (or horse's) education, it may be necessary to go into more detail when explaining theory during this stage. This increased understanding, combined with attention to the rider's developing sense of "feel," can often bring home the importance of fixing the problems from earlier stages. Once students can see the positive benefit to themselves and their horses from correcting past mistakes, they tend to jump on the "let's fix it" bandwagon with renewed energy, vigor, and hope.

INSTRUCTOR'S REMINDER

It can be helpful to "assign" the student the incorrect feel or position once they have experienced the more correct response. By asking the student to move back and forth between the "right" and "wrong" feel, you can bring home a strong sense of the correct feel. In other words, by asking for the incorrect response (with awareness), you help your student discern the difference between what is correct and incorrect through feeling it, not just intellectually understanding it! 🐎

3. It is vitally important that lessons lay the foundation for muscle intelligence, rather than just mental intelligence. Chart 43 contains a list of supplemental skills and techniques that can help students develop awareness, and the sense of being "present in the moment," which is required for riders to acquire a solid sense of feel when riding.

| Support the Learning Process | |
|---|---|
| Help students develop present-mindedness | |
| **Cross Training Skill** | **Benefit** |
| Visualization | Helps students reproduce good feelings related to a new skill being learned, and decreases learning time. |
| Meditation | Teaches students how to let their minds be in the present. |
| "On-hold" | Helps students be able to put their busy lives and responsibilities away ("on hold") during their riding time. |
| | Chart 43 |

# PRACTICAL APPLICATION
## Step 1 – Introduction to Aids in Action

*Objective:* To help students gain more refined control by riding with energy, straightness, a sense of reference feel, and adding the half halt to their skill toolkit.

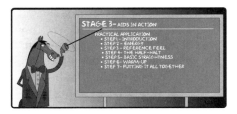

*Theory:* Review the concepts of Forward Energy, Reference Feel, and Half-Halt. Provide as much theory as is appropriate for the student's age, maturity, and interest level.

**Toolkit**

🐎 Explain the BIG PICTURE of this stage with a demonstration of the main elements; forward energy, reference feel, and the half-halt. (Keep your explanations brief - focus on the elements associated with these concepts you believe are important for your individual student's needs).

🐎 Ask questions to determine the student's comprehension of what was learned from Stage 2 and of the concepts of forward, straightness and reference feel. How the student answers you will give you the starting point for further discussion.

INSTRUCTOR'S REMINDER

The steps in this stage are not necessarily linear! The instructor must evaluate each horse and rider combination and introduce the steps in the order appropriate for each pair's base of knowledge and ability. The steps are presented here in the order they would be presented in the ideal world. 🐎

*Test to move to Step 2:* Ask students to articulate their understanding of the BIG PICTURE of this stage and outline a plan for moving forward that is clear, logical, and based upon correct rider and horse education principles. Does the student know the ideal program and what is the best plan for her and her horse?

## Step 2 – Forward Energy

*Objective:* Create in the rider an understanding and awareness of receiving energy from the horse's hind leg into an elastic hand.

*Theory:* Review the concept of forward energy in the Theory Made Simple chapter. Forward energy is energy that, once created, is ready to be directed by the rider. No energy, no performance. Developing a sense of rhythm while separating speed and true forward energy is an important distinction for the student to understand and experience during this step. Speed can be differentiated from forward by helping the student recognize how speed is typically difficult to direct, while forward energy is not.

### Toolkit

- Have a conversation with your students to understand what they are currently feeling in their hands, their legs and in their seats. Begin with their awareness and expression of what they feel. Ask your students lots of questions, such as: "What are you feeling?" "Where?" "What would feel better to you?" When the student does develop true forward energy, as them questions such as: "How does this feel different than before?" "How would you describe this feeling?" "Okay, I'm following you, but tell me more." "Why?" and so on!

- Use your communication and diagnostic skills to uncover how best to describe energy to each individual student. Receiving energy is an abstract concept that is vague and confusing for many people so it is important for instructors to find a clear way to explain it to their students. One visual example that I (Jill) have found helpful is to imagine an ocean wave. It starts at the ocean floor, gains power, rises up through a curve and lands with power on the ground. The beginning of the wave with the ocean's push is like the horse's hind leg, and the rider's hand is the landing spot of the wave.

- Exercises to teach the concept of FORWARD to riders in a GROUP LESSON

  Exercise 1 – What does "forward" look like? This is the cognitive understanding of "forward."

  1. Explain the theory behind "forward" in a way that is appropriate for students' ages, cognitive abilities, and attention spans, using just enough details to get the idea across. Metaphors, visual im-

agery, etc. make it easier for students to conceptualize.

2. Have one rider walk a horse around the group in a circle, no smaller than 20 meters.

3. Ask the rider to allow the horse to walk in an uninspired fashion, slowly and lazily. Have the observers watch where the horse's hind footprints fall. They will probably fall behind the horse's front hoof prints.

4. Now ask the rider to have the horse move faster with no contact on the reins (unless the horse tries to trot).

5. Have the observers watch the horse's hind legs - the horse will probably take the same size steps, but be moving at a faster speed. The horse's hind foot will probably not be landing on or in front of his front footprint. When the horse does step into or in front of the front hoof print with the hind foot it is called 'tracking up.' A note: Some naturally good movers will track up even when being lazy, but as they move truly forward, they will increase the distance they track up by quite a bit.

6. Now have the rider on the circle pick up the reins, ask the horse to walk actively, with energy, but keep a steady feel on the rein (half-halt if the rider knows this aid) so that the horse can not speed up. Have the observers watch what happens to the length of the horse's stride behind. It should get longer, so that the hind hoof print falls on or in front of the front hoof print.

Once the first rider has done this exercise, repeat again with another rider so that the first rider can observe the above sequence of footfalls. Try to keep the explanation clear and simple. Many riders' sense of "forward" comes from combining this visual understanding of what the horse's hind legs are doing, with FEELING the difference between forward and not forward. The next exercise addresses how to teach the "feel" part.

Exercise 2 – What does "forward" feel like? The kinesthetic understanding of forward.

1. Begin by having the riders sit the trot around the ring. Ask them to rate their "feeling of forward" on a scale of 1 – 10.

2. Now have the riders canter around the ring. Have them come back to trot, re-establish a steady tempo, and ask the riders to again rate their "feeling of forward" from 1 – 10.

3. Have each rider trot in a 20-meter circle around you. Using a long dressage whip gently encourage the horse to take bigger steps behind while the rider maintains a steady tempo – not allowing the horse to speed up (if the rider knows the half-halt, this is the aid to prevent the horse from picking up the pace). Again, have the rider rate the "feeling of forward" from 1 – 10.

4. To finish the exercise, have the riders ride around the ring again and bring their horses back to the lowest level of forward that they felt. Now ask them to try to increase the forward feeling gradually until they reach the highest number they felt.

- Ask riders to do transitions with their eyes closed, feeling the horse respond to their leg aids, feeling the energy go forward and receiving it in their hands.

- Have riders walk, prepare to trot, and feel the energy of the hind leg pushing forward and filling out the rein. Then have riders prepare to return to walk in the exact same way they prepared to trot, feeling the energy begin to go forward, and then walking with that forward energy moving towards the hand.

- Have students jump a course and describe the energy between and over the fences. Listen carefully and see if they felt like it was controlled energy or fast energy. Help them define the difference via feel. This is also a great exercise for a group. Each rider describes what they feel, and the students observing describe what they see. The instructor then comments on what has been said and what actually took place.

These are just a few examples of how to help riders develop a feel for FORWARD. There are many others. Be creative! The important thing is that riders learn this concept; it is critical for riders not only to understand it intellectually, but also to FEEL it. Riders will continually develop their understandings of this feeling, refining it over years of practice. Be careful not to discourage the beginning rider - praise and enthuse over the small changes - it is one small change after another that brings riders closer to a full and rich understanding of FORWARD

*Test to move to Step 3:* Ask riders questions about the concept and have them demonstrate an understanding of and beginning feel for forward energy. Have students demonstrate the difference between forward and fast.

## Step 3 – Reference Feel

*Objective:* Create awareness for riders of the feeling they would like to have consistently in their hands and under their seat and legs. Awareness is the key word here, as the reference feel is that "wonderful" feeling that all riders describe feeling on occasion, but rarely do they get asked to define it, stay aware of it, and pay attention to its disappearance.

*Theory:* Having a reference feel allows students to know when a half-halt (or adjustment) is needed. It is the rider's consistent awareness of the presence and absence of this ideal, desired feeling in the hands, seat, and legs that gives the cue that a half-halt (adjustment) is needed.

*Important Points*

1.  Once a rider is consistently aware of the feeling of a steady, regular, light connection between hands, seat, and legs, it becomes "home base," the origination point for the changing dynamics, which occur in each ride. When this reference feeling changes, the rider knows it is time to half-halt, and when the horse responds to the half-halt, the reward for the horse is the rider's 'bugging off' by returning to the pre-established reference feel. This feeling needs to be identified in the three major parts of the rider's body; legs, hands, and seat.

### Toolkit

- **Leg**: Ask students to describe the connection between their legs and the horse in two places: 1) their thighs and the saddle, and 2) their calves and the horse's barrel. Continue to ask until you come up with an acceptable, simple descriptive word that they can think of to check if their reference feel is on track. Examples from students: thigh hugs saddle like uncooked sirloin steak, calf fits horse like boot fits leg.

- **Hands:** Ask students to do the same with the reins, describing how many ounces they have in their hands (examples might be: a dinner fork - about 1 ounce, or a Campbell's soup can - about 10 oz.). You can even take objects of different weight with you to help them identify a comparable weight. Once they identify an amount with your help, and you agree that it is acceptable, remind them that this contact needs to be consistent and elastic, receiving energy from the hind leg. Practice some ring figures and ask students how many ounces they have in their hands at various times.

- **Seat:** Ask a student how the horse feels under his or her seat, and more importantly how his or her seat feels. Is it glued to the saddle, does it swing with the horse's motion? Where is the student sitting – on the front, back, or middle of the pelvis? Make sure the seat is in the middle of the student's "rocking chair."

- Do exercises and ask questions related to students' reference feels. The goal is to bring their attention to their chosen descriptive words.

- Sometimes instructors need to help student understand feel by putting your hand between the rider's leg and the horse and/or saddle and thigh to help them establish an ideal feel. Another way of doing this is to get on the horse and let the rider feel the instructor's connection between the horse, saddle and the related body area.

It is essential to explore words with your student to find his or her own descriptive word and use it when working on maintaining reference feel. ⚘

*Test to move to Step 4:* Ask riders questions about their reference feels and have them demonstrate what is meant and what they intend their reference feels to be.

## Step 4 – The Half-Halt (Adjustment)

*Objective:* To: 1) help riders understand the concept of the half-halt, and its relationship to the horse's ability to engage his hind end while maintaining rhythm and tempo, and 2) help riders develop the timing and coordination of their seat and hand aids so they can ride the half-halt effectively.

*Theory:* The half-halt is an adjustment a rider makes to create balance and engagement or to prepare the horse for a transition, ring figure, corner, or movement. All half-halts are accomplished in three steps, ending with a release (saying "thank you" to the horse):

- Push with seat and/or legs,
- Hold with hands and/or seat,
- Release the hold.

| Half-Halt (adjustment) --- 3 Steps & 3 Basic Uses | |
|---|---|
| hold–push–release | For horses who get strong in the hand |
| push—hold—release | To prepare a horse for a change in direction or gait |
| push—hold—release | To create more engagement |
| | Chart 44 |

*Important Points*

1. Many riders think that once they have felt the half-halt work once or twice, they "have it." Emphasize that the half-halt is **communication** between rider and horse, and thus the horse has a say in whether it wants to answer. Sometimes horses ignore the half-halt, and what may work down the long side of the ring may not work in the corner. Riding is a sport that is constantly changing, moment-to-moment, thus the half-halt is used for continual adjustment, **not as a tool that is guaranteed to work JUST BECAUSE the rider asks.** The rider must always be establishing the prerequisites for the half-halt to work. These are: relaxation, rhythm, forward energy, straightness, and bend.
2. Students need to become comfortable with experimenting with adjustments. Many half-halts (i.e., 20, 30, 40, and up!) are given in a single training ride. It is time to do a half-halt when the horse gets heavy against the rider's hand or leg, leaves the route, or speeds up.

3. Half-halts are most effective when the rider relies on muscle memory and an intuitive sense of "feel" when applying the aids, which requires much practice (and patience!).

Toolkit

Half-Halt Exercise: This is *one way* to begin to teach riders the feeling of this important, but ever so elusive aid. Explain that you are going to teach the concept of the half-halt – an aid that is the rider's unique way of communicating with the horse "body to body." There are three parts to this exercise: first, the practice of slowing down without using the reins. Second, developing an understanding of slowing down while increasing engagement of the hindquarters. Third, practicing the simultaneous application of "slow down" aids (hand and seat) with the driving aids (leg).

**Part 1:** Practice slowing down without reins
- Start off at walk, have rider "ask" horse to halt without using the reins – it might take a few attempts if the horse has been desensitized or is dull, but often it works quickly. Riders get pretty excited by this; they are often amazed that it works. When it does not work right away, stress that it will with practice - that just because a horse ignores the rider's body does not make it right. Also, if the horse ignores the rider's early attempts to slow it down or halt from body communication, the instructor can explain and empathize with why the rider has to resort to "pulling" on the reins to get a response.
- Ask students lots of questions to get them thinking about what they are doing with their bodies! For example, "How were you able to accomplish this?" Make sure the rider keeps the correct position and does not fall back into a driving seat. Ask "How do you think the horse 'heard' you?" This opens up the opportunity for a brief, but clear discussion of how horses respond to a rider's shifting weight (because the horse wants to have the rider stay over his center of balance, the horse will slow down or move forward to "catch up" with the rider).
- Continue this exercise, moving into trot and canter as the rider begins to get more consistent responses from the horse. Only when the rider can consistently get the horse to decrease his gait in response to the seat (weight, back, or whatever term the instructor chooses to use) is it time to progress to the next step.

**Part 2:** Understanding the idea of how to **simultaneously** slow the horse down while increasing energy from behind (through the increased engagement of the hind legs).
- Ask students why pulling backwards on the reins does not work (namely because the horse WILL SHORTEN THE SWING OF THE

HIND LEGS when the rider takes a backward feel or pull, preventing the engagement of the hind legs necessary for a correct half-halt).

- Ask students questions to help them discover the answers for themselves. This discussion often becomes an "Aha" experience for many students. For example, the instructor can ask, "Why can't we just pull on the reins to slow down? Doesn't this work the best?" And continue on from there.
- Once students understand that pulling on the reins stops the hind legs, ask them how they can slow the horse down without pulling. They will explain to you what they just did in the above exercise. Now ask them how they can slow down WHILE INCREASING ENGAGEMENT AT THE SAME TIME. Most riders will smile and say something to effect of, " Use my leg and say slow with my body at the same time." Ta-da! They are ready for the next step.

**Part 3:** Practice the simultaneous application of "slow down aids" (hand and seat) with driving aids (leg).

- Explain to students that when they use their legs to create energy, many horses initially respond by speeding up. The simultaneous use of their bodies (as they did in the first exercise) AND the reins can prevent this from happening. Important point: ***The hand can not pull back, but instead can only "hold" as much as the rider is "holding" with the seat, and then releases when the rider relaxes the seat.*** Many different words and images are used to help the rider understand the need to stay upright and tall in the saddle while half-halting, and not slouched back into a driving seat. Some instructors use the phrase, "hold with your back," others say "take a deep breath," while others talk about the use of the abdominal muscles. The most important point here is that the rider stays balanced over the horse, *with the pelvis in the center of the saddle,* not tipped forward or dropped back.
- Allow the rider to practice on a circle at the walk. Using a long dressage whip, the instructor can gently encourage the horse to take active steps behind while the rider asks the horse to "slow down" using body language (and hand if needed, but only in a holding and releasing fashion). It helps to keep reminding the rider to breathe deeply, stay sitting up tall, and release any tension from his or her arms. The half-halt ideally is done with a soft and relaxed rider, not a rider who is tense and stiff from trying to drive and hold at the same time. Emphasize the need for experimenting and practice. The half-halt requires a high degree of coordination of the aids, which comes from trial and error and a lot of practice. Reward the small successes so that the rider feels the progress!

If the horse does not listen to the leg in the half-halt; students can do a transition to remind the horse of the expected response. Similarly, if the horse does not respond to the flexion, overbending is the horse's reminder. ⚑

Have the student ride ring figures and over jumps with the intent of putting the student in a position of needing to do a half-halt. Practice doing the figure or fence without the half-halt, then with the half-halt, and then without the half-halt again. Have the student verbally describe what they are feeling across the different situations. Help the student become aware of how differently the horse responds in different situations, even though the rider is using the same aids for the half-half each time. Feeling the result during practice and over jumps is a confidence building experience for riders.

*Test to move to Step 5:* Ask the rider to demonstrate making adjustments to the horse's way of going through using half-halts while riding simple figures and transitions, maintaining an accurate feeling of receiving energy and a consistent reference feel in rein, legs, and seat. Riders ready to move to Step 5 exhibit the following characteristics:

- They make quick, light, accurate responses; rather than slow, heavy, misguided reactions.

- They remain steady and quiet in between half-halts.

- When not getting a desired response, they know to first reference their own position, relaxation, and technique; and then either adjust themselves or intensify the primary aid needed. The horse is the last place they look for the source of their problems.

- When problems persist, they are aware of the need to trace the steps of the communication cycle (what was asked for compared to the answer the horse gave them), and make appropriate corrections.

## Step 5 – Basic Straightness

*Objective:* To teach the rider the role of basic straightness, its effect on performance and its value as a diagnostic tool.

*Theory:* This is the time to develop the concept of straightness. Basic straightness, in its classical definition, means that when performing basic movements such as circles, half-circles, serpentines, and figure-eights, the horse travels in such a way that the hind feet follow in the track of the front feet (see advanced straightness and the discussion in Stage 4 for a definition of straightness in lateral movements). When a horse does this, it is said to be traveling straight. Review the concepts of basic straightness, bend and flexion in the Theory Made Simple chapter and teach students the information they need to understand based on their ages and ways of thinking and learning.

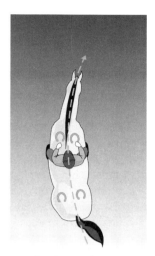

Straight on Curve

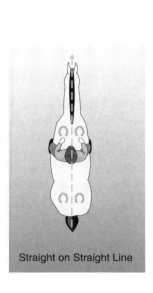

Straight on Straight Line

*Important Points*

Focus on the route with basic straightness using flexing, bending and over bending as needed. At this point students understand how to ride consistently from the inside leg to the outside hand, but they may not be consistent. Now it is time to understand staying on route with the horse lined up correctly on the direction of travel. By doing this with a clear understanding and feeling for the individual aids that were taught earlier, students can begin to use the appropriate aids to stay on route with the front of the horse correctly lined up with the rear of the horse whether on the flat or over fences.

**Toolkit**

Exercise (to help students understand straightness and give them the feeling)
1. Have students walk toward you and away from you, asking them to rate (1-10) how straight they think the horse is. Then you rate the straightness. Continue this exercise until both you and your students come close to agreeing on the degree of straightness.
2. Now let the riders allow the horses to walk "naturally" and ask about the degree of straightness. The riders will probably tell you that the horses are trying to swing the hindquarters in, and/

or the shoulders out. It is good for the riders to be able to feel this!

3. Ask the riders to now make the horses walk straight, and ask what they had to do to make that happen. The riders will find that it takes lots of little corrections and that they need to keep the outside rein and the inside leg on pretty consistently. If they can come to this conclusion themselves, it will be much more valuable in the long run.

☞ Transitions with flexion or while over-bent a specific number of inches to one side or the other.

☞ Doing transitions on the wall with an inside bend is a wonderful diagnostic tool for checking the horse's balance and lightness to the leg aids. Begin transitions on the long side while maintaining bend and flexion. If the rider has difficultly doing this with an inside bend, start with an outside bend. During the transition, tightness or resistance is demonstrated when the horse is unable to remain on route or lacks straightness. The transitions also check the ability of the horse and rider to maintain flexion and lightness of connection through a change.

☞ Ride corners with inside bend and giving with inside rein.

☞ Ride up and down hills.

☞ Ring figures with counter flexion and inside flexion.
  • 20-meter circles, figure eights and serpentines with inner flexion and counter flexion.
  • Half-circles and half-voltes.
  • Cavalletti, grids, single fences and a short course.

> *"The correct use of the inside hand is necessary, because without flexion there is no outside hand. Before I can ride with my outside aids, I have to come through with my inside aids and the horse has to respond to them."*
>
> —**Stephan Kiesewetter**

 Students can be taught that if the horse does not respond to the rider's request for inside flexion to prepare for the corner, overbending is an effective correction. ☞

*Test for moving to Step 6:* Student understands basic straightness and can demonstrate it riding a specific route, using over bending and transitions while staying straight and on route at walk, trot, canter and over a small jumping course.

## Step 6 – Warm up

*Objective:* To develop a consistently effective warm-up and understand its importance through awareness and comparison with the warm-up from the previous day's ride. Use the information collected to determine the appropriate training program for the day.

*Theory:* Warm-up allows rider and horse to assess how they are feeling that particular day and to work out any stiffnesses or blocks. The correct way to begin each ride is for the rider to immediately establish contact with the horse through the leg to a light, receiving hand. Although walking around on a loose rein does warm up a horse's muscles, it does nothing to prepare the horse for the actual work that is going to be performed. With this light, consistent contact the rider helps establish the horse's focus while walking the horse to loosen it up. Being attentive to the warm-up is a very important part of each ride.

---

**WARM-UP OVERVIEW**

√ Horse and rider are FOCUSED on each other
√ Rider checks POSITION
√ Rider checks HORSE responses
√ Rider compares horse's responses to yesterday's warm up
√ Rider compares horse's responses to yesterday's training session
√ Rider decides what to include in 1st training set

Chart 45

---

*Important Points*

1. Teach students to follow a systematic checklist for their positions and their horses' performances. The personal position checklist is the first check your student should make while walking the horse and letting it loosen up. Whatever shows itself as a problem during this check is to be identified and fixed immediately, if possible. If it is not possible to fix it right away, a portion of the training time should be dedicated to its repair.

2. Usually challenges that are recognized in warm-up will show themselves periodically during the training session. A useful technique is to decide on a simple, short reminder of the position issue to include as part of each half halt made during the ride. **Example:** One day Mary arrived for her lesson abnormally distracted. She soon shared the problem with me; her son was ill and she was worried about him. While Mary was usually past her position struggle of having her weight go down through her thigh, her worry and distraction on this day caused it to resurface. During the warm-up Mary identified the tightness with 'hard thighs.' We practiced a few transitions with 'softening the thighs' and

then went forward with our program of working on a course of jumps. My job was to remind Mary to include "soften my thigh" with each half-halt (adjustment) she made between her fences.

| RIDER'S PERSONAL DAILY WARM-UP CHECK LIST | |
|---|---|
| **Position** | Straight line ear-shoulder-hip-heel |
| | Straight line elbow-bit |
| **Suppleness** | Elastic, centered spring from head down through heel |
| | Equal spring in each ankle |
| | Relaxed, supple joint check |
| **Relaxation** | Freedom, looseness of body |
| | Calmness and presence of mind |
| **Focus** | Balanced attention to horse & environment |
| | "Get on horse's page" |
| **Effectiveness** | Respond promptly to horse |
| | Expect prompt response from horse |
| **Mood** | Content, happy, attentive to horse/riding |

Chart 46

3. Once the students have gone through their personal checklists it is time to move on to the horse. During the warm up the rider feels the horse's rhythm and follows it. It is important that the rider also establish a mental connection with the horse, keeping the horse focused on the work being asked. In addition to acute awareness of the horse's natural rhythm, the rider must be alert to staying on a pre-determined route. During this check the riders have some evaluations to make. We need to teach the student to record the results in their mind from one warm-up to the next and from the end of one ride to the next. There are two comparisons committed to memory: the comparison of this warm-up to the previous day's warm-up and the comparison of this warm-up to how the horse felt at the end of the previous day's training/ schooling session. These important comparisons provide vital information on the progress of the training program as well as serve as prerequisites for each movement that will be performed during the training session.

**Example:** Tom is very skillful in his warm-up. After he quickly executes his personal checklist he takes Night Air, his event horse, through a warm-up program. Tom walks and trots in both directions, first asking Night to do a few transitions from walk to trot to test Night's response to Tom's leg aids. Satisfied, Tom then begins neck bending 2", sometimes to the inside, and sometimes in counter bend. Tom is evaluating Night's response to his rein aids and his inside thigh as well as Night's suppleness. Intermixed with this work Tom does a few twenty-meter circles in

| RIDER'S DAILY HORSE WARM-UP CHECK LIST | |
|---|---|
| **Leg** | Prompt forward response to each leg |
| | Prompt response to move shoulder to opposite side |
| | Prompt response to move hindquarter |
| **Rein** | Soft, quick submission to rein aid |
| | Flex equally on both sides |
| | Equal response on each side |
| | Accepts elastic soft contact |
| **Focus** | Attentive to rider |
| **IMPORTANT**: ride equally in both directions and frequently change directions (rule of thumb...not more than one time around the arena without a change of some sort). Compare the 'feeling' of the horse going in both directions. | |

Chart 47

both directions, evaluating Night's rhythm, relaxation and straightness on this pattern. Night loves to canter, so within a few minutes Tom adds the canter with a few twenty-meter circles in both directions. Depending on how Night feels (compared to his previous warm-up and training session), Tom will decide how many transitions and ring figures he will do, as well as how much neck bending. He always does the transitions along the straight side of the arena, so he can more easily feel any resistances that might occur. When he is finished with his warm-up and evaluation, he decides where to begin his training session based on his intermediate plan.

**Toolkit**

☞ Encourage riders to use exercises and evaluate the results as they follow their checklists. The following exercises are for use during warm-up to help evaluate the horse's responsiveness and flexibility. Students are encouraged to decide what order is best for their horses.

**Warm-up EXERCISES**
- Transitions with light contact
- Maintaining bend and changing directions
- Changing bend when changing directions
- Transitions with light contact and bend

Chart 48

*Test to move to Step 7:* Have the rider demonstrate an effective warm-up and explain what he or she did and why, and whether the rider thinks he or she is appropriately prepared for the training session.

The instructor needs to insist that students use warm up effectively. Watch until you feel certain that this important preparation for the ride is consistent and well attended to by the rider. The correct warm-up influences each day's training sessions as well as progress of the training program. ✈

## Step 7 – Putting it All Together

*Objective:* Once each concept has been adequately learned individually, it is time to put them all together. The rider now needs to be able to demonstrate the timely, proper and effective use of aids at all three gaits and over fences while maintaining the correct position. This level of competence is only achieved by combining the rider's thinking mind with the feeling body.

*Theory:* A good understanding of all of the concepts discussed through Stages 1, 2, and 3 are required for this step to be sufficiently accomplished. The theory behind equine movement and "feel," along with the concept of consistency are particularly of relevance for this step.

*Important Points*
1. Students need to learn to take into consideration both their own roles and the horse's role in creating performance results and problems. Instructors can help develop, through the active use of the question and answer technique of communication, their students' awarenesses of the circular effects of rider on horse and horse on rider responses.
2. In order for all the aids to work together, students must feel the response of one aid at a time. Once each aid is felt and practiced until it becomes a habit individually, THEN all the aids can be used together to ride figures, corners, transitions, and correct movements.
3. Allow students their learning curves, and help them enjoy the process, showing them joy in the struggle. Most importantly, revel in students' small accomplishments. Learning to ride at this level is truly a challenge, but also is a gift and true joy— exude this and your students will too!

### Toolkit

☞ Ask a lot of questions to help students understand the how, why, and feel of such concepts as the reference feel, forward energy, straightness and half-halts when performing figures, a dressage test and a jumping course.

- Use questions to help students begin to diagnose performance flaws.
- While students are performing basic ring figures, jumps and courses, ask questions that bring awareness to what is good.
- Similarly use questions to bring students' attention to what needs to be corrected, and ask them to correct it, making certain they understand what they are correcting and why.

**Keep order and simplicity to the questions, so students gain confidence in the process.**

*Test for moving to Stage 4:* The rider can maintain a correct position while using the aids in a coordinated manner, and remaining in control of the horse. The horse begins to perform comfortably and with ease, moving into the rider's light, receiving hand and legs, maintaining a consistent performance at the walk, trot, canter, over caveletti, grids, single fences and a course.

*Specific test:* Ask the student to ride a correct corner with preparation, giving on the inside rein through the corner, and being able to correctly diagnos balance problems if the horse does not stay correctly bent around the inside leg when the rider gives with the inside hand.

Jumping in Harmony

Time for another celebration as you and your student have achieved a sound foundation! Achieving the skills through this level is equal to a high school education. The next stage, Transition 1, is designed to guide instructors in helping their students make the choice of what direction they want to go next with their rider educations.

# TRANSITION 1 – CHOICES

*The time to review accomplishments and plan for the next step*

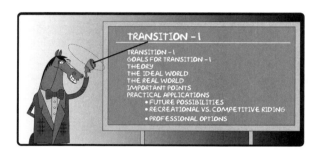

Stages 1, 2 and 3 of the Rider Education System focused on developing important fundamental rider skills, including the establishment of a correct, basic, balanced position; a following, educated seat; and a developed sense of feel acquired from the sensitive and correct application of the aids. A rider spends many years learning the art of riding through these stages and now has reached the level of proficiency of many amateur riders in the USA. Riders who have gained the skills to begin a partnership are also ready to decide what in particular they want to do with their riding time. This is a time to consider the choice of a specific competitive sport that correlates with the rider's individual skill and interest level; others may choose to continue with their rider educations; and others might want to combine the two. It is very much like the celebrated graduation from high school with the excitement of preparing for the next stage of life. Graduating with solid skills from Stage 3 opens the doors to many opportunities.

## GOALS OF TRANSITION 1: (for instructors)
1. To help guide your students in making a realistic decision about the next step as they pursue their love of riding.
2. To help your students evaluate their interests, time, skill level and money related to life and their horses.

3. To help your students create a plan to follow their decisions.

4. To help your students enjoy the competency they have achieved.

## THEORY

Instructors combine their professional and ethical responsibilities and their knowledge of the horse world with the reality of the student's skill, time, money, aptitude, talent and goals to create a plan that ensures a future filled with satisfaction, quality and growth.

## THE IDEAL WORLD

At this point in our American System of Rider Education, we deviate a great deal from the classical, systematic approach to rider development as is seen in Europe with the German Scale of Education. In this classical system, riders reach this transition stage after Stage 5, not Stage 3. Stage 5 riders' skills are highly developed and fine-tuned, and they have well-established basics in both rider and horse education, making these riders ready to pursue a career in the horse training profession. In Europe, partly due to each country's cultural and financial support, horse sports are quite popular, making them viable and respected professions. As a result, professional horse trainers are expected to proceed through the system, and the availability of the many riding schools and well-educated instructors and horses make this possible. In addition, entrance to the horse training profession is closely monitored, and is strongly linked to the formal system of education. In the United States there exists a different reality than the one in Europe, which for many reasons prevents us from following this classical approach to rider development.

## THE REAL WORLD

In the United States, there are many reasons why our riders do not progress through all five stages of the classical riding program, but four reasons stand out as the most salient. One, there is a serious lack of training opportunities for the American rider due to the vast size of our country and the limited numbers of classically educated horses and instructors. Two, the horse training profession is not regulated in America, so there is little incentive to pursue the time-consuming and expensive education beyond Stage 3. Three, many American riders' goal is to pursue riding as a sport and hobby, not as a profession. And four, many riders are hampered in their goals by limitations and constraints such as time, talent, horses, and money. For these reasons, and many others, students at the end of Stage 3 are faced with decisions to make, and realities to consider when it comes to their riding careers.

At the end of Stage 3, students have developed sufficient proficiency on their horses to create a foundation that enables them to pursue their individual interests and passions. This is a wonderful situation to be in, as there exists in America many options for our students to pursue in their enjoyment of their horses. At this point, instructors' jobs become two-fold; to help students find an enjoyable safe outlet for their love of riding while they continue to work on their basic foundation, and/or prepare them to move to Stage 4. Perhaps, because of all the various options available to our students, instructors need to take care that they are honest and straightforward with their students as they help them think through all the issues presented by this transition stage. It helps to keep the BIG PICTURE in mind, so that you do not unintentionally encourage your student to move forward unrealistically. In addition, instructors need to be certain that their students have both the proper foundations and the resources to meet their intended future plans. If students are missing skills it is the instructor's professional and ethical responsibility to point them out (kindly, and with compassion) and help the students create a plan to remedy these gaps so that they become solid through Stage 3 and fully prepared for the next step, whatever it might be.

## IMPORTANT POINTS

1. Many times riders progress through their riding educations in such a way that they arrive at a fairly advanced level of riding with significant "holes" or weaknesses in certain areas. This can happen for a number of reasons, including:
   - Lack of good or consistent instruction
   - Inadequately or incorrectly trained horses
   - Not enough practice time to develop the needed sophisticated degree of "feel"
   - Progressing too fast up the levels
   - Imbalance in the "cognitive" versus "feel" elements of learning
   - Too much emphasis on the horse's performing movements, without the prerequisite rider skills firmly in place
   - Horse problems that are beyond the rider's understanding or ability to correct
2. In the "real world," riders present instructors with many different kinds of "holes" in their educations. Yet many of the problems fall into the categories of: a) position issues, and/or b) horse issues. Each will be discussed below.

### POSITION ISSUES

Many of the "holes" that riders have today stem from inconsistencies and weaknesses in their basic positions. Many students have not had (or availed themselves of) the opportunity to work on the lunge line for any extended period of time. If lunge line work is done at all, it is only for brief or inconsistent periods of time. While lunge line work often results in important corrections no matter how little is done, short time periods prevent the rider's muscle memory from replacing old habits with new ones. It takes time for the body to relearn well-established patterns of behavior. This is why it is so important to be careful what is taught at the beginning. What is learned first goes onto the "hard drive" of the brain, and becomes difficult (but not impossible!) to modify. To help these students, it is important that instructors become comfortable with moving back and forth between stages during their lessons. Yes, students need to fill in their weak areas but it helps so much if they can maintain a sense of progressing forward while they do so. Once students grasp how their

---

*Perhaps most importantly, students need help from the instructor to understand the need for going back to earlier stages (such as "position issues" in Stage 1) in order to move forward.*

---

position issues are connected to their training problems, they tend to be eager and motivated to change. Those students who are not interested in working through their position issues, despite a clear understanding of the consequences, are revealing much about their own motivations for riding – which may or may not settle well with you as their instructors. Therefore, as the instructor, you have a choice to make. Either continue teaching this student, or refer the student elsewhere. Before you reach this difficult decision, you may want to get a consultation from a respected fellow instructor or consulting service. For many instructors, getting rid of the occasional student who does not quite "fit with the program" brings about a huge sense of relief. Going against your personal values and belief system is a sure fire way to increase your stress and risk of burnout!

### HORSE ISSUES

Other common problems stem from the horse's lack of proper training. Riders on such horses may put together the correct sequence of aids, but the horse, because of a lack of education, does not always respond appropriately. These riders are then in the unenviable position of trying to learn advanced skills by "hunting in the dark." They are trying to figure out what they are looking for, but not really knowing for sure what it looks (feels) like! If by chance the rider does stumble upon a correct response from the horse, the rider often misses it because there is no way to recognize it as a correct response! The horse then becomes confused and mistrustful, and the negative cycle begins. When faced

| COMMON EVASIONS | | |
|---|---|---|
| **Nose behind vertical** | Rider | Heavy or hard hands<br>Backward action of arms<br>Seat not following |
| | Horse | Does not accept bit<br>Lack of muscle in back |
| **Dropping contact** | Rider | Non elastic hands<br>Tight arms<br>Stiff back |
| | Horse | Does not accept bit<br>Lack of engagement |
| **False bend** | Rider | Lack of understanding<br>Too much hand, not enough leg |
| | Horse | Lack of understanding |
| **Leaning on bit** | Rider | Heavy, holding hands<br>Ineffective aids<br>Inappropriate driving seat |
| | Horse | Longitudinally stiff |
| **Above bit** | Rider | Lack of understanding<br>Tight, non-following seat<br>Stiff hands or seat |
| | Horse | Stiff in back<br>Lack of engagement<br>Does not accept bit |
| **Running** | Rider | Holding<br>Driving<br>Stiff |
| | Horse | Does not accept aids<br>Lack of balance |
| **Blocking** (refusing to go forward) | Rider | Slow in answering horse's response<br>Stiff |
| | Horse | Not off leg<br>Lack of engagement<br>Attitude, confused<br>Stiffness |

Chart 49

with this situation, instructors must uncover ways to help the horse become educated within the rider's skill level. Students need to understand the need for this process and again be willing to return to a lower stage to help educate their horses through slow, simple exercises. The team cannot move forward without each partner's having a solid foundation that allows them to respond to each other.

**INSTRUCTOR'S REMINDER**

In situations where holes in the rider's position or the horse's education interferes with progress, issues are best addressed by an instructor who is flexible in the order and approach taken to address these problems. For example, sometimes correcting the horse problems opens the way for the rider to make progress on long-standing position faults, and sometimes it is the other way around! ◢

## PRACTICAL APPLICATION
### Future Possibilities

*Objective:* Review the qualifications of the horse and the rider, and the rider's motivation, interests, and future goals and dreams; then guide the student to investigate the possibilities as an educated consumer.

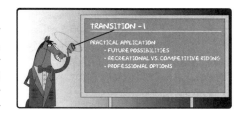

*Important Points*

1. Before you begin, review "Active Listening" so you can help your student "think out loud" and come to his or her own conclusions and decisions via the guidance of your well timed questions.
2. Review the Counseling Skills chapter, in terms of helping students think through their ambivalences, and being able to be a good sounding board.

**Toolkit**

↝ Set up private sessions with your student and the family to discuss the options. It is perfectly acceptable to charge your hourly teaching rate for this time. Spending time with your student during this critical period is as valuable as a riding lesson. Some of the points to discuss:

- Review and realistically evaluate with your student his or her skills, abilities, strengths and weaknesses.
- Resources (financial, social, emotional, and horse-wise) available to the student.
- Review student's interests and passions.
- Discuss limitations and constraints facing the student in terms of real life in a positive way.
- Discuss student's short- and long-term goals.
- Review the success, motivation and educated consumer chapters with your student.
- Give the student ideas and contacts to explore, and then discuss the results after the student has explored each option.

- Take the time to develop the student's confidence in taking the next step by including the student in discussions and listening carefully to expressed concerns, fears and loves.
- Encourage the student to come to you for guidance whenever it might be needed.
- Let your students know you are proud of them and happy for whatever they choose.

**Example:** Eva represented her region on the event team at Jr/Yr's; she was going to graduate the following June, so was thinking about what her next step would be. Her instructor and respected clinicians suggested she become a working student and develop her riding talents further. Eva loved horses and took this advice with respect, but was not sure that she really wanted to become a horse professional. Her parents helped Eva explore different options by encouraging her to seek out career-counseling services. Eva did so, and brought to the counselor both her instructors' recommendations and her uncertainty. Eva had the horse, the talent and the skills to become a sound professional. After all options were considered, Eva decided to pursue both her riding and another profession. In order to do this she had to dedicate twice as many years to her education so she could continue with college part time and horses part time. Eva planned to devote eight years to this, but ended up finishing her degree in six years and was able to get a job she enjoyed in the advertising field while also keeping a small competitive barn. The process of uncovering and exploring all these possibilities required considerable time and interaction between counselor, parents and Eva as they carefully considered all her possibilities from the long term goal to the day to day detail required with the various choices.

## Recreational versus Competitive Riding

*Objective:* To help student explore the options and requirements for each possibility.

**Toolkit**

🖙 Discuss ideas that your student might enjoy. Encourage students to investigate several choices that might be of interest to them; endurance riding, appropriate level of competitive riding, hunter/jumper, eventing, dressage, or fun with horses via foxhunting, polo and of course there is just general learning for FUN!

**Examples:** Two very different examples come to mind. Abby started riding again as an adult, when her youngest child was 8. They rode together, and Abby's love of riding was rekindled. She had been a successful hunter/equitation rider as a junior and her daughter was pursuing the same direction. Abby decided to not only support her daughter's hobby, but to join her. She decided to begin work with a local trainer. Abby worked hard for two years to reestablish her skills. She finally felt ready to make the move from lessons to the show ring. She met with her instructor to discuss purchasing a horse and to her surprise her instructor suggested she explore some different options before she decided to buy a show hunter. Her instructor suggested she explore endurance riding and foxhunting. Surprised, but intrigued by the suggestions, she followed her instructor's advice. After considerable investigation she decided to take up foxhunting. Abby was able to enjoy hunting two days a week and go to shows with her daughter on the weekends. Abby had the best of both worlds.

Tara, on the other hand, was graduating from high school and had reached her Pony Club "C-3" rating. Because her parents had invested so much time and money in Tara's riding they wanted her to continue her riding and pursue riding in college. Tara, however, wanted to experience a social life at college. Tara's instructor spent time with the family and helped them find a solution, which was an appropriate lease for the horse she loved, just in case she changed her mind. During her second year in college Tara realized that she missed her horse, but did not want the stress of lessons and competition. Instead, she decided to trail ride and enjoy the time with her horse for fun.

## Professional Options – Trainer and/or Instructor
### BECOMING A TRAINER

*Objective:* To help the student understand the requirements of becoming a trainer, the life of a trainer and what level and type of horse the student wants to train.

**Toolkit**

> Discuss ideas to investigate and explore training options. Explain to students that it will be necessary to begin the learning process over again with lots of review of what they have learned. Becoming a trainer is the same as graduating from high school, selecting a career and then beginning to educate for that career. The training the rider has had up until now equals their education from grade school through high school (see Stages of Rider Education). Specialization for training horses requires additional education.

**Example:** Tom loved horses, and when he finished high school he was a Pony Club "B." In particular Tom loved to back and start young horses. Tom and his instructor discussed the dangers both physically and financially. Once it was clear that Tom was not to be deterred in following this love, Tom's instructor put him in touch with several farms that had young horses. Tom contacted the farms and found the ideal intern position. He started out as an apprentice to the head trainer and over the next two years gained knowledge and experience. Today Tom is a well-respected handler and backer for young horses.

### Becoming an Instructor

*Objective:* Discuss the requirements and options for pursuing a teaching career.

- Review Career Development chapter with the student.
- Help student explore the requirements of becoming an instructor. Suggest different ways a student can pursue a career in teaching (see career development).
  - Equine College
  - Regular College, taking education courses and riding on side
  - Apprentice with a qualified instructor

**Example:** Brenda, a successful hunter/jumper rider loved teaching at summer camp. Brenda had the skill to become either a trainer or an instructor. Without a doubt, after discussing options with her instructor, Brenda was certain she wanted to teach. Since Brenda had ridden almost every day of her life since she was six years old, her instructor helped her see the possibilities of keeping more avenues open. Brenda decided to enter a college with an equine science program so she could get her college degree, pursue her competitive riding and learn more about teaching. When Brenda graduated she was able to get a job that required some training and some teaching. Over the next few years she was able to create a balance she really enjoyed. Brenda rewarded her instructor with a nice letter, "Sally, thank you so much for helping me pursue my career choice. I love my job and have you to thank for it."

It is very important to help students become aware of their assets as well as their limitations, so they will be able to make a choice that leads to success and carries the ethical standards of excellence. We do not want riders to think they can become instructors or trainers without the well-rounded skills.

For students who want to continue their education as trainers, instructors or in competition to levels higher than low hunters, novice eventing, or training level dressage, Transition 2 following Stage 4, is the time that instructors ideally help their students decide if they have the time, talent, money and aptitude to continue on to Stage 5. Students making the choice to move on to Stage 4 must be dedicated to learning, have a firm foundation in the skills of Stage 3 and must recognize that moving through the next stage of riding requires considerable time and money.

We strongly urge all trainers, instructors and students motivated to jump higher than 3'6" or train 3rd level or higher in dressage to become familiar with both the theory and the practical stages of the proven German Scale of Education and Stages 4 & 5 of Rider Education. Anyone can learn theory but only a few can enjoy the practical application of this theory. **Example:** I (Jill) am frequently frustrated by this situation and Cari is a typical example of the challenges facing many American riders. Cari, a thirty five year old college and pony club graduate came to me for guidance to become a certified instructor. She believed in having proof of proficiency in all areas and wanted to pursue this in the field of rider education. She was a professional educator who also taught in the local pony club and owned her own horse. The challenges Cari faced were limited finances and an older horse who was at his peak at first level dressage. We discussed the reality of her situation and Cari decided to accept her limitations and continue to expand her knowledge and skills as much as her situation allowed. Today Cari attends as many clinics and workshops as she can, is one of the most popular pony club instructors, and is now preparing students for their "B" tests with good results. Since she could not get her USDF certification, she is carefully selecting professionals to do clinics with the pony clubbers, watching her students' lessons, asking lots of questions and integrating what she is learning into her own riding and teaching.

No matter what path your student chooses, instructors in this Transition Stage have an important job to do. Just as you guided and supported your students through the personal development of their riding abilities, you are now in a position to support and guide your students through the decision of how to continue with their love of riding. You have the opportunity to help them maneuver their ways through the numerous opportunities and challenges facing them at this critical juncture of their lives.

# STAGE 4
# THE 1ˢᵗ PHASE OF PARTNERSHIP DEVELOPMENT - WHERE RIDER EDUCATION AND HORSE EDUCATION MEET

*Stages 1, 2 and 3 of the Rider Education System focused on developing important fundamental rider skills including the establishment of a correct, basic balanced position; a following, educated seat; and a basic sense of feel acquired from the sensitive and correct application of the aids. Riders are now ready to move on to more advanced stages of a classical education, where their own education and the horse's education come together. This process culminates in a true horse and rider partnership.*

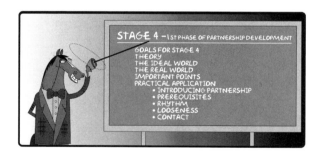

## GOALS OF STAGE 4

During this stage, the teaching emphasis now shifts from being focused primarily on the rider to focusing on the rider and horse combination. Instruction now emphasizes the *quality* of the beginning partnership that is developing between horse and rider. With Stage 4 students, instructors will find it helpful if they can stay aware of the separate goals for the rider and the horse that are specific to each one's role in the partnership.

**Rider Goals:**
- To develop a deeper understanding of the mechanics and psychology behind classically correct horse training.
- To develop an understanding and appreciation for, and a recognition of, a true partnership between rider and horse.
- To learn and consistently use the training prerequisites and preparatory half-halt.
- To understand how rhythm, looseness, and contact interact and develop together to produce an energetically forward, round horse that offers his energy into the rider's elastic, receiving hand.

**Horse Goals:**
- To develop and maintain a consistent, natural rhythm in all three gaits and over fences.
- To develop and maintain the quality of looseness in all three gaits and over fences.
- To develop an elastic, consistent contact through which the rider receives the energy created from the forward movement.

## THEORY

The concepts of rhythm, looseness, throughness and a more defined contact are introduced and developed in this stage. Instructors will find it helpful to review these sections in the Theory Made Simple chapter.

## THE IDEAL WORLD

As has been stated in each previous stage, the ideal situation is one where students enter Stage 4 having established solid skills from the previous three stages. In this wonderful, ideal world students have developed a keen sense of "feel" when riding, and have learned the proper coordination and application of aids, so that they can confidently address horse problems that arise when riding trained horses. Their timing is good, as is their body control and awareness. These riders are now ready to approach the training of a young or green horse under supervision. (Reminder: This is the *ideal world*; in reality, many riders either learn on green or young horses, or seek them out to "train" much earlier on in their riding educations!)

*IDEALLY, riders are not asked to work with green horses until they have reached Stage 4 because in the earlier stages their abilities are not well-enough established to be of service to the horse.*

Horse training, like rider education, proceeds most quickly and comfortably (for both rider and horse) when one member of the team is wiser and more educated than the other. For young, green horses, this team member should be the rider. Horses, like riders, learn best when one of the two team players can be the mentor, guiding the greener one through the learning process with tact and sensitivity. Horses are fairly simple creatures in terms of how they respond to their environments. When first exposed to a new situation, their brains are wired to remember results that either produce pain (so as to avoid in the future) or pleasure (so as to approach in the future). If a well-schooled rider is riding a horse and asks the horse clearly for a certain response, and then rewards the horse promptly for the correct response, the horse's brain fires "voila!" and learning is in progress. The same situation in the hands of a less experienced rider produces inconsistency in either the asking, the rewarding, or both – causing the horse's brain to either record the "wrong response" or to become confused, recording many different responses. This results in frustration, anxiety, and possibly pain and fear for both the horse and the rider. *Therefore, the fastest, most comfortable, and effective way to train young or green horses is to have them ridden by riders who have reached Stage 4 (or above) in their riding educations.*

*In the German Scale of Education, riders would not begin to train horses until they have acquired the skills from Stage 5.*

## THE REAL WORLD

It is truly exciting for riders to ride at the Stage 4 level. The wonderful feeling of moving as a team with the horse, and the focus on improving the quality of the horse's performance – these are powerful motivators for riders during this stage. Despite the considerable amount of knowledge and skills these riders demonstrate, the reality is that a considerable number of Stage 4 students who enter lesson programs or attend clinics also present significant core weaknesses in their basics. Many of these weaknesses involve position problems that contribute to the lack of an independent seat and hand. Moreover, many of these riders misunderstand classical riding and training theory. Some Stage 4 riders are even mounted on green or incorrectly trained horses! As a result, one of the biggest challenges in riding instruction in the United States today is the need to retrain many of the basic skills in riders who have moved beyond the early stages of their riding educations. These students skipped the ideal learning progression through the basics for one reason or another, resulting in very accomplished and often competitively sophisticated riders, who also have significant weaknesses in their riding skills. Today's instructors of Stage 4 students are challenged in some critical ways: they must correctly evaluate and diagnose the core weaknesses in their students' basics and rebuild those basics without demoralizing the students, while also continuing to help the students progress forward and meet their goals. The struggle of how to do this is one of the factors that instructors find frustrating and stressful, and is one factor in creating instructor burnout. The System of Rider Education presented here is designed for American students and instructors to allow flexibility when working through the stages. There are ways to work simultaneously on issues from two different stages.

> *Think outside the box and be willing to intermix skills from different stages and steps as needed.*

Thinking outside the box is essential when teaching riding to today's students. It is also helpful to ask other instructors for ideas and suggestions to get a broader perspective and valued input for particular challenges.

**Example:** Amy was two weeks away from the Regional Dressage Finals. Her instructor knew something was wrong as Amy's horse was inconsistent in the bridle and Amy could not sit the trot. Amy and her instructor tried several approaches to solve the problem, but nothing worked. Amy's instructor asked me (Jill) to consult with them for advice. Two problems became apparent as I watched Amy warm-up and asked her to review her warm-up. First, she was so focused on her problems that she was unable to see anything positive; and second, her horse was heavy on the left shoulder and Amy was constantly holding on the right rein, preventing him from moving correctly through to her hand, as well as causing her to lock up in her body. We had a short talk about a positive point of view and being able to recognize when the performance was better (not necessarily perfect). Then I had her work on getting her horse's shoulders equally light at the walk. By the end of the lesson Amy felt comfortable sitting the trot and felt her horse moving forward to her hands. A fresh point of view and different vocabulary enabled Amy to have a breakthrough. Both instructor and student gained some valuable input and Amy placed well at the finals!

Instructors must always be aware of the potential need to review or even re-introduce certain steps in the stages of rider education. The challenge is to avoid doing this in a way that discourages the student. It can help to explain some basic learning theory (for example, two steps forward, one step back) to let students know that it is normal to have periods where they have to rebuild the foundation of a skill. Returning to the missing step and rein-stating it correctly is the only way to ensure that proper develop-ment continues to take place in the long term. 🐎

Many riders have learned the basics without riding horses that are correctly trained. At this stage it is important to discuss with students how you (instructor and student together) are going to educate their horses. If students are resistant or do not under-stand, the instructor may need to ride the students' horses, de-scribing what aids are being used at each point, to help students begin to develop their eyes and their "feel." 🐎

## IMPORTANT POINTS

1. This book spends considerable time providing instructors with an understanding of classical theory through descriptions, definitions, and illustrations of the important concepts and terms associated with the German System of horse training. What is presented here is based on this system and adapted for the American culture and the realities that instructors face teaching in America.

2. During this stage instructors are now introducing the concepts of classical horse training principles to their students. The theory be-hind Stage 4 of the rider's education is based on the successful Ger-man System, specifically the first Phase in the Scale of Education for the horse. In order for instructors to successfully teach the com-plex and demanding skills required in Stage 4, they need to be thor-oughly grounded in the order and foundation of this classical infor-mation themselves (see the German Scale of Education in the Theory Made Simple Chapter).

3. If instructors are clear in their minds about the theory behind the classical system of rider and horse education, they are free to be creative and flexible about how they intermix the stages in this American system to help their students advance (see Introduction – Wheel). It is when instructors are not clear on the 'big picture' that the seeds of confusion, frustration, and incorrect riding are planted, fertilized and grown.

4. When teaching, it is the instructor's responsibility to identify whether a lack of correct response from the horse is a problem with the rider, the horse, or a combination of both.  In all cases, it helps if the instructor can take the student or horse back, step-by-step, and reestablish the missing pieces in their educations.

5. No matter whether it is the horse or the rider that has a problem, returning quickly to a step that the horse and rider understand en-sures progress. Sometimes this means jumping back and sometimes ahead, but the important piece is to always return to a successful experience for horse and rider. This keeps the learning process fun and encouraging so riders stay open and receptive to new challenges.

If a rider issue presents itself, the instructor needs to use good communication skills (see psychology and communication chapters) to engage the student so that the student *wants* to return to the previous steps in order to uncover the problem, and is willing to add the time needed to fill in the 'hole' that is preventing further advancement. 🐎

# PRACTICAL APPLICATION

## Introducing Partnership

*Objective:* To teach the student: 1) to understand and recognize the factors that make up a partnership, 2) to recognize the difference between having a partnership and not having one, and 3) to connect the role of position,

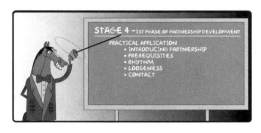

use of aids, and the need for "feel" in the development of that partnership.

*Theory:* The development of a partnership between horse and rider involves looking at the qualities of each individual member of the team honestly and realistically. This means identifying the needs, strengths and weaknesses of both rider and horse. In addition, it means identifying those areas where individual strengths and weaknesses will affect the team's development and performance. It is important to take into consideration each individual's mental and physical attributes. Once these have been evaluated, a plan can be made to enhance the strengths and to strengthen the weaknesses using previously learned skills and new skill sets that will be introduced in this stage.

*Important Points*

1. The increased focus on the partnership between rider and horse means that the instructor needs to be sensitive to the needs of both. There must be clear, specific explanations of what the partnership as a whole needs in order for the pair to advance towards their long-term goals. This can be difficult, if it means that the rider or horse needs something the other cannot provide. **An example**: Sam has had Shiloh since he was a 3-year-old colt. He did almost all the training himself, and did an impressive job. Shiloh is now 8 years old, and the two are preparing for Sam's Pony Club "B" rating later in the summer. Sam, while attending prep clinics, received feedback that his horse was not truly "through" in his back, mainly because Shiloh was crooked. After observing the pair in motion, it soon became clear that Sam had a habit of locking his left arm, and dropping his shoulder in response to Shiloh's locking of his inside jaw and shoulder. The habits were so ingrained with each member

of the team that we decided to temporarily break up the partnership. Sam rode another horse for two weeks, working on straightening his position, feeling the "correct response" to his rein aids, and improving the quality of his contact. Shiloh was ridden by a rider who did not have Sam's particular set of position problems, and soon learned how to move forward and straight, with proper bend and flexion. When the pair was reunited two weeks later, it was like watching a completely new partnership in motion. Sam and Shiloh were not feeding off of one another's bad habits, and as a result they were beautiful to watch. The strong connection and good will between them was evident, and they made rapid progress in a short time. Sam not only passed his B that summer, he exceeded the standards on his flat work!

**Toolkit**

- Help your student to identify performances that reflect qualities of a good partnership using videos, horse shows, tapes, pictures, and demonstrations. Compare and contrast with performances that do not reflect such qualities.

- Have your student watch a well-executed warm-up done with proper rhythm, sufficient looseness, and correct contact. Ask questions about throughness such as, "When do you think this horse is "through"? "What are you seeing?" and "Why?" Then, have students watch a warm-up without these qualities. Ideally, this should be done on the same horse. Students need to see movements done both with and without throughness in order to develop their eyes.

- Video portions of your student's ride, and play it back with your student. This can be a whole separate lesson if needed. This is a powerful learning tool for developing your student's eye, and helping match what is felt with what is observed.

- Ask your students questions to help them connect the role of each of the skills they have learned in previous stages to each of the steps in Stage 4. Stay attuned to the balance of intellectual versus body learning. Try to keep their minds and bodies engaged in the learning process.

*Test to show understanding of Partnership:* Ask a lot of questions! Ask students to describe how what they have learned previously (in Stages 1, 2 and 3) is coming together in Stage 4, and how they understand the developing partnership between rider and horse. This is an ideal time to get a clear picture of each partnership's assets and weaknesses at this stage in their training, and to share this information with the rider.

To help expand students' awareness of "feel" and use of aids, instructors need to give students opportunities to evaluate what is going on with the horse before they jump in and correct them. As students refine their awareness, their overall confidence in their riding abilities and senses of feel will increase. ⚘

## Prerequisites

*Objective:* For students to 1) learn and use the four prerequisites (Energy, Inside Flexion, Contact, and Straightness and Balance) that need to be in place before a rider can prepare horses for doing a movement, and 2) learn to know when and how to use the half-halt to prepare the horse for each action or movement.

*Theory:* One of the main goals of Stage 4 is teaching students how to refine the use of the aids, especially the half-halt. Although the half-halt is used for many purposes, one of its most common uses is to prepare a horse for a movement, change of direction, turn, or any other shift or transition. The "preparatory half-halt" works best when the rider has established certain training prerequisites, but in another one of the many circular actions of horse training, the preparatory half-halt can also help establish the prerequisites.

*Important Points*
1. The ability of the rider to consistently develop the prerequisites during a ride depends a great deal on the instructor's own consistent use of systematic training and reminders.
2. Students whose education has progressed in an orderly fashion through a System of Rider Education will find this prerequisite step to be a reminder of what they have already learned in previous stages. Students who are new to this system of rider education may require some shifting back and forth between stages and steps to learn these new skills in order to create effective riding habits. It is consistent practice that creates the prompt reaction of the rider.
3. Students must become aware that they need to use the preparatory half-halt both to prepare horses to enter an exercise or movement, and to exit the exercise or movement. **Example**: Kim wanted to supple her young horse, and did a good job of preparing him to go onto the circle. However, when she finished the circle she just let him go around the arena. She could not figure out why he speeded up after every circle. After watching her and asking her a few questions, she realized that she had just assumed he would come out of the circle on his own and go around the ring. Once she began to prepare him to leave the circle with a preparatory half-halt, she discovered he was able to maintain the same rhythm as he went off the circle.

The preparatory half-halt is so versatile that it is used both before and after the establishment of the prerequisites! ⚞

 Remind students often of the need to establish the prerequisites throughout the steps in this stage. ⚞

## Toolkit

⚞ Introduce the prerequisite steps that are needed by the horse for all movements, including transitions. These important points will be a review for the student who is moving through the stages in an orderly fashion. These concepts will be new or unfamiliar to those students who have missed some of the basics from earlier stages. If this information is new to your student, review the relevant concepts from the Theory Made Simple chapter.

- Energy: sufficient energy from the horse's hind leg in prompt response to the rider's leg and seat,
- Inside flexion: achieved from the rider's inside leg with help of inside fingers,
- Contact: consistent and elastic connection in the outside rein,
- Straightness and Balance: maintain balance and straightness through the horse's body without losing the outside hind leg.

⚞ If you find yourself introducing a new movement into your student's repertoire, first teach the theory, purpose, and the expected change of the horse's body position related to route for each movement. Then let the student ride the horse in the new movement. After they have tried the new movement a couple of times, discuss what they liked and what they need to change, paying particular attention to the presence or absence of the prerequisites before, during, and after the movement.

⚞ To introduce students to using the preparatory half-halt, have them first perform simple, familiar exercises while focusing on preparation. For example, ask the student to prepare for a circle and see if the horse moves onto the circle with ease and comfort, or does the student just turn the horse onto the circle, resulting in possible loss of balance by the horse. If the horse is not comfortable, ask the student how he or she prepared for the circle.

- Use the same procedure with transitions. Transitions with flexion on the long wall are very useful in helping the student properly prepare the horse. Example: Each time Andrea did a transition to canter she began her canter and her circle at the same time. I asked Andrea why she did it that way and she replied, "It is easier." She was correct but she did not know why it was easier.

Also, she was not preparing her horse properly for the transition. We discussed how to properly prepare a horse for a transition using a slight inside flexion, energizing the hind leg and then asking for the transition while the horse remains on the outside track. The first time Andrea went from walk to trot she felt her horse move against her inside leg instead of bending around it and remaining on the track. It took only six transitions between walk and trot for Andrea to learn the benefit of preparing her horse for the transition.

🖋 To begin teaching the habit of preparation, have students practice using the preparatory half-halt after all the prerequisites are in place. First check straightness, then engage the horse, and then ask for the response (Review the preparation steps of a half-halt in Stage 2 and 3).

As students develop their timing and coordination with this aid, have them begin using the preparatory half-halt to help establish the prerequisites.

**Q:** What if one of the prerequisites is lost when we ask for the intended movement?

**A:** Instructors need to help the student make a decision:
a) Correct the problem during the movement or, b) return to an earlier exercise to reestablish the lost prerequisite.

It is not acceptable to continue on as if nothing has happened.

**Example:** Before Mary cantered her horse, she checked on the engagement of his hind legs, his inside flexion and his connection to the outside rein. She prepared him for canter by asking for even more engagement and holding the increased energy in her outside hand. As she did this, he swung his hindquarters to the outside. Mary chose to correct this evasion as she continued to ask him to canter. On a less experienced horse, who might be new to cantering, she would abort the canter depart and rebalance the horse to prepare him to canter. Instructors need to help their students learn to make these decisions. Experience combined with the input from the instructor provides the student with the tools to experiment.

🖋 Use the following list of exercises, in this order, for each day's ride - while maintaining the above prerequisites. These exercises progress from straightforward, easy to execute movements to more complex ones. It can be detrimental to the learning process for both rider and horse if they are allowed to move on to harder exercises before they have been successful with the simpler ones.
- Basic ring figures
- Transitions with bend/flexion
- Lateral work with correct bend
- Transitions in lateral work

To help solidify a rider's sense of feel, compliment their moments of success. Likewise, when riders are not getting it, clarify the desired response through demonstration, explanation, and/or feel. 🐎

Even when riders know the importance of preparing horses for ALL actions, and then preparing them to end the action, they need constant reminders to develop the habit of consistently preparing the horse. 🐎

**Test to show understanding of Prerequisites:** Ask the student to list the prerequisites for any movement, and then have the student demonstrate riding ring figures and lateral movements with proper preparation. Ask the student how to recognize when a rider is, and is not, using proper preparation for a movement. What signs would the horse exhibit? The rider? What happens to the horses' balance and throughness when riders properly prepare horses for movements versus when they do not?

## Rhythm

*Objective:* For riders to understand, recognize, maintain and develop consistent, natural rhythm in the horse.

*Theory:* Rhythm is the backbone of the entire classical training program for the horse. The concept of rhythm is easy to understand for the musically inclined, but for many it must be learned. Rhythm is the regularity of the strides in each gait, with each stride covering equal distances and with equal duration of time between footfalls. From the time riders get on their horses, it is their responsibility to feel their horses' rhythms and get on the 'same page' as their horses. Each horse has his own unique rhythm. Rhythm needs to be maintained during transitions, movements, turns and straight lines.

*Important Points*

1. Instructors discuss with students the role of rhythm and its effect on everything they do while riding. The factors that influence rhythm, such as looseness and contact, need to be explained so the student understands the interactions between them. This is where the instructor's comfort level with the theory behind these concepts becomes important. If the instructor is not clear, or is confused, the student will be also!

2. "On Route." Often horses will deviate from route rather than maintain rhythm and balance. Riders often miss this evasion because they do not want to interfere; they 'feel' that their performances will be disrupted if they ride through the corners, so they allow their horses to cut the corners and thus miss a training opportunity. Some riders just ride around, unaware of the importance of using the 'whole' ring and riding accurate figures. Staying on route

and being consistent with this awareness provides for more accurate training sessions, more balanced horses and faster training progress. This is one of the things that riders are most often unaware of. When driving our cars, we do not wander around...why do this on a horse?

*At all times and in ALL movements a consistent rhythm is essential.*

**INSTRUCTOR'S REMINDER** Effective riders strive to maintain the exact same rhythm at all times; through curves, transitions, and straight lines as well as through ring figures and lateral movements. 🐎

## Toolkit

🐎 To help your students identify their horses' natural rhythms, ask your students questions as they ride at walk, trot, canter and over jumps. Some good questions include: "What is natural in terms of movement for this horse today? (For example: stiff, slow, excited, fast, etc.)," "What can you do to help this horse at this moment? In two moments from now? In three?" "Do you like this rhythm?" "Is this the horse's natural rhythm?" "Do you have to make a lot of adjustments or not?" "How many steps do you get between adjustments?" And so on. As a result of this awareness, riders will begin to put together the word "rhythm" and a feeling. This is success!

🐎 To help your students learn how to synchronize their own body movements to a horse's natural rhythm, have your students close their eyes and then answer questions as described above. Allow periods of silence as the student tries to feel the natural pace of the horse's rhythm. Instructors often feel very 'boring' at this time, but riders need this quiet time to really focus on what they are doing. The students are not bored as they are very busy 'feeling' their horses' rhythms! It is essential that the rider learns to adapt to the horse's natural rhythm, rather than expecting the horse to adapt to the rider. The natural rhythm of the horse can only be changed through training and exercises building on this natural rhythm.

- As students learn to feel the horse's rhythm, this is a good time for instructors to help students understand the difference between rhythm, being forward, and going fast. This takes time to understand both visually and through feeling, and is one of the challenges in teaching rhythm with forward energy. An ideal time to help students feel this is **after** the canter. Ask students to go forward to trot from canter, reestablish the same rhythm in the trot that they had before the canter and then feel the trot. When the same rhythm is established riders can feel the increased engagement. This is a good time to find out how they would describe this feeling, as well as the difference between these three concepts. As the instructor, help your students find the 'right' questions to ask themselves during practice sessions so that they can tune into the correct feeling regarding rhythm and forward energy, and not speed.

🏇 Have your students jump caveletti, grids and courses with the focus on identifying the differences in their horses' rhythms, and how they can maintain a steady rhythm. When jumping, the rider's aids often need to be applied faster, and with more coordination than when riding on the flat because of the horse's increased energy and excitement level. Similar questions can be asked as described above, but the focus may be on recognizing how the horse changes as the circumstances change. If the rider feels out of control or uncomfortable with the horse's pace or speed, go back to single fences, lower fences, or both, and build upwards from there.

The instructor's role in helping students develop their senses of 'feel' is of utmost importance. No matter what level rider, the reality is that the person on the ground can sometimes see more than the rider can feel, and having regular input from a ground person will help the rider continue to refine a sense of feel. Instructors can keep the student's mind on track with positive reminders and questions that expand awareness and planning skills. It is important to tell your students what is good so they can attach a feeling to it. This helps them make corrections when it is not correct, thus time is not wasted practicing the incorrect feel.>

*Test to show understanding of Rhythm:* Have the student identify and maintain the horse's natural rhythm while on a route that includes simple ring figures, and a course of jumps.

## Looseness

*Objective:* To gain an understanding of what looseness is, to recognize its presence and absence, and to learn exercises that create and develop looseness in the horse while maintaining rhythm.

*Theory:* Looseness is often referred to as relaxation or suppleness. When the horse is loose, he is working through his back, with muscles that are free of tension, and joints that bend and straighten equally on each side of the body with each step. Stretching is essential to the concept of looseness, both as an exercise and as a test. As an exercise, stretching makes a horse become more longitudinally supple. As a test, once moving with looseness, horses will want to stretch.

INSTRUCTOR'S
REMINDER

In order to allow the horse to be loose the rider must establish a deep, elastic, following and independent seat. Often riders need to loosen themselves up too, preferably off the horse. Suppling exercises found in yoga, tai chi or Pilates can be useful rider supplements for this purpose. As soon as both partners are as loose as possible, it is time to decide what exercises will help the horse advance his training throughout the training session. ◀

*Important Points*

1. Horses do not develop looseness when they are "higher than a kite," anxious, or otherwise distracted by the environment. Only when the horse is in a relaxed state and mentally focused on the rider can looseness occur.

2. The feeling of a horse that is moving with looseness is where the horse is using his whole body in a relaxed way while coming forward with a round back, with energy, and in rhythm.

3. The concept of the circle of muscles helps riders understand how looseness is achieved.

4. Although the three concepts of rhythm, looseness, and contact are described and talked about separately, it is important to re-member that, in practice, they are all closely interlinked. These three concepts are attended to in each ride, at all levels of horse training, from green youngsters to older schoolmasters. Most im-portantly, rhythm, looseness, and contact are the foundation of the classical training system. As horses develop in one area, such as rhythm, this automatically improves the other two areas. For example, the more we develop looseness/relaxation, the more improvement we will see in rhythm and contact, and vice versa.

5. Each horse's state of looseness and relaxation depends upon his unique conformation traits and degree of natural balance. The addition of a rider to the equation can be either an enhancement or an obstacle for the horse. The positive or negative effect of the

rider on the horse's natural looseness and relaxation depends upon the rider's own level of skills, balance and relaxation.

6. Horses can resist moving with looseness in two ways, by slowing their rhythms down or by speeding up. In order to maintain the forward rhythm on a slow horse, the rider may need to use forward, driving aids to keep the hindquarters active. For a horse that speeds up the rhythm, the rider may need to use a lot of half-halts.

**Example:** Tim and Snowman were a new team. Snowman moved with a lot of body stiffness, especially through his back. As a result, Snowman was always trying to avoid the corners. The corners require some degree of bend, thus making him use his body, which Snowman did not want to do. I asked Tim, "Does Snowman feel 'loose' to you"? "I don't know," Tim replied. I tried another question, "Tim, how do you know if Snowman is using his muscles?" Tim's response was, "I have no idea." This honest and direct answer made me think that Tim could benefit from a simple explanation of what muscles we pay attention to when riding, and how they work. "Tim, lets discuss what muscles a horse uses and for what purpose and then practice some exercises." Once I gave Tim an overview of the Circle of Muscles he understood more of what was making it hard to get Snowman into the corners. He began to understand that when Snowman brought his hind legs up under himself, especially in corners, he was made to use his back, which Tim felt in the increased swinging of Snowman's pelvis. Tim now understood the need to really ride his corners, as they helped get Snowman to use more of his body, which helped him to become relaxed and loose! After an explanation of the bending exercise from Stage 2, we began practicing riding around the ring, using corners and circles to link Tim's intellectual understanding with the ridden 'feeling.' Within half an hour Tim was able to feel some of Snowman's back and neck muscles begin to work, and was able to feel the difference between times when Snowman was tight and stiff, and when he was more relaxed and loose. Success!

### Toolkit

To help riders develop looseness on horses that are stiff, have your students perform exercises that use overbending (neck bending) while remaining on route. Most stiff horses struggle to do this. When asked to stay on route with contact and maintaining their rhythms while overbending, horses are made to use their bodies and thus stretch and relax. All the rules taught in Stage 2 about overbending are used in this exercise. If the rider can use the overbending exercise (for short periods only) while riding various exercises, this will help the horse work through his stiffness by stretching each side of his body, thus promoting looseness. Be careful that the rider uses these overbending exercises correctly and can easily and correctly shift between an overbend and a correct bend, so that the horse does not learn to stay in the overbend, thus using it as an evasion.

It is very important not to get 'greedy' here. Once horses submit and understand that they can move their bodies, they begin to use muscles that have been without motion for a long time. Attention must be paid to keeping the initial working sets short, and only gradually increasing the work time and demands so the horse can slowly become accustomed to using his body in this new way.

- Have your students ride "correctly ridden" circles. Done well, circles actually promote looseness in much the same way that correctly riding corners does – by increasing inside leg engagement, roundness in the back, and body bend. That is, by asking the horse to maintain straightness on a curve, the rider is encouraging the horse to use his inside hind leg further engaged under his body, which requires the horse to use his back muscles and stretch all along the outside of his body, all of which promote looseness! Caution: when a rider uses a circle to balance or control the horse rather than using the circle to bend/supple a prepared horse, it is a sign of loss of control. This is frequently seen when the instructor asks the student to canter, and as soon as the horse canters, the student falls onto a circle. Work with the student so that he or she either begins the circle in the trot and then asks for the canter, or canters while going straight and balances the horse *before* starting the circle.

- Help your students identify the "feeling" of looseness by riding various exercises with a focus on describing looseness. Ask your students to provide you with "feeling words" of their own choosing to describe the feeling of looseness throughout the different movements.

- Review with your students the purpose of different exercises so that they can learn when, how, and why they should use them in their quests to develop rhythm, looseness, and contact (See Chart 51). By teaching your students to understand the specific benefits of various exercises, you develop their awareness of the blocks and stiffness in the horse, as well as the confidence to experiment with the exercises. Ultimately you want your student to have the knowledge, feel, and understanding that will allow them to know when, and how, to use a specific gymnasticizing exercise.

- Play with grid work and jumping exercises. The very act of the horse's jumping and basculing (rounding) over the fence helps horses become "loose" through their backs (and other muscles as well). Varying the distances between the grids can encourage a horse to jump from a shorter or longer frame, and can help riders learn to feel this difference. The shorter the distance between the jumps (but take care not to make the distances too short!), the more the horse has to come to the base of the fence, sit on his hocks, and round his back over the jump. The longer the take off distance, the flatter the horse can jump, as the bascule is not so pronounced. Some riders learn the "feel" of their horses' roundness more easily over fences than they do on the flat.

🐾•Stretching is a useful exercise to encourage looseness. The rider takes the elastic feeling that is created by the horse's moving properly forward into the rider's hand, and asks for the horse to take the rein forward and down as much as he can, until the rider is on a long, *but not loose,* rein. It is critical that the rider not lose contact – loss of contact will teach the horse to "root" the rein out of the rider's hands by pulling his head down. This is not proper stretching! When done correctly, stretching requires the horse to elongate his frame from back to front. In essence, stretching helps a horse supple his body longitudinally; similar to how shoulder-ins and leg-yields help horses to supple their bodies laterally. One good way to encourage horses to stretch is to have the rider do small overbending exercises within transitions. Help your students identify other exercises that work for their horses and then ask them to practice these until they develop some consistency in their abilities to ask their horses for a proper stretch. The key is preparing the horse to stretch by riding him forward and straight into a soft, elastic connection to the rein. Horses need to learn how to stretch at all three gaits.

A common question riders ask is, "How do I know if the stretch is enough?" This is a hard question to answer, as the amount a horse stretches in any given moment is relative to the horse's level of training, balance, and degree of looseness. Basically, you want the horse to stretch frequently between training sets, remaining aware to maintain rhythm, bend, or straightness.

🐾•The length of time the horse is asked to remain in the stretching position depends on the individual horse and what it has been doing prior to stretching, The main goal is to be able to have the horse move in and out of stretching with ease and no changes in rhythm, thus allowing it to be a relaxation exercise for the horse during the training session in addition to the other values. It is

important to note that the horse should wait for the rider to ask him to come back to the working frame.

Corners: Each corner is a training opportunity; it is essential to teach riders to prepare the horse *before* the corner, trust the horse *in* the corner, and prepare to *leave* the corner. 🐎

| EXERCISE BENEFITS FOR HORSE & RIDER | | |
|---|---|---|
| **Circle** | Rider | Stay "on route" with horse following directions without aid of wall |
| | Horse | Balance by carrying more weight on inside hind leg |
| **Corners** | Rider | Coordination, use of inside leg, release on inside rein, feeling of energy of inside hind leg going under seat with energy going to outside hand. |
| | Horse | Balancing and stretching body, engaging inside hind leg |
| **Neck Bending** | Rider | Use of reins independently |
| | Horse | Supples stiff horse, acceptance of bit |
| **Transitions "on route" with Bend** | Rider | Feel straightness vs. resistance / Coordination of inside leg to outside hand |
| | Horse | Supples and separates shoulder from hind leg |
| **Riding Cross Country** | Rider | Improves balance, coordination and timing |
| | Horse | Supples, builds muscle, encourages forward energy |
| **Stretching long & low** | Rider | Feeling of energy going forward, elastically through back |
| | Horse | Stretching and relaxing back muscles |
| **Leg Yield** | Rider | Coordination of aids |
| | Horse | Supples horse via response to sideways, pushing aids |
| **Turn on Forehand** | Rider | Coordination, one aid at a time |
| | Horse | Suppleness, response to aids |
| **Shoulder-in** | Rider | Coordination of aids |
| | Horse | Engagement & strengthening of inside hind leg Stretching of outside muscles |
| **Grids & Jumps** | Rider | Increases feel, confidence in forward movement, speeds up reactions |
| | Horse | Forward, supple & FUN |

Chart 51

*Tests to show understanding of Looseness:*

- Have the rider work the horse with the purpose of evaluating the degree of rhythm and looseness in the horse. Ask the rider to articulate what he or she is thinking and feeling during the ride.

- Ask your students to explain the benefits of the various exercises related to the development of looseness.

- Stretching is also used as a test of looseness. Before moving to the next step, the

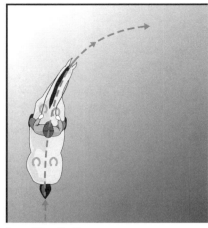

Correct Bend in Corner

horse needs to stretch down at least until the mouth is at the level of the elbow. The nose must always remain on the vertical or slightly in front. The rider will feel the horse stretching while maintaining the same route and rhythm. The horse may go as low as he is capable of going as long as rhythm and route remain the same. If route or rhythm change then the horse needs more supling exercises.

Once a horse is 'loose' and can correctly stretch without running, changing rhythm or route, and moves freely forward through his whole body in a natural rhythm, then the rider will find the horse easy to sit as well as accepting of the aids. 🐎

## Contact

*Objective:* To help the rider: a) develop an elastic, consistent rein connection with the horse that is capable of directing the forward energy created by the horse, and b) to maintain this elastic, consistent rein connection (receiving reference feel) while doing the ring figures listed in Step 4.

*Theory:* Up to Stage 4, contact has developed from a light contact, as we would ride in a hunter class, to light contact with the horse being round. For this Stage, riders learn how to ride their horses with increasing degrees of forward energy while maintaining the quality of the contact. The quality of the rider's contact is directly related to the horse's route (direction), roundness, looseness and rhythm. Most importantly, contact is never the result of a backward action by the rider's hands, but instead always results from forward action beginning with the horse's hind legs. Contact is never the result of a backward action by the rider's

hands, but instead always results from forward action beginning with the horse's hind
legs.

*Important Points*

1. For this stage, instructors build upon
   the skills of the steps in Stage 2 (receiving energy, reference feel and
   half-halt (adjustment) and Stage 3.

2. As the energy of the horse improves
   as well as his rhythm, the rider's
   ability to maintain a quality contact
   becomes increasingly difficult. Caution must be taken to help riders ride
   the increased energy and muscle
   strength of the horse without getting
   stiff and tight, which tends to result in riders holding and even
   riding backwards, from hand to leg. Keep riders focused on riding
   forward to a receiving hand.

> *Contact is never
> the result of a
> backward action
> by the rider's
> hands, but in-
> stead always
> results from
> forward action
> beginning with
> the horse's hind
> legs.*

| CONTACT through the STAGES | |
|---|---|
| Stage 1 | Practice without interfering with hands |
| Stage 2 | Develop light following hand |
| Stage 3 | Develop Reference Feel, light contact with some energy |
| Stage 4 | Energy into receiving reference feel, with consistent contact – horse develops roundness |
| Stage 5 | Roundness develops to 'on the bit' |

Chart 52

**INSTRUCTOR'S REMINDER**

The instructor's role during this phase is more often that of a
coach than an instructor, helping students discover how to use
what they know and gain confidence in making corrections (see
Coaching – Fundamental Teaching Skills). ⚞

**Toolkit**

- Discuss with your students the elasticity of their contact. Ask them
  to identify words that they can use as a reference point for the correct feeling of a quality contact.

- Encourage your student to be aware of the horse's hind leg energy
  coming through to a receiving hand. Ask them to articulate how
  they are directing this energy – for example, are they using an elastic-like contact or do they feel the contact becomes less flexible,
  more inconsistent, or backwards?

- Have your students evaluate for themselves the level of consistency of the contact as they ride their movements and half-halts. Do they find that the contact is better during simple movements, but becomes stiffer when other demands are placed upon them? The first step for students in learning how to be consistently steady and relaxed in their reins is to be aware of when they are not. . .and why.

- Have your students ride occasionally with "bungee-type" reins so they can feel the degree of "elastic" they are trying to achieve with their leather reins.

- Ask your student to compare and contrast the quality of the contact when riding a trained horse versus a green one. Help the students develop an awareness of how a horse's stiffness can unwittingly make the rider stiff in turn.

- When jumping, begin teaching your students how to use the "advanced release" (following contact) over small fences and grids. This release is designed to provide the most control when jumping, but must not hinder the horse's use of head and neck in any way. Ask riders to pay attention to the horses' behaviors over the fence and on landing. If horses are being restricted by the riders' releases, they may do some (or all) of the following behaviors: pin their ears back, stop basculing over the fence (jump flat), minimize the use of their heads and necks, and most commonly, shake their heads upon landing, trying to pull the rein free from its restrictive position. Riders often find it helpful to use slow motion playback on video of their jumping lessons so that they can see how well they are able to maintain contact over the fence, without restricting the horse.

*Test to move to Stage 4:* Rider can maintain rhythm, looseness and quality of contact while performing any first level dressage test or riding a course of fences.

The move from Stage 4 to 5 is similar to choosing a graduate degree; very few riders have all the requirements of talent, time, money and desire. For this reason, the transition from Stage 4 to Stage 5 is one of the biggest steps a rider can take. It takes a lot of self-reflection, understanding, drive, and determination for a rider to make the decision to move forward towards Stage 5. For this reason, we place the second transition stage, Transition 2, after Stage 4 and before Stage 5. Instructors are encouraged to explore carefully and thoroughly the requirements for Stage 5 with their students. Stage 5 students need to be independent in body and mind and have the necessary skills to make decisions and put them into effect. Some degree of natural talent and quick, feeling reactions are needed for Stage 5. No matter what your student's decision is, the Stage 4 student has now entered the beginning of the "elite" levels of riding, where the degree of skill and talent needed is considerable. This is an enormous accomplishment that reflects much hard work, sacrifice, and "blood, sweat, and tears" on both of your parts! Again, celebrate with your students as they develop real competency at Stage 4.

# TRANSITION 2
# SELECTING A SPECIALTY AND MOVING ONWARDS

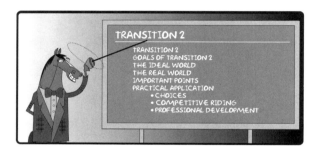

Once they "graduate" from Stage 4 in the Stages of Rider Education students enter another transition phase, where decisions are made about their equestrian goals and how they wish to pursue them. Riders desiring an advanced education, which can be equated to entering graduate school, will proceed onward to Stage 5. Other riders, for various reasons, will choose to stay at Stage 4, and enjoy the fruits of their labor. Regardless of your student's choice to stay at Stage 4 or move on to Stage 5, the partnership with their horses will continue to develop and grow. For all these riders, reaching a Stage 4 level of riding competency and skill is an inspiring accomplishment. The dedication, effort and time these riders have invested in reaching this goal are considerable, and we applaud all students who strive to attain this level of riding education.

The decision about the next stage of their riding education often requires riders to seriously consider the demands, requirements, and resources available to them as they pursue such an advanced education. Instructors can be a real resource for their students at this time, helping them to review and evaluate their talents and skills honestly and fairly.

# GOALS OF TRANSITION 2

1. To guide students in making realistic decisions about the next step that will lead to success.
2. To honestly evaluate students' interests, time, skill, aptitude, talent and money related to their goals and desires.
3. To create a plan with students to meet the agreed upon goals.
4. To enjoy and celebrate with students the level of competency they have reached.

## THE IDEAL WORLD

Ideally, all students who get to Stage 4 would be able to make their riding career decisions based solely on personal desire. For those who want to continue to Stage 5, they would, ideally, be sufficiently talented, dedicated, and well mounted enough to make this a realistic goal. These riders would have a solid background in classical riding and training and if competing, they would be doing so on appropriate horses at appropriate levels. Their learning progresses would have been orderly and gradual; their skills honed by spending long, correct hours in the saddle. These riders would also understand that, in order to pursue such goals as higher levels of competition, the training of horses beyond 1st level, or becoming an instructor of Stage 3 students and beyond, they would need to obtain a more advanced education. In this ideal world, these students could choose between traveling to Europe, taking on internships or apprenticeships here in the United States, or training privately with a qualified trainer.

There is also an "ideal" situation for those Stage 4 riders that would choose not to go forward with their educations. These riders could decide, for reasons of their own, that the skills they learned in Stage 4 were sufficient for them to enjoy their chosen equestrian pursuit. They would then choose to engage in horse activities that they found enjoyable and challenging, at safe and appropriate levels. These riders may also choose to pursue specialized training in a specific activity, such as starting young horses, retraining older or spoiled horses, or becoming a beginning and intermediate level instructor. In this ideal world, no matter what options these Stage 4 riders took, they would continue to develop and learn, while staying aware of their educational limitations.

## THE REAL WORLD

There are two common problems that crop up in the real world for riders who have reached Stage 4 in their educations. First, not all riders who desire to become highly educated riders have the talent, time, resources, dedication, or attitude to do so. Everyone has limitations and constraints imposed by their "everyday lives," and for some riders these can negatively impact their available options. For example, most instructors know of very talented riders who for many different reasons are unable to proceed with their riding educations. Often, it is due to a lack of finances and support. In the United States, riding at the upper levels is a very expensive proposition and sponsorships are limited. There are also those situations where riders dream of making the Olympics, but lack sufficient natural talent to make this goal realistic. Other obstacles can also get in the way, including internal factors like personality style and degree of people skills.

**Example:** Barbara loves horses, has reasonable talent, and a wonderful education gained through six years as a working student with a top professional. Barbara's dream is to be a horse trainer. The only problem is that Barbara's personal strengths are not in the area of people skills. She dislikes "playing the game" of attracting sponsors and owners, and her personality makes it hard for her to be flexible and compromising. As a result, Barbara had considerable difficulty making her dream a reality, despite the effort and time she put into doing so. Top riders and trainers tend to have highly developed interpersonal skills in addition to exceptional talent. This is important as they are constantly competing for the limited financial arrangements needed to attain and maintain upper-level performance. After much self-reflection and thought, Barbara decided to accept herself as she was rather than trying to change her personality. She modified her dream, and today Barbara is enjoying the training of a few select horses at the lower levels for customers that are grateful and appreciate her efforts.

 One of the harder things that Stage 4 students have to do is find a way to satisfy both their love of the sport and future educational desires within the limitations and constraints that "real life" imposes. This means being flexible and realistic enough to consider different approaches and avenues than what they initially desired or expected. ⌐

A second common problem that crops up with some Stage 4 riders is that they are allowed to proceed onward with their educations despite having significant gaps in their knowledge and/or abilities. The motivation for many of these riders (and instructors) is a desire to compete at the upper levels of competition. Unfortunately for these riders, when placed in this situation they are forced to "specialize" too soon. The demands of upper-level competitions often require some modifications in the basics. Without a firm riding education through Stage 5, riders asked to perform at these levels are forced to learn how to "break the rules before they know the rules." A creative instructor can teach students what they need to know to pilot a trained horse around a jumping course or dressage test, all the while bypassing the core principles taught in Stage 5. What this accomplishes is the development of a lot of "good passengers." However, these students are not, in the classical sense, "good riders." Some of these riders learn how to "passenger" quite well, developing high levels of coordination, balance, and skills; and succeed competitively. Despite these strengths, they are missing the firm classical foundation of an independent seat and knowledge and understanding of fundamental horse training principles.

Perhaps the biggest problem with this situation is that these riders mistakenly believe that the skills needed for competition and for training are one and the same. For classically educated riders, this can be true - these skills do have significant overlap. Unfortunately, for the riders who have missed some of the fundamental skills in their educations by progressing too fast up the competitive ladder, they are not the same. When riders skip up the levels and then enter the horse training profession, they do so without the prerequisite fundamental skills and understandings needed to properly educate and bring along young or green horses to the upper levels. Of course, the big losers in this situation are the horses and riders who develop under such a program. A vicious cycle begins, where horses and riders do not receive a solid, classical education; but then go on to teach and train others who then do not get a solid, classical education either, and so on.

## IMPORTANT POINTS

1. We continue to advocate that instructors have the theory and practical knowledge to ride two levels above what they are teaching. This means that those instructors who teach at Stage 4 or beyond need to have a solid grounding in classical education themselves. Only then are they in a position to mentor and guide their students through the demanding skills required at these levels.
2. Those instructors who do not have the needed qualifications to teach at the upper levels owe it to themselves and their students to recognize and accept their limitations. They can help guide their students through the difficult process of finding another instructor with a more advanced range of experience.
3. At this level students need to be independent learners and educated consumers. Instructors can help their students by teaching them to take the lead in planning their educational futures, as well as continuing their educations by integrating information from a variety of sources, such as books, videos, outside clinics, conferences, and so on.

# PRACTICAL APPLICATION

## Making Choices

*Objective:* To help students carefully evaluate the various educational opportunities available to them to decide which best fits their desires and situations.

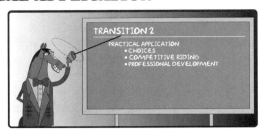

*Important Points*

1. Riders who have faced the accomplishments or challenges of Stage 4 are in a position to truly understand the time and devotion required to continue progressing up the levels of education.

2. Students have the same choices as in Transition 1, except they may choose to continue riding and competing at a higher level.
   - Recreation/Competition
   - Professional
   - Combination of both

**Example:** Dale graduated from pony club as a "B" and had a very competitive event career. Dale realized, with the help of her instructor, that she did not have the time or money to continue progressing up the competitive levels. However, she knew she loved horses and wanted to do something with them. She decided to work with project horses, capitalizing on her love of and patience with horses. Dale became a flight attendant to earn her living and had one project horse at a time that she brought along. Dale was very successful doing this and had many requests to take horses. Not having her own barn, Dale she realized she could not earn enough money to support herself this way full-time. With this realization, Dale remained happy with what she could do and enjoyed giving a few horses a good start.

### Toolkit

Enter into a realistic, honest discussion with your students about their goals and desires. Allow them the chance to say they don't know yet. As they begin to bring up different options, be honest about what each option requires, without being negative. Encourage students to give you a list of the pros and cons associated with different options, along with their own descriptions of their strengths and weaknesses.

Encourage your students to do much of their own research. You can provide real-life stories and experiences to supplement the information they find, making the experience come alive for them. Be careful not to take on too much of the responsibility for getting the information for your students. What they do on their own will have a stronger effect and greater impact than what you can tell them.

Try to encourage your students to do some "imagining" work. For each option they express a true interest in, have them envision their lives one year from now, two years from now, and then five years from now. Then ask them to project where they would want to be ten years from now. This is a difficult task for older teens and young adults to do, but it can be a very valuable one. At this age, young people do not want to really look at their options in "black and white," as it is more enjoyable to feel that all doors are open, and everything is possible. This exercise injects reality into the students' perspectives, which is something that they may be actively trying to avoid. As students come face to face with the reality of their situations, especially regarding something as important to them as horses and their riding, there might be a sense of loss if they see that what they want might not be able to happen, at least in the way that they want it to happen. An important part of growing up involves tolerating this loss of all possibilities. Instructors can help this process along as decisions around riding, education, college, and horses are often some of the most intense and important decisions students have had to make up until this point in their lives.

## Competitive Riding

*Objective:* To explore the requirements of the rider's chosen sport through the levels and decide if all the ingredients are in place to realistically pursue this sport competitively (see "The Real World" above).

*Important Points*
1. If a student intends to advance through the levels of a particular sport he or she needs to understand clearly the demands that sport places on the horse, the level of risk involved, financial requirements, and time required to be competitive. For example, competing in the hunter divisions will require a different level of fitness (thus time commitment) than competing at the intermediate or advanced levels of eventing. It is helpful to have your student watch upper-level competitions to see up close and personal what it is like.
2. It is important that the student understands that advancement through Stage 5 towards specific competitions requires working with a good professional who has had competitive experience at the level the student aspires to. Many students believe that their instructor can take them wherever they want to go, no matter what the instructor's background is because students are used to seeing the instructor as "the expert." It takes the intellectual part of the mind longer to figure out that one is a "better rider" now than one was a year ago. Despite students' progress and high levels of skill, students may still see themselves as disciples of a particular instructor, and will not want to voluntarily break

the bond. Students may need explicit permission from the instructor to do what is best for them, as they may feel selfish, or that they are abandoning the instructor.

3. Have an honest discussion with students to evaluate their skill levels and abilities. This can be a difficult discussion, as few riders are truly objective about their own riding. As well, many instructors find it hard to be objective about their students! It may be helpful to get an outside opinion from a trusted, neutral source- for both you and your student. Include parents in these discussions if appropriate. Remember to be sensitive yet fair. No one really wants to hear the truth if it is negative, no matter how much they say they do.

**Toolkit**

- Identify a rider's competitive interests and motivations behind the interest. For example, you can ask your student, "Why are you involved in this sport?" It may be because friends are doing it. Or, the student may be interested in the sport because it is all the student knows or has been exposed to. Some riders choose to specialize in a particular sport because the only qualified instructor around participates in that sport. Riders even choose sports because it is what their horses excel at. None of these motivators are necessarily bad, but it helps if the riders can be upfront and honest with themselves about why they are pursuing a particular activity.

- Have a realistic, honest discussion regarding the horse's skills and abilities. Some riders fail to take their horses' talents (or lack of) into consideration when choosing a sport or level of competition. Sometimes a rider's desire to advance is in direct conflict with the reality of his or her "best buddy's" limitations. This can be a trying and emotional time. Many times in a rider's life the rider will come to a place where what is good for them is different than what is good for the rider's partner – and vice versa. As well, riders at this stage think about getting a young horse to train to the upper levels, mainly because it is initially less expensive to go this route. It is important to have a frank discussion about the reality of a Stage 4 rider taking a horse all the way through the levels.

- Have a realistic and honest discussion about the demands and requirements of the sport. Some riders become spell bound by the thrill of competition and the glory of success. Yet for any sport, the day-to-day grind associated with the preparation is intense, and equestrian sport is no exception. It can be very helpful to encourage students to attend the big events or shows, and to go into the schooling areas and barns to see the "less glamorous" sides to the sport. In addition, it can be eye opening to have students talk to top competitors to see what their daily lives are actually like. Students can groom for instructors or other competitors they know. As in most cases, knowledge is power, and the more factual information students have about their sport of choice, the better.

## Professional Development

*Objective:* To help students understand the importance of continuing their educations and experiences under the mentorship of a qualified professional - whether they choose a career in teaching or training.

*Important Points*
1. Honest evaluation of skills, both riding and personal.
2. Students who want to become professionals must continue under qualified mentorship and experience to become well-qualified professionals.

### Toolkit
- Read career development chapter
- Explore internship possibilities
- Explore advanced education opportunities

#### CHOICES ARE NEVER EASY

Riders and instructors often have a long history that has developed into a solid, bonded relationship. The process of creating the relationship was rewarding, but more rewarding is knowing that you have helped develop a well-rounded and skilled rider who is ready to move on. As the instructor you can be proud, whether a student's riding turns into a profession, avocation, sport, or art. Students who have achieved the Stage 4 level of riding have something to celebrate, as both instructor and student have accomplished a great deal, and achieved success. During our teaching careers, some of the most rewarding moments occur when students call to share with us their personal and professional successes. We continue to take great pride in helping students make the decision to take the next step, despite knowing that the dynamics of our relationship will change. As instructors and clinicians, we are frequently called upon to help Stage 4 riders think through their career development plans. Many of our students struggle with these important life decisions, such as choosing between continuing college education, riding (or doing both); whether to live at college or become a working student and take college courses on the side. Each student is different, and our rewards come when the student, after careful consideration, completes what he or she started out to do, and finds joy and satisfaction in life. **Example**: Writing this brings to mind Alix, a gifted rider. During high school Alix rode several horses while working after school. She became a 'B' in Pony Club, and competed successfully. In my heart I wanted her to continue her horse career and develop her talent. However, during our discussions about her future, it became clear that while she loved the horses and what she was doing, she wanted to enjoy being a 'normal' young person and pursue the social aspects of college. I will always remember our conversation and the restraint I summoned to be quiet and listen. Now, 20 years later, I can enjoy the benefits of my restraint as Alix has a vital job in the medical field and enjoys her love of horses as a hobby.

# THE 2ND PHASE OF PARTNERSHIP DEVELOPMENT

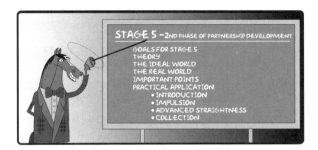

Riders who choose to proceed on to Stage 5 will now be working on the 2nd phase of partnership development, where the focus is on learning the skills necessary to work horses through the last three phases of the German Scale of Education; impulsion, straightness, and collection. Theory takes on considerable importance during this stage, as both rider and instructor need to have a clear understanding of balance and its complex relationship to straightness in order for the rider to put together the pieces that ultimately lead to collection. Please note: in this stage we do not go into as much practical, how-to detail as we do in previous stages. Students who have reached Stage 5 in their educations are quite competent in the basic technical skills, and thus need actual riding experience and time in the saddle under a qualified trainer's eye to develop the advanced abilities required by this stage. Therefore, we offer in this section only a general overview of Stage 5 requirements. There are some excellent books that delve thoroughly into the complex concepts in this stage, such as impulsion and collection (see the list of books in appendix). However, for riders to truly develop their skills to this advanced level, the two most important tools needed in this quest are: 1) a qualified instructor, and 2) a capable horse. With these two pieces in place, the stage is set for riders to experience the wonderful process of becoming equal partners with their horses as they learn to move together with cooperation, communication, and grace.

## GOALS OF STAGE 5

During this stage, the emphasis is on developing the horse's ability for self-carriage, which demands more from both rider and horse than in any previous stage. Instructors oversee the correct order, use and application of aids to assist students in improving their partnerships and performances.

**Rider Goals:**

- To develop a more advanced understanding of straightness and its relationship to impulsion, balance, and collection.
- To become increasingly sophisticated and educated in the application of the aids for more advanced and complex exercises.
- To improve a horse's performance using appropriate training exercises in a logical order.
- To become skilled at the more advanced exercises that develop impulsion through attention to straightness, leading to collection.
- To use and maintain these skills while jumping more advanced courses over a variety of terrain.

**Horse Goals:**

- To build and maintain correct muscle development through consistent and correct work under saddle and on the lunge line.
- To achieve a greater degree of suppleness, resulting in the offering of a more elastic contact.
- To develop increased power, energy and thrust while maintaining straightness, which leads to the ability to collect.

## THEORY

In Stage 5, riders are ready to learn the fourth, fifth, and sixth steps in the German Scale of Education (impulsion, straightness, and collection) and put them into practice.

For riders to progress into and through this stage, it **is now critical for the instructor to pay attention to the rider's position and "feeling" skills as they developed from the earlier stages.** Significant weaknesses in either of these areas will cause a rider to unknowingly hinder the horse in his ability to respond properly or to perform an exercise or movement correctly.

Instructors and riders should review the theory behind the concepts of impulsion, straightness, balance, and collection in the Theory Made Simple chapter.

# THE IDEAL WORLD

In the ideal world, students have moved up through the stages of rider education on correctly educated horses under the guidance of a classically trained instructor. When this is the case riders will have developed correct habits and the 'right' feel. Their "muscle memories" are correct because of many repetitions of the 'right' position and the 'right' feel. As a result, these riders climb up the learning curve faster and are stronger than those who do not have the ideal education.

**Example:** Lorraine began riding at camp in the summers. Her craving to learn was a delight to the well-educated instructor. Lorraine wanted a horse, but accepted her instructor's guidance to wait until she had advanced through Stage 1 and started Stage 2. After her second season at camp, Lorraine's parents purchased a solid, well-schooled 12-year-old horse, Willy. His background was easily able to take Lorraine through Stage 3. Under the guidance of her instructor and the correct responses of Willy, Lorraine was able to move through Stages 2 & 3 in two years. Lorraine sought out one of the few working student situations that enabled her to ride some well-schooled horses and feel the concepts in Stages 4 and 5. Since Lorraine had developed a well-educated sense of feel from the beginning, she and Willy developed well in the more advanced partnership, and Lorraine was able to use her feel to train younger, less experienced horses and riders.

The perfect combination is an educated horse and an open-minded student with a clear understanding of what he or she really needs as well as what he or she wants to do. The challenge for today's instructors is to promote this awareness and balance in their students. When this balance is achieved, it provides both rider and instructor with many rewarding experiences. ⚞

# THE REAL WORLD

As students progress upwards in their riding educations, the 'real world' problems become more complex and difficult. At Stage 5 horses and riders are, by definition, quite advanced in their training. They are working on upper-level movements and/or jumping big courses. Riders who have not had the advantage of being educated in the ideal world tend to fall into two different categories. The first includes those riders who, inspired by the beauty and/or thrill of upper level competition, become motivated to purchase well-trained (and expensive) horses. These riders are typically not well grounded in classical horse education principles, or in the basics of riding theory. They may have a lot of enthusiasm (and sometimes raw ambition), and approach equestrian sport as they do other endeavors in their lives where drive and determination was all that was necessary to succeed. They mistakenly believe that sitting on advanced horses and competing at the upper levels qualifies them as "advanced" in their educations. Unfortunately, what these riders have learned is how to perform (sometimes quite competently) the movements, but not to **train the movements.** Professional trainers are frequently used to maintain the training of these highly schooled horses because their owners cannot themselves maintain the high degree of training needed to consistently perform at these advanced levels. These riders are missing a detailed theoretical background, a well-developed sense of feel, a classically correct and balanced position, and most of all, an independent and educated seat.

The second category of 'real world' issues that show themselves in Stage 5 riders are those who have trained their own horses to this level. This is quite an accomplishment, and one that deserves admiration and respect. However, as with any learning process, mistakes are made along the way. These horses, because they were learning as their riders were learning, frequently exhibit training problems stemming from a lack of solid basics. This is similar to the situation riders find themselves in when they proceed through the stages incorrectly. What is missing for these horses is a confirmed sense of "throughness," which can only come about as a consequence of habitual practice of the basics of rhythm, looseness, and elastic connection. These horses tend to be tight and restricted in their bodies, especially through their backs. As a result, their riders suffer from position issues related to riding stiff horses. It is such a cycle! Rider influences horse, horse influences rider - this circle works both positively and negatively!

For instructors at this level, the challenge is not so much physical as psychological in nature; how to help these riders and horses unlearn incorrect habits. Instructors have to *motivate these Stage 5 students to 'buy into' the need for remedial work.* This is where training in psychology can come in handy (see psychology section in book). Once the instructor and student are able to "get on the same page," instructors find that they are once again on firm ground. They can now proceed by shifting back and forth between teaching Stage 5 skills and working on the skills needed from previous stages. Once the basics are firmly established (for both rider and horse), progress can go quite quickly because of the education and experience the rider does have.

Here is one example of this dilemma in practice: Ida came to a clinic with the desire to work on impulsion in preparation for her "B" test. Ida and her off-the-track thoroughbred, Tiger, had been together for a year. Before that Ida had ridden a variety of horses, none properly schooled. Ida had sound technical knowledge in her mind, but was unable to actively use what she understood. When they entered the ring there was no way to know who was the stiffest, but it was clear we could not work on impulsion. Ida had her lower leg about 2 inches away from Tiger's side and her back was as stiff as an iron pipe. Tiger was a very nice horse but lacked the rhythm and looseness required in his training, and Ida's stiffness did not help him. The stiff, uneducated horses in Ida's riding career had taught her muscles to be stiff. In order for Ida to move forward we had to return to Stage 1 and reclaim the basics of a relaxed and deep seat. After agreeing to postpone the "B" test, we agreed on a two-track program that involved reeducating Ida and educating Tiger. Ida went on a program of fixing her position starting with her lower leg, and worked on suppling Tiger at the same time. Since both were serious students, they were able to pass the "B" with flying colors the next year. Reeducation takes time, as students must replace incorrect muscle memory with the new feel.

Sometimes instructors find that their students respond negatively to attempts at correcting the basics. These students either are not aware of or do not want to be aware of the gaps in their educations. To handle this situation, please refer to the Counseling Skills for Instructors chapter, which provides some tools for working through resistance. ⚞

Psychology skills allow instructors to help their students learn how to return to a previous step without feeling defeated. ⚞

### Important Points

1. Because the training of the horse is so exciting, riders and instructors get tempted to focus singularly on the horse's performance as evidence of progress. It is important that the diagnosis of a problem and its correction takes into account BOTH rider and horse issues. That is, it helps to remember that few problems at this level are "one-sided," involving only the rider or the horse. The nature of equestrian sport is that we can rarely separate rider and horse - they move together, as one unit, thereby constantly influencing one another.

2. Instructors need to be sensitive to any sign of the rider's developing a backward action in the use of the contact; even the slightest presence of a tight or restrictive hand can cause numerous evasions in the horse.

3. Many training problems are first observed in the horse. Instructors need to be skilled at determining where the problems begin, with the horse or the rider. For new Stage 5 students, a problem might be the result of the rider's natural learning curve, such that when learning new feelings, movements and power, old habits

*Riders now focus on issues of impulsion and straightness, which improves balance, which leads to collection.*

may return. Again, return to the faulty skill and intermix your teaching based on the individual student's need.

# PRACTICAL APPLICATION

## Introduction

*Objective:* To help students identify visually, and through feel, the qualities necessary for the development of a working partnership between rider and horse.

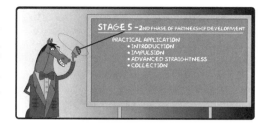

*Theory:* In order for students to ride effectively at this level, they need to know the basics behind both equine and human anatomy and movement. They also need to understand the 'big picture' in terms of horse training. All of the concepts in the Theory Made Simple chapter can be reviewed, with special attention paid to the concepts of impulsion, balance, advanced straightness, and collection. Integration of knowledge, skills, and techniques from other areas becomes increasingly important as students develop their riding educations to this level.

### Toolkit

- Demonstration: Using videos or by watching a demonstration, have your students observe the concepts of engagement, impulsion, straightness and balance in action. If students have been educated to use imagery, they may be able to increase their senses of "feel" by watching and "imagining" themselves to be the actual riders.

- Discussion: Discuss what students are seeing and how engagement relates to impulsion, how impulsion relates to straightness and balance, and how they all lead towards collection. Revisit the circle of muscles and their development using visuals, such as a chalkboard, drawings, articles, video's, etc.

*Test to show understanding of the Introduction:* Ask the student questions about the expanded understanding of partnership between horse and rider in Stage 5 and have the student describe the concepts of engagement, impulsion, straightness, and balance.

## Impulsion

*Objective:* Building on the Stage 4 awareness of basic straightness, instructors will help students become consistent and use exercises and figures to build impulsion, or forward thrust, in the horse.

*Theory:* Impulsion is when a horse moves energetically from the hind end forward with power and thrust. That is, energy moves from the hind legs, over the back (which is round), up through the withers, neck, poll and into the rider's receiving hands. Review the section on Impulsion in the Theory Made Simple chapter.

*Important Points*

1. Mixing lateral exercises with transitions builds the power for forward thrust.
2. Impulsion and straightness complement each other and are developed together. This takes expanded feel, awareness, quick timing and a clear understanding of desired outcome by the student.
3. Instructors need to stay aware of the rider's quality of contact. The work at this level requires an educated, quality contact that is consistent and elastic.

## Toolkit

🔸 To develop the thrust that is necessary for impulsion, have your students work on transitions between gaits, within gaits, and within their lateral work, all while maintaining rhythm and straightness.

🔸 As the rider and horse team performs transitions with rhythm and straightness, ask the rider to be aware of maintaining forward contact to the hand. Video replays of a student's rides can help identify reactions by the horse that signal tension in the shoulder, back, arm, or hand.

🔸 Students can use jumping exercises to improve impulsion without changing the prerequisites. The increased skill level of the student, combined with a well-muscled, stronger horse, means that there can be more balance developed in the horse's canter. This allows the rider/horse team to jump higher fences and/or answer more difficult jumping questions.

| MORE ADVANCED EXERCISES FOR HORSE & RIDER | | |
|---|---|---|
| **Rein back** | Rider | Forward motion directed to step back |
| | Horse | Obedience<br>Increased longitudinal suppleness<br>Increased engagement |
| **Turn on Haunches Half pirouette** | Rider | Coordination |
| | Horse | Improves engagement<br>Obedience to leg |
| **Jumping a course** | Rider | Improves timing<br>Ride forward with control<br>Think quickly<br>Respond automatically |
| | Horse | Balance<br>Engagement<br>Forward FUN |
| | | Chart 53 |

Exercises in Chart 51, Stage 4 are also used with less time between each exercise.

Instructors are encouraged to remain aware of the role of position and the use of the aids during this stage of learning. As riders are challenged to 'feel' and use their aids appropriately, they may lose some of the fundamental basics and allow the horse to alter their positions or challenge their confidence and thus alter their consistency of route, rhythm, and/or balance. It is essential for instructors to encourage students to take regular instruction during this phase of learning, as there is room for many bad habits to develop. 🐎

*Test to show understanding of Impulsion:*
- Have students ride transitions and ring figures in order to develop an increased amount of impulsion in the horse.
- Ask students questions to show the depth of their knowledge and degree of understanding and feel for the degree of impulsion their horses are capable of at this level.
- Have your students describe a training plan to continually increase impulsion. Ask students how they would recognize impulsion in horses they are watching from the ground.

## Advanced Straightness (leading to balance)

*Objective:* To help students develop a more advanced understanding of straightness and how it leads to the level of ridden balance that is needed for collection.

*Theory:* At this level, straightness is concerned with the quality of a horse's weight distribution during movements. Review the section on Advanced Straightness in the Theory Made Simple chapter.

*Important Points*
1. It takes increased muscle strength for horses to travel straight in all movements, especially lateral ones. As horses become stronger, riders will feel this increased power in their seats and through their hands as they first create, and then receive this energy.
2. Adding more advanced exercises that require increased coordination in the rider and greater strength in the horse often allow room for faults (both rider and horse) to infiltrate the work. Instructors need to stay very attuned to problems that may arise through the learning process and correct them before they become ingrained and well established.
3. Due to the circular nature of rider and horse influence, instructors need to experiment with what to focus on first, the rider or the horse, when presented with a training challenge.

4. When riders start attending to issues of advanced straightness, they are increasingly dealing with the concept of balance. Riders trying to achieve true straightness must attend to the way their horses are distributing their weight on either side of an imaginary line dissecting the horse into two equal parts.

5. As riders work to develop Stage 5 skills, they will be increasingly asked to understand the circular and interconnected relationships between all theoretical concepts. They will need help in learning how to multitask and stay aware of more than one concept at a time, while developing refinements in their coordination that allow them to respond quickly and accurately with more than one aid at once.

*Learn how to be flexible as you teach in order to uncover the core of any training challenges. Results speak louder than words.*

**Toolkit**

🖎 Instructors begin to ask their students to perform all of the exercises learned in the earlier stages, only now with more frequent transitions.

🖎 Instructors spend less time in each movement; rather they emphasize frequent changes using all of the gymnasticizing exercises learned in previous stages.

🖎 When jumping, riders at this stage now are asked to focus on the horse's balance before, during, and after the fence and on the immediate strides upon landing. The focus is less on the rider's ability to jump correctly over high and difficult fences (this is assumed), but is more on helping the horse get to the fence with the proper pace, balance, energy, and attitude in order to be successful in negotiating the obstacle. As the fences get higher and more difficult, there are fewer opportunities for horses to save a rider when an error is made; so more demands are placed upon the rider's being very correct in their positions.

See Chart 49 for some common evasions.

**INSTRUCTOR'S REMINDER**

It is essential to remember that at all points in training, if one of the basic ingredients is missing, instructors must return to what the horse and rider understand, accept and can perform, and then move on again. 🖎

*Test to show understanding of Advanced Straightness:* Ask students to describe the process of developing straightness and balance in a horse through all of the stages. Have students demonstrate riding a horse with advanced straightness and evaluate the horse's balance while riding ring figures and doing gymnasticizing exercises.

## Collection

*Objective:* To develop the quickness and comfort in the rider to be able to create, receive, and contain the increased power that develops from all earlier work, and which results in collection.

*Theory:* Combining the advanced carrying power of a balanced horse with all the necessary prerequisites of rhythm, looseness, contact, impulsion and straightness, along with the rider's ability to create and hold all this energy, makes horses shift their weight back onto their hind ends while maintaining forward energy and thrust. This is collection. See the Collection section in the Theory Made Simple chapter.

*Important Points*

1. Students who are successful in creating true collection are aware, confident riders who have developed the ability to diagnose by 'feel' and use the appropriate well timed adjustments and exercises to maintain balance through transitions and lateral work.

2. When students begin asking their horses for collection, whether between jumps or on the flat, they find their horses becoming rounder and more powerful athletes to work with, which may be both good and bad!  Stronger horses move with more energy, power and expression, and can become a bit explosive at times. They also can resist more forcibly as well.

3. It is also important for students to understand that the increased stress of the work requires careful observation and consideration of the length of each training session. Like any athlete, if regular training sessions are too long, too short, or improperly designed, injuries will occur. Students must develop and maintain a regular, systematic training program that considers the long-term mental and physical development of their horses.

**Toolkit**

✎ The best way to learn collection is to ride collection!  Ideally, riders can first learn the complex sequence of aids on a trained horse; and then as they develop increased tact, timing, and coordination, they can work with horses less educated to the collection aids.

- When riding collected work, the exercises from earlier stages and steps are done with increased frequency, more change, and quicker response from both horse and rider.
- Transitions within and between gaits mixed with lateral work.
- Collected work is done in short, frequent training sets. If too much is asked for too soon, or for too long, horses lose their confidence and enjoyment of their work.

INSTRUCTOR'S REMINDER

An experienced instructor with a good eye is essential. It is very easy for both horses and riders to develop bad habits because there are more demands on both partners. With a good ground person bad habits are avoided or dealt with and the end result is a partnership marked by beauty and harmony.

Once riders are accomplished at this stage, they are ready for specialization. Students are now ready to use their advanced skills to learn how to ride a horse at the upper levels of dressage, cross-country or show jumping, depending on the student's area of interest. In addition, Stage 5 students are also ready to advance in their professional teaching and training skills if they have not already started this during Transition 1 or 2. Riders who have accomplished the skills of Stage 5 can consider themselves to be at the "elite" levels of their sport. They have truly come far in the mastery of the art of equestrian riding. A toast to Stage 5 riders everywhere – may you continue to inspire others, and be inspired by the beauty and nobility that defines the true human/horse partnership.

Jumping in Harmony

# CONCLUSION

*Equestrian Education* is filled with valuable information for both how to teach and what to teach. It is designed to guide instructors who want to improve their lessons as well as remain refreshed and up-to-date. It is not designed to overwhelm instructors with too much information.

No matter how you use this book, we hope you will remember these Important Points:

1. Keep it simple but thorough.
2. Move freely between the stages and steps, but keep the BIG PICTURE (the System) in mind.
3. Expand your overall education and integrate what you learn.
4. Develop your students' independence and confidence by creating independent thinkers.
5. Present information so that students commit skills to muscle memory.

We hope you enjoy using *Equestrian Education* as much as we enjoyed writing it!

# ABOUT THE AUTHORS

### JILL K. HASSLER-SCOOP

Jill is an instructor, coach and clinician. She is author of *Beyond the Mirrors, In Search of Your Image, Equestrian Instruction* and co-author of *My Riding Goal JOURNAL* as well as numerous articles in equestrian magazines. Jill has a wide background; forty two years teaching, thirty-five years managing Hidden Acres Farm and then Hilltop Farm, twenty-five years of service to the United States Pony Clubs, twenty years experience with disabled riders both locally and nationally, and twenty years of educational consulting. In her riding career Jill showed successfully in the hunter and equitation arena, and at USPC Regional and National Rallies, and graduated as a B pony clubber. Retired from Hilltop Farm in April of 2001, Jill is devoting more time to her love of horses and education via Equestrian Education Systems, which provides a wide variety of educational services.

### KATHY KELLY Ph.D.

Dr. Kelly is a clinical psychologist, USPC National Examiner, instructor, and clinician. As a psychologist, she has specialized training in the areas of eating disorders, equine-assisted psychotherapy, and sport psychology. In addition, Dr. Kelly is a popular motivational speaker who travels nation-wide helping groups and organizations benefit from fun and practical applications of psychology. As an instructor and clinician, she teaches adult amateurs and prepares pony clubbers for their upper-level testings. In her riding career, Dr. Kelly is a graduate A pony clubber, has competed successfully in the areas of dressage, eventing, and hunter/jumpers, and has had considerable exposure to the European riding and training systems.

### ELIZABETH CLARKE

Elizabeth Clarke has been involved with horses all of her life, and has been a serious student of dressage for many years. A graduate of Smith College with a degree in Economics, she worked as a commercial banker for several years before attending the University of Virginia Law School. After practicing law for a few years and a brief tenure as Director of Dressage for the United States Equestrian Team, Beth established an organizational and business management consulting service with a client base made up largely of horse related businesses. She has been a regular columnist for *Trail Blazer* magazine and an occasional contributor to *Dressage Today* magazine's "Ask the Experts" column, and has given business planning and risk management seminars for equine professionals around the country. Having lived in locations as diverse as Annapolis, Maryland; London, England; Northampton, Massachusetts; Palo Alto, California; and Salzburg, Austria, Beth now teaches equine law, business management and facility design in the Equine Science Department at Otterbein College.

### NICHOLAS FOWLER

Nick Fowler and his wife Dawna share a journey of enlightenment through responsibility, self-awareness and commitment. Nick brings these same commitments into his relationships with other people and horses. He works as a manager and personal/executive coach for a large manufacturing company, and in his spare time consults with non-profits and individuals who want to make changes in how they relate to others. Many of the ideas expressed here grew from conversations with his daughter – a rider and instructor - as she grew with her horses and students and in her skills at relating with them both.

# LIST OF CHARTS

# SUGGESTED READING

This list contains a few recommended books, but the list is not all-inclusive as there are many, many valuable books and videotapes available.

## PROFESSIONAL DEVELOPMENT

*An Introduction to the Tellington-Jones Equine Awareness Method*
*(The T.E.A.M. Approach to Problem Free Training)*
  by Linda Tellington-Jones & Ursala Bruns
  Published by Breakthrough Publishers, 1988
   One of the first to write about the importance of understanding horse behavior from an 'inner' perspective. This is an important book to read as you evaluate all the information on 'natural horsemanship'.

*Buddhism Without Beliefs: A Contemporary Guide to Awakening*
  By Stephen Batchelor
  Riverhead Books, 1997
   Here are valuable lessons in awakening, integrity, friendship, compassion, freedom, etc., each condensed to a few thought-filled pages.

*Centered Riding*
  By Sally Swift
  A Trafalgar Square Farm Book, David & Charles Inc., 1985
   *Centered Riding* shares the imaginative and innovative philosophy of Sally Swift. We are guided, step-by-step, through wonderfully accessible ideas and visualizations. Based on years of experience as a successful instructor, the author gives a refreshing contrast to the all too often mechanics-only school of training. Harmony of human and horse, mental and physical, is offered as the guiding principle. This book will appeal to riders of all levels, especially those who seek to merge the visual mind with the physical self. Includes photographs, diagrams and often delightfully humorous illustrations.

*The Consultant's Calling: Bringing Who You are to What You Do.*
  Jossey-Bass, 1990
  By Geoffrey M. Bellman
   A very successful consultant talks about the importance of knowing who you are and taking the critical time to reflect on the results of your interactions with others.

*Dialogue - and the Art of Thinking Together*
   By William Isaacs
   Currency, 1999
      A wonderful model for effective communications - applicable in many
      situations - this builds on the pioneering work of David Bohm and
      the hundreds of primitive societies who had not forgotten how to
      communicate effectively.

*Heads Up! Practical Sports Psychology For Riders,*
*Their Families & Their Trainers*
   By Janet Sasson Edgette
   Doubleday, 1996
      One of the first books written about the role of sports psychology for
      the rider, Dr. Edgette gives some practical stories about its role in a
      rider's life. This book offers an interesting and relatively new ap-
      proach to horsemanship.

*Insights into Personal and Team Effectiveness*
   Insights Training and Development, Ltd, Dundee, Scotland.
   www.insightsworld.com
      Insights is a personal profile (similar to Meyers-Briggs) that helps an
      individual better understand and communicate their personal needs
      for interaction with others and to appreciate the needs of others who
      may be very different.

*Motivational Interviewing*
   By William R. Miller and Stephen Rollnick
   Guilford Press, 1991

*Riding Towards the Light: An Apprenticeship in the Art of Dressage Riding*
   By Paul Belasik
   J.A. Allen, 1990
      A beautiful story of integrating and the development of ideals.

*Reading People, How to Understand People and Predict*
*Their Behavior — Anytime, Anyplace*
   By Jo-Ellan Dimitrius, Ph.D. and Mark Mazzarella,
   2nd edition, 1999

*Six Pillars of Self-esteem*
   By Nathanial Branden
   Bantam Books,1995
      This book condenses a lot of information about Self-awareness, Liv-
      ing Consciously, Self-assertiveness, living responsibly, and integrity.
      It includes a powerful 32-week program of reflective exercises.

*That Winning Feeling! A New Approach to Riding Using Psychocybernetics\**
   by Jane Savoie
   Trafalgar Square Publishing, 1992

A book full of concepts and ideas on how to change luck, worry, dreams, criticism & frustration into positive thinking. An excellent book for competitors in dressage, eventing and show jumping, about the power of POSITIVE THINKING and how attitude affects success. Endorsed by Sally Swift, Robert Dover and Anne Kursinski.

*To Know as We are Known: Education as a Spiritual Journey*
By Parker Palmer
Harper, 1993
A small, but acclaimed book opening a door to understanding the importance of heart in all that we do - especially teaching.

*The 7 Powers of Questions, Secrets to Successful Communication in Life and at Work*
by Dorothy Leeds
A Perigee Book, 2000

*The Way to Perfect Horsemanship*
By Udo Burger
Trafalgar Square Publishing, 1998
Training principles based on the horse's biomechanics and psychological make up.

*The Zen of Groups*
By Dale Hunter, Anne Bailey, and Bill Taylor
Fisher Books, 2nd edition 1995

### PROFESSIONAL DEVELOPMENT AND FUNDAMENTAL SKILLS

*Equestrian Instruction: An Integrated Approach to Teaching and Learning*
by Jill K. Hassler-Scoop and 16 additional contributors
Goals Unlimited Press, 2000
Equestrian Instruction is an excellent source of comprehensive information for aspiring instructors, accomplished instructors, and riders of any discipline. This handbook reveals the process of successful learning and teaching. The ideas and techniques presented create independent, confident, well-balanced riders on happy, comfortable horses performing optimally to the delight of their inspired instructors.

*In Search of Your Image: A Practical Guide to the Mental & Spiritual Aspects of Horsemanship*
by Jill Keiser Hassler
Goals Unlimited Press, 1993
This practical book requested by readers of Beyond the Mirrors, is positive, encouraging and full of suggestions on how to increase your 'mental skills tool box'. The more 'mental skill tools' we have the more we can enjoy our riding, improve our horsemanship and get the results we want. It will help you understand yourself and through

your work with horses overcome some of the obstacles in riding and maybe life!

*In Search of Your Image: WORKBOOK*
    by Jill Keiser Hassler
    Goals Unlimited Press,1993
        The Workbook helps you learn the 'mental tools', map your progress, and get new ideas, thus becoming more aware and confident about your training. It also offers practical 'how to' exercises to speed up learning and develop a strong foundation. A popular book that serves as a great annual journal format!

## FOR NEW INSTRUCTORS

*Beginning English Exercises*
By Cherry Hill

*Beginning Western Exercises*
By Cherry Hill

*Basic Horsemanship: English & Western*
By Gaydell Collier

*The Riding Instructor's Handbook*
    By Monty Mortimer
    Redwood Books, 1998
        An easy to use book filled with the basics for riders Intro to Stage 2, with lots of very good exercises recommended.

*USPC Manual of Horsemanship: Basics for Beginners*
by Susan Harris

## FUNDAMENTAL SKILLS

*Becoming An Effective Rider: Develop Your Mind and Body*
*or Balance and Unity*
    by Cherry Hill
    Storey Books, Dec 91
        Manual for the American Association for Horsemanship Safety. A good book for both instructors of all levels and students who want to know more about what safe instruction should include. Includes useful sections on selection of school horses and legal concerns and precautions for an instructor.

*Development First - Strategies for Self-development*
*Leader as Coach - Strategies for Coaching and Developing Others . . .*
    By David B. Peterson and Mary Dee Hicks
    Personnel Decisions International, 1999
        These two books by Personal Decisions, International, a large corporate executive coaching firm, summarize concisely the basic elements of coaching.

*The Songs of Horses, Seven Stories for Riding Teachers and Students*
   By Paul Belasik
   J.A. Allen, 1999
      Seven lovely stories that give instructors ideas on the variations that
      can be used to help the individual student.

### STAGES OF RIDER EDUCATION

*Anne Kursinski's Riding & Jumping Clinic*
   By Anne Kursinski
   Doubleday, 1995
      Vital information, easy to use from basic flatwork through jumping.

*Balance in Movement - The Seat of the Rider*
   By Susanne Von Dietze
   Trafalgar Square Publishing, 1999
      Easy to read, excellent for all riders to better understand the relation-
      ship between the horse's movement and position. Includes basics of
      building a good seat. Fantastic diagrams and photos, clear text.

*Cavaletti, The Schooling of Horse and Rider Over Ground Poles*
   By Ingrid Klimke
   Lyons Press, 2000
      Excellent book on the details of using cavaletti.

*The Complete Training of Horse and Rider; In the*
*Principles of Classical Horsemanship*
   By Alois Pokhajsky
   Doubleday and Company, 1967
      Based on his love of horses, the book is filled with the classic infor-
      mation for training the rider and the horse.

*Dressage in Harmony: From Basic to Grand Prix*
   By Walter Zettl
   Half Halt Press, 1998
      A training book based on the love of the horse, this book is a real
      treat to those who are interested in the art of dressage. With love of
      the horse at the heart of the writing, Zettl covers rhythm, relaxation,
      contact, straightness, suppleness, and collection. Dressage in Har-
      mony is a must for all dressage riders and great for those who want
      to delve into the classics.

*Hunter Seat Equitation*
   By George Morris
   Doubleday, 1990
      This is a classic in its field

*Lunging: The German Riding and Driving System; Book 6*
   Kenworth Press, 1990
      An excellent guide to lunging horses. Simple to use and understand.

*Major Anders Lindgren's Teaching Exercises:*
*A Manual For Instructors & Riders*
    By Major Anders Lindgren
    Half Halt Press, 1998
      Well-illustrated exercises arranged according to difficulty, in the same order as introduced in AHSA dressage tests.

*The Classic Rider: Being at One with Your Horse*
    By Sylvia Loch
    Trafalgar Square Publishing,1997
      A study of classical dressage training including the horse's physiology and psychology.

*The Classical Seat: A Guide for the Everyday Rider*
    By Sylvia Loch
    Trafalgar Square Publishing, 1988
      A small, easy to use guide for seat, balance, rhythm and feel.

*The Principles of Riding: The Official Instruction Handbook*
*of the German National Equestrian Federation*
    Kenworth Press, 1997
      An easy book to use; a must for all serious instructors.

*Training the Three Day Event Horse and Rider*
    By James Wofford
    Derrydale Press, 2000
      Filled with practical advice on all aspects of training for a three day event horse and rider. Filled with illustrative photographs.

## VIDEO

*The Visible Horse*
    By Susan Harris
    Trafalgar Square Publishing
      An easy to understand study of how horses' bones and muscles work while moving.

*The Visible Rider*
    By Susan Harris
    Trafalgar Square Publishing
      An easy to understand study of how a rider can follow the horse's movement. It includes common riding faults and the effect on both horse and rider.

# INDEX

281

282